STUDIES IN MODERN BRITISH RELIGIOUS HISTORY

Volume 4

Christabel Pankhurst

Fundamentalism and Feminism in Coalition

STUDIES IN MODERN BRITISH RELIGIOUS HISTORY

ISSN: 1464–6625

General editors
Stephen Taylor
Arthur Burns
Kenneth Fincham

This series aims to differentiate 'religious history' from the narrow confines of church history, investigating not only the social and cultural history of religion, but also theological, political and institutional themes, while remaining sensitive to the wider historical context; it thus advances an understanding of the importance of religion for the history of modern Britain, covering all periods of British history since the Reformation.

I
Friends of Religious Equality
Non-Conformist Politics in mid-Victorian England
Timothy Larsen

II
Conformity and Orthodoxy in the English Church,
c. 1560–1660
edited by Peter Lake and Michael Questier

III
Bishops and Reform in the English Church, 1520–1559
Kenneth Carleton

Christabel Pankhurst
Fundamentalism and Feminism in Coalition

TIMOTHY LARSEN

THE BOYDELL PRESS

© Timothy Larsen 2002

First published 2002
The Boydell Press, Woodbridge

ISBN 0 85115 905 2

The Boydell Press is an imprint of Boydell & Brewer Ltd
PO Box 9, Woodbridge, Suffolk IP12 3DF, UK
and of Boydell & Brewer Inc.
PO Box 41026, Rochester, NY 14604–4126, USA
website: www.boydell.co.uk

A catalogue record of this publication is available
from the British Library

Library of Congress Cataloging-in-Publication Data
Larsen, Timothy, 1967–
   Christabel Pankhurst: fundamentalism and feminism in coalition / Timothy Larsen.
   p. cm. – (Studies in modern British religious history)
   Includes bibliographical references and index.
   ISBN 0–85115–905–2 (hardback)
   1. Pankhurst, Christabel, Dame, 1880–1958.   2. Evangelicalism – History – 20th century.
3. Fundamentalism – History – 20th century.   4. Feminism – Religious aspects –
Christianity – History – 20th century.   I. Title.   II. Series.
   BR1643.P36 L37 2002
   269′.2′092–dc21
                                                              2002010742

This publication is printed on acid-free paper

Printed in Great Britain by
St Edmundsbury Press Limited, Bury St Edmunds, Suffolk

Contents

For Jane

Preface

The British have never forgotten Christabel Pankhurst (1880–1958). Alongside her mother, Emmeline, she led the Women's Social and Political Union as it pursued its militant campaign to obtain votes for women. Christabel Pankhurst had personally inaugurated the civil disobedience phase of the campaign and was therefore, together with Annie Kenney, the first – but by no means the last – of the Suffragettes to go to prison. Pankhurst's tactical mind was a major force behind the waves of militant feminist action which marked that dramatic period in British history. Her name was on everyone's lips for the most important years of the campaign, not least those of the prime minister, members of the cabinet, and MPs. The outbreak of the Great War followed by the granting of votes for (some) women in 1918 permanently ended Pankhurst's role as a militant leader in the women's struggle. Around twenty years later, however, her nation remembered her formally. In the 1936 New Year's honours list it was announced that she had been created a Dame Commander of the Order of the British Empire. When Dame Christabel Pankhurst died on 13 February 1958 at her home in Santa Monica, California, the British nation responded to this loss by adding a permanent memorial to her next to the one of her mother that stood near the House of Lords. Less than twenty years after that act of remembering, women's rights came to the fore once again, and Pankhurst's name has become familiar to generations of British schoolchildren ever since. Historians have also become aware in recent decades that history writing in the past had largely excluded women and have endeavoured to introduce the lives of women and the experiences of women into their narratives. Today it would be hard to imagine any general account of British history in the twentieth century that would leave out the name of Christabel Pankhurst.

On the other hand, although Pankhurst is often named, she is rarely studied. In fact, in an age when very impressive scholarly biographies are continually appearing of women that most well-educated people have never heard of before, and many well-known women seem to find a new biographer on a triennial basis, no academic has ever written a biography of Christabel Pankhurst. Indeed, David Mitchell's *Queen Christabel*, published a quarter of a century ago, is the only attempt that has ever been made by anyone to write a full biography of Christabel Pankhurst and, as will come out in the course of this study, it is a seriously flawed work.[1] Martin Pugh has recently written a study of the Pankhurst family, but it relies on Mitchell's research for the section on Christabel's religious work, thereby perpetuating some of that earlier study's errors and failing to redress its main limitations on this subject.[2]

This study is not a biography of Christabel Pankhurst. It is not even a biography of the second half of her life. It is a study of her Christian ministry and thought. Although even the first half of Pankhurst's life has been surprisingly neglected by scholars, the second half has been left as a completely open field. There has not even been an article or a thesis or a chapter in an edited volume on it, let alone a book-length study.[3] Nevertheless, Pankhurst achieved a remarkable level of fame, influence, and success in her religious work. She began to study the Bible and to take seriously evangelical theological ideas in 1918, and by 1922 she was ready to emerge as a Christian teacher. She joined the fundamentalist movement and became an enormously popular preacher, teacher, and evangelist, both in Britain and in North America. She was numbered among the elite on the biggest fundamentalist platforms, the great annual Bible conferences that brought thousands of the faithful together from across the country, and she repeatedly preached from the pulpits of some of the most important flagship churches in major cities. Her ministry was highly respected by an impressive array of the most well-respected leaders of fundamentalism at that time, as well as by innumerable rank-and-file supporters of the movement. She wrote a succession of popular religious books, and numerous articles by or about her appeared in evangelical newspapers. No story of fundamentalism in the 1920s is complete that fails to take notice of her popular and influential ministry.

Fundamentalism and feminism are not usually thought of as in coalition. It is sometimes said that militant feminists behave or think like fundamentalists, but the charge is made precisely because it is intended to jar, if not wound. The conventional wisdom is that fundamentalists hate feminists and feminists hate fundamentalists. A thesis of this study is that it was not always so. In the early decades of the twentieth century, it was possible to be both a feminist – in the sense of believing in gender equality in society (votes for women being the concrete goal) and in the church (women preachers being the concrete goal) – and also a fundamentalist, that is a conservative evangelical Protestant making a stand for 'fundamental'

---

[1] David Mitchell, *Queen Christabel: A Biography of Christabel Pankhurst*, London: Macdonald and Jane's, 1977.

[2] Martin Pugh, *The Pankhursts*, London: Allen Lane Penguin Press, 2001.

[3] Those interested in a more detailed discussion of the existing historiography are directed to the epilogue, as well as those places in the main body of this book in which particular scholarly works are critiqued in the course of discussions of specific themes.

doctrines such as the inerrancy of the Bible and the literal, bodily resurrection of Jesus Christ in defiance of modernist or theologically liberal
ideas and trends. Christabel Pankhurst embodied this coalition between
fundamentalism and feminism, but she was not a singular case. Her
ministry was supported by some of the most powerful fundamentalist
ministers of her day, men who believed in votes for women and women in
ministry. In fact, far from being an exceptionally restrictive place, fundamentalism was perhaps the best place to be in the 1920s if you were a
woman who felt a call to ministry.

The writing of this book was made much easier by the helpfulness of
numerous people. I owe a special debt to the Revd Glen Taylor of
Eastbourne, the editor of the *Prophetic Witness*. Not only did he allow
me – a complete stranger on an even stranger quest – access to his
complete set of the *Advent Witness*, but he also handed over his office and
his photocopier to me, and he and his wife gave me gracious hospitality
in their home. I am grateful for the help provided by my research assist-
ants, Stephen Barkley and Jon Vickery. Sandy Finlayson, the former
Director of Tyndale's library, and Hugh Rendle, its Public Services
Librarian, cheerfully put up with my ceaseless requests, not to mention
my perpetual schemes to circumvent normal library policies. Many of my
former colleagues at Tyndale College & Seminary, Toronto, were stimulating conversation partners: beyond the core faculty, who were both
enthusiastic and useful, I also need to express my thanks to Donald
MacLeod. Mary Hall gave an evening of her holiday to proof-reading.
My brother, the historian and librarian, David K. Larsen, has been a
valuable interlocutor throughout the whole of this project, as well as
procuring sources for me and commenting on an early draft of the manuscript. June Purvis and David Bebbington kindly read an early draft and
offered astute comments on it, but as many parts of the text were altered
thereafter, and as I stubbornly failed to heed their advice on certain
points, they can hardly be blamed for the defects of the work as it now
stands. Stephen Taylor and Arthur Burns, two of the editors for this
series, have both supported and improved this project. On a more
personal note, my life has been immeasurably enriched by three generations of women: my mother, Pearl, and my mother-in-law, Pauline,
comprise the first, and my two young daughters, Lucia and Amelia, the
last. Jane, whom I dearly love, stands at the centre, and to her this book
is dedicated.

Timothy Larsen, PhD, FRHists, is Associate Professor of Theology at Wheaton
College, IL, USA.

Chapter One

CHRISTIAN MINISTRY

The Suffragettes

On 13 October 1905 Christabel Pankhurst may or may not have spat in a policeman's face. If, as she later insisted, no actual saliva was involved, then, in any event, she feigned this transaction with such verisimilitude as to achieve her calculated aim of being arrested for a technical assault. In high spirits, she had announced when leaving the house that day, 'I shall sleep in prison to-night!' Her loyal follower, Annie Kenney, had been her accomplice, and was also arrested. Thus the militant phase of the British campaign for women's suffrage began.[1]

Pankhurst was a founding member of the Women's Social and Political Union (W.S.P.U.), and although her mother, Emmeline Pankhurst, was considered its titular head, her eldest daughter was often considered its primary strategist and decision-maker. Sylvia Pankhurst, Christabel's younger sister, testifies, 'Mrs Pankhurst, to whom her first-born had ever been the dearest of her children, proudly and openly proclaimed her

[1] This section is meant as a way of rehearsing the basic outline of the Suffragette movement for the benefit of those approaching this book from an interest in religious history. It is written largely from the perspective of Pankhurst's own account. Those wishing to pursue this subject further should consult the secondary sources that have addressed this theme at length such as Andrew Rosen, *Rise Up, Women: The Militant Campaign of the Women's Social and Political Union, 1903–1914*, Boston: Routledge & Kegan Paul, 1974. The following are noted for those wishing to understand the latest scholarly interpretations of the women's movement in Britain during this period: June Purvis and Sandra Stanley Holton (eds), *Votes for Women*, London: Routledge, 2000; June Purvis, 'Christabel Pankhurst and the Women's Social and Political Union', in M. Joannou and J. Purvis (eds), *The Women's Suffrage Movement, New Feminist Perspectives*, Manchester: Manchester University Press, 1998; June Purvis, 'A "Pair of . . . Infernal Queens"? A Reassessment of the Dominant Representations of Emmeline and Christabel Pankhurst, First Wave Feminists in Edwardian Britain', *Women's History Review*, 5, 2 (1996); Martin Pugh, *The March of the Women: A Revisionist Analysis of the Campaign for Women's Suffrage, 1866–1914*, Oxford: Oxford University Press, 2000; Martin Pugh, *The Pankhursts*, London: Allen Lane Penguin Press, 2001; June Purvis, *Emmeline Pankhurst: A Biography*, London: Routledge, 2002.

eldest daughter to be her leader.'[2] The W.S.P.U. inaugurated militancy – a euphemism for civil disobedience – as a tactic in the campaign and, continuing in this vein, succeeded (along with a few other organizations that left it or were purged out of it) in dominating the subsequent discussion of the politics of women's suffrage, and in capturing the attention of the public. Pankhurst, looking back on the fight once it had been won,[3] commented on an interview she and other W.S.P.U. members had had with A. J. Balfour, the Conservative leader, in 1905. They had asked him why his party had not done anything for them:

> 'Well, to tell you the truth, your cause is not in the swim,' was his reply. Never again should a political leader, whatever his party, make that the excuse for having refused or neglected to give votes for women. Peaceful pleading had continued for more than forty years, and still the votes for women cause was 'not in the swim!' Militancy kept it in the political swim, till the harbour was reached.[4]

The new approach by a largely younger group of women prompted the *Daily Mail* to find a distinguishing name for them, the 'Suffragettes', a sobriquet which W.S.P.U. women were happy to own. Pankhurst recalled:

> There was a spirit in it, a spring that we liked. Suffragists, we had called ourselves till then, but the name lacked the positive note implied by 'Suffragette'. Just 'want the vote' was the notion conveyed by the older appellation and, as a famous anecdote had it, 'the Suffragettes [hardening the 'g'] they mean to get it'.[5]

The W.S.P.U. decided to focus much of its efforts on hounding members of the Liberal cabinet. Pankhurst later admitted, 'The Liberal Government was in fact the enemy.'[6] Unwilling to be heckled at every stop, the ministers were driven to more and more elaborate security measures which, in turn, were matched by the cunning of the Suffragettes. Sylvia Pankhurst chronicled the way that the situation escalated:

> Cabinet Ministers had long ceased to address open meetings; their audiences were now only admitted by tickets, carefully distributed

---

[2] E. Sylvia Pankhurst, *The Suffragette Movement: An Intimate Account of Persons and Ideals*, London: Virago 1977 [originally 1931], pp. 191–2.

[3] Pugh's *March of the Women* is a recent work that argues what has become the new orthodoxy, that votes for women were secured more by the work of the constitutional suffragists than that of the militant ones. This is not a debate that needs to be entered into in this study: rather than an attempt at an objective assessment of the situation as a whole, Pankhurst's perspective is setting the tone for this account.

[4] Dame Christabel Pankhurst, *Unshackled: The Story of How We Won the Vote*, London: Cresset Women's Voices, 1987 [originally published posthumously, in 1959], p. 58.

[5] Pankhurst, *Unshackled*, pp. 62–3.

[6] Pankhurst, *Unshackled*, p. 61.

amongst their supporters. The W.S.P.U. early resorted to the printing of forged tickets. The Liberal organizers then excluded women from the meetings, issuing only a few special women's tickets to guaranteed supporters, and bearing the name and address of the holder. To circumvent this move, the Suffragettes set themselves to enter the meetings by strategy, climbing in through windows and lying concealed. . . . Elegantly gowned women, mingling unsuspected among the guests in famous houses, suddenly seized Ministers by the shoulder and raised their cry. . . . As Suffragettism spread, the women who accosted Ministers at parties and receptions were, more and more often, duly invited guests.[7]

During a 1908 by-election, the W.S.P.U. put considerable effort into campaigning against Winston Churchill, who was a Liberal MP for the North-West Division of Manchester, and who had recently been made a member of the Privy Council. Pankhurst moved to Manchester for the duration and personally ran the W.S.P.U. campaign against him. Churchill duly lost the seat, and it was widely believed that the work of the Suffragettes had contributed to his defeat. Pankhurst relished this victory as if she had been elected herself: 'In 1906 the Liberals won the election in North-West Manchester. In 1908 the Suffragettes won it.'[8]

1908, however, also saw Herbert Asquith, a wily opponent of women's suffrage, become prime minister. Emmeline and Christabel became a kind of Moses and Aaron, relentlessly demanding the immediate emancipation of their people, with Asquith taking on the role of a Pharaoh, wanting relief from their plagues but still evasive, deceptive and, at his core, implacably stubborn.[9] Therefore the militant tactics were destined to escalate, as were the measures used by the government to deal with the perpetrators.

The years ahead brought confrontations in which the stakes rose higher and higher. For the opening of the new Parliament on 13 October 1913, the W.S.P.U. planned a mass demonstration which was advertised by handbills that read: 'Men and Women, Help the Suffragettes to Rush the House of Commons'. In response, a court summons was issued for Emmeline and Christabel Pankhurst, and their co-worker (known in the W.S.P.U. as 'the General') Flora Drummond. Ignoring the summons, they went to the demonstration anyway and spoke in Trafalgar Square. They were then arrested and spent the night in prison. Christabel Pankhurst, who had studied law at Victoria University, Manchester, obtaining a L.L.B. degree with first-class honours in 1906, decided to defend their

[7] Sylvia Pankhurst, *Suffragette Movement*, pp. 275–6.
[8] Pankhurst, *Unshackled*, p. 91.
[9] Christabel Pankhurst, 'Politicians I Have Met: Tussles and Flattery', *Weekly Dispatch*, 17 April 1921, p. 5.

case herself. She was in her element and made the most of it. In a particular stroke of genius, she called two members of the cabinet, Lloyd George – whose curiosity had prompted him to be in the crowd on the day – and Herbert Gladstone, who had seen the handbill. Sylvia Pankhurst gave an account of the spectacle:

> Lloyd George obviously disliked the ordeal and constantly appealed to Curtis Bennett to forbid the questions fired at him by Christabel. Wrote Max Beerbohm in the *Saturday Review*: 'His Celtic fire burned very low; and the contrast between the buoyancy of the girl and the depression of the statesman was almost painful. Youth and an ideal on the one hand, and on the other middle age and no illusions left over.'[10]

They were convicted none the less. Emmeline Pankhurst and Flora Drummond received three-month prison sentences, and Christabel Pankhurst was given ten weeks, allowances apparently being made for her comparative youth. They were released at the end of the year straight into inspiring celebrations organized by the movement.

A steady stream of rank-and-file W.S.P.U. members was also being arrested. In 1909, Marion Wallace Dunlop, who had been sent to prison for pro-women's suffrage acts of graffiti, introduced a new tactic: the hunger strike. The government was well aware that some of the Suffragettes were ready, quite literally, to die for the cause, and that if one died in prison the movement would have a martyr and the government a scandal. Wallace, therefore, managed to secure early release after having served only four days of her month-long sentence. Having produced such a result, this tactic was then generally adopted by Suffragette prisoners. Moreover, their tactics out-of-doors, as it were, had also been evolving.

In 1909, vandalism emerged as a standard method for making their point, beginning with throwing stones through the windows of government buildings. The government now responded to the hunger strikes with forcible feeding: a cruel, painful, revolting, and dangerous procedure. Scores of women had repeatedly undergone this ordeal before the year was out. With the situation mounting dangerously on both sides, in 1910 Parliament seemed finally to have a concrete scheme for women's suffrage in hand, the Conciliation Bill, which, if it had become law, would have enfranchised some women. The W.S.P.U. responded to this hopeful turn of events by calling a 'truce', that is, a cessation of militant activities.

This hiatus was short-lived. After complicated manœuvres by various politicians that aroused the suspicions of the Suffragettes, any immediate hopes were brought to an end when Parliament was dissolved. A wave of militancy was the response, especially window-breaking, including the

---

[10] Sylvia Pankhurst, *Suffragette Movement*, p. 290.

windows of some of the homes of cabinet ministers. The level of participation is indicated by the fact that within three days 285 arrests had
been made. The police responded to the mass demonstrations of the
women with spiteful, unnecessary violence; moreover, sexual assault now
became one of the hazards of participating in a W.S.P.U. demonstration.
'Black Friday' was the name given to the day (18 November 1910) that
marked this new turn of events. It was a massive clash with the police
from which numerous women returned with injuries and reports of
ill-usage. Such outrages only added fuel to the militant fire. Pankhurst
offered the following rationale for the move to vandalism: 'The women
would not yield. But that Black Friday struggle made them think again
that property, rather than their persons, might henceforth pay the price
of votes for women.' And again: 'our women were insisting that a broken
window was a lesser evil than a broken body'.[11]

After receiving additional evidence that the government was not going
to allow a women's suffrage bill to become law, the W.S.P.U. expanded its
tactics yet further. Moving beyond the property of the government and of
members of the government, window-breaking on a massive scale was
now undertaken in commercial districts of London. Sylvia Pankhurst
narrated with relish a major exercise along these lines which took place in
1912:

> On Friday, March 1st, at 4 p.m., whilst a conference was actually
> being held at Scotland Yard to devise measures for the protection of
> shopkeepers, an unadvertised outbreak occurred. In Piccadilly,
> Regent Street, Oxford Street, Bond Street, Coventry Street and their
> neighbourhood, in Whitehall, Parliament Street, Trafalgar Square,
> Cockspur Street and the Strand, as well as in districts so far away as
> Chelsea, well-dressed women suddenly produced strong hammers
> from innocent-looking bags and parcels, and fell to smashing the
> shop windows. There is nothing like a hammer for smashing plate
> glass; stones, even flints, are apt to glance off harmlessly. The
> hammers did terrible execution. . . . Jewellers were not spared. In
> fashionable Bond Street few windows remained. Police reserves were
> hurried out, shopkeepers were warned all over London, police
> stations were besieged with complaints. Mrs Pankhurst had mean-
> while driven to Downing Street in a taxi and broken some windows
> in the Prime Minister's residence.[12]

The response of the police was to put out warrants for the chief leaders of
the W.S.P.U. on the charge of conspiracy to commit damage to property.
Of the five persons so cited, Emmeline Pankhurst and Mabel Tuke were
already in police custody. Frederick and Emmeline Pethick Lawrence were

[11] Pankhurst, *Unshackled*, pp. 166, 169.
[12] Sylvia Pankhurst, *Suffragette Movement*, pp. 373–4.

picked up by the police at the headquarters of the W.S.P.U. The Pethick Lawrences were a wealthy couple who helped to bankroll the W.S.P.U. as well as to lead it, although Frederick would point out at his trial that as a man he was technically not a member: as a male who played a direct role in the W.S.P.U. his situation was *sui generis*. Christabel Pankhurst, however, was not there at the time. Writing after the struggle was over and subsequent to her Christian conversion, Pankhurst recounted the plot against them in biblical language: 'The Government's purpose was to hold the shepherds captive, while they did their utmost to scatter and suppress the flock.'[13] Her rather pedestrian narrative gains a burst of energy as she recounts her thoughts and movements at this time. First she went to a nursing home that the movement used for helping its members recover from hunger strikes and forced feedings:

> An inspiration came to them. They dressed me as a nurse! So dressed I went with one of them to the home of friends of hers, sympathizers, who lived in a flat not far away. They welcomed me. I had found a haven. Not long after I left the nursing home, where my too-well-known hat had just been reduced to ashes in the drawing-room fire, the police arrived to search for me! . . .
>
> I did not sleep at all that night for thinking. Suddenly, in the small hours, I saw what I must do! Escape! The Government should not defeat us. They should not break our movement. It must be preserved and the policy kept alive until the vote was won. My law studies had not been in vain. They had impressed indelibly upon my mind the fact that a political offender is not liable to extradition. . . . I must get to Paris, control the movement from there – and from there keep the fight going, until we won![14]

It is possible that she is over-egging all this in order to justify why she ended up living a life of comfort in Paris while her mother's health was being broken as her tally of hunger strikes mounted up to ten, with forced feedings now added to the ordeal. It may have even been that it was a pre-arranged plan between the mother and daughter that Pankhurst would relocate to France, but that she chose to recall it as an expedient of the moment. Nevertheless, the results were the same: Pankhurst remained in France until the Great War changed everything, leading the movement from there, writing articles for the W.S.P.U.'s newspaper, *The Suffragette*, and giving orders via faithful couriers, especially the ever loyal Annie Kenney. Pankhurst herself gave a blunt assessment of the resulting shift in power: 'I was now in solitary command of the W.S.P.U. and its movement.'[15] Although Pankhurst has subsequently been censured by some for her flight

---

[13] Pankhurst, *Unshackled*, p. 202.
[14] Pankhurst, *Unshackled*, pp. 203–4.
[15] Pankhurst, *Unshackled*, p. 216.

to Paris, it seems clear that at the time the police were very annoyed indeed to not be able to lay their hands on her, and the rank-and-file members of the W.S.P.U. were jubilant that she had so outwitted the authorities.

Militancy had not yet reached its zenith. W.S.P.U. members now set about vandalizing up and down the country, with arson, in particular, being added to their arsenal. Once again, Sylvia Pankhurst has provided a vivid inventory:

> golf greens all over the country scraped and burnt with acid. . . . Old ladies applied for gun licences to terrify the authorities. . . . There was a window-smashing raid in the West End club-land . . . Boat-houses and sports pavilions in England, Ireland and Scotland, and a grand-stand at Ayr race-course were burnt down. Mrs Cohen . . . broke the glass of a jewel-case in the Tower of London. Works of art and objects of exceptional value became the target of determined militants. Thirteen pictures were hacked in the Manchester Art Gallery. . . . Empty houses and other unattended buildings were systematically sought out and set on fire . . . Bombs were placed near the Bank of England . . . Lloyd George's new house in process of erection at Walton-on-the-Hill was injured beyond repair by a bomb explosion. . . . That this was the work of the Suffragettes was usually made evident by literature deposited in the vicinity.[16]

For its part, the government strove to find a duly heightened response. Its new weapon became the Prisoners (Temporary Discharge for Ill-Health) Act, the so-called 'Cat and Mouse' Act, which was made law on 25 April 1913. From then on, prisoners who obtained release by going on a hunger strike would have the clock stopped on their sentences and as soon as they had recovered – which would be amply demonstrated by, for example, attending a public meeting of the W.S.P.U., if not merely attempting to leave the house where they were staying – they would be re-arrested and their sentence would continue where it had left off. Therefore they would be subjecting their bodies to a continual tortuous cycle of hunger strikes with the seemingly inevitable effect of perman-ently damaging their health. Moreover, the government tried to drive *The Suffragette* out of existence by letting it be known that any publisher who took it on would be immediately arrested. One publisher was pros-ecuted for allowing a biblical quotation to be printed in *The Suffragette*, 'The people that walked in darkness have seen a great light' [Isaiah 9:2], a text that took on a rather different connotation in the context of an arson campaign! The playwright Bernard Shaw noted dryly:

> The Suffragettes have succeeded in driving the Cabinet half mad. Mr McKenna [the Home Secretary] should be examined at once by

[16] Sylvia Pankhurst, *Suffragette Movement*, pp. 434–5.

two doctors. He apparently believes himself to be the Tsar of Russia, a very common form of delusion.[17]

There were only two ways left to escalate militancy, either assaults on persons or a self-sacrificial death. The former was ruled out, but the latter now came. Emily Wilding Davison had already committed several acts that might have resulted in her own death while imprisoned for her efforts in the women's movement. Some said that she was unstable; others that she was an attention-seeker. Nevertheless, given the realities of the situation, it does seem to strike a note of grace that Davison was preserved from the banal prison deaths she had originally courted and allowed to extinguish her life in a brilliant piece of macabre choreography that would ensure that her name is remembered to this day along with the handful of other women who are deemed to have played the greatest roles in the movement. On Derby Day (4 June 1913), at just the right moment, Davison threw herself in front of the King's horse. She had sewn the W.S.P.U. colours (purple, white and green) on to the inside of her coat as a posthumous testimony to the cause for which she became a martyr.

Vandalism continued as well. On 10 March 1914 Mary Richardson slashed the Rokeby *Venus* in the National Gallery. She claimed at her trial that she had done it because the government was slowly murdering Emmeline Pankhurst. When the judge complained that the picture was irreplaceable, Richardson retorted that so was Mrs Pankhurst. Asquith continued to be harrassed. George Dangerfield noted:

> Mr Asquith's car was held up at Bannockburn, and he himself attacked with a horse-whip; while his visits to important cities were so invariably attended by false fire alarms, smashed windows, attacks on letter boxes, and other varieties of militancy that it grew positively unsafe to invite him.[18]

Moreover, Emmeline Pankhurst had appealed to the King (George V), and when word came back that he had been advised not to meet her, on 21 May 1914 she none the less led a deputation to Buckingham Palace that was also a mass demonstration, and that provoked another brutal clash with the police – as well as gangs of malicious men – reminiscent of 'Black Friday'. Thereafter, His Majesty was considered a fair target for heckling as well. At least on three occasions he was subjected to declaiming Suffragettes, including finding himself addressed across the audience at a theatre as 'You Russian Tsar!' by a woman who had taken the expedient of chaining herself to her seat before commencing her performance in order to hamper attempts to remove her. On 11 June 1914, while the Home

---

[17] George Dangerfield, *The Strange Death of Liberal England*, New York: Perigee Books, 1980 [originally 1935], p. 205.
[18] Dangerfield, *Strange Death*, p. 206.

Secretary, Reginald McKenna, was explaining to the House his policy for dealing with militant women, the Suffragettes set off a bomb in Westminster Abbey that damaged the Coronation Chair.

And then this low-level war was swept away by the Great War. The government ordered the release of Suffragette prisoners. Alive with patriotism, Emmeline Pankhurst and her eldest daughter were delighted to call another 'truce', give up militancy for the time being, and throw themselves and their organization wholeheartedly into the war effort. Christabel Pankhurst returned to England in September 1914 and promptly gave a speech on 'The German Peril'. *The Suffragette* newspaper was even renamed *Britannia*. Sylvia Pankhurst, who was naturally inclined to work for peace rather than victory, commented on her older sister's new outlet for her strategic mind in this considerably larger campaign:

> Christabel received the commendation of many war enthusiasts. Lord Northcliffe observed that she ought to be in the Cabinet. Lord Astor told me, when I happened to be seated beside him at dinner, that he had received two letters from her; he had sent one of them to the War Office, the other to the Minister of Blockade. Undoubtedly he was much impressed by their contents.[19]

A measure that allowed some women to vote in a British General Election became law on 6 February 1918.[20] Some measure was needed in order to deal with the nature of the existing legislation because its residency clause effectively disqualified servicemen and those who had moved in order to do war work on the home front from voting. According to Pankhurst's perspective, the government apparently had come to the conclusion that votes for women were inevitable and that it was better to take the lead during a 'truce' than to wait for a renewal of militancy. Asquith argued that the contribution which the women had made to the war effort had strengthened their claim. Thus in 1918 both of Christabel Pankhurst's great causes ended in victory – and a new cause came to her attention for the first time.

Sexual Intercourse

Pankhurst never married, nor is there any evidence that suggests that she ever showed any interest in having a romantic or sexual relationship with

---

[19] Sylvia Pankhurst, *Suffragette Movement*, p. 594.
[20] It is important to recall that men did not have adult suffrage at this time either. Nevertheless, the provisions of the bill deliberately made the qualifications for women more restrictive than those for men in order to ensure that women did not become the majority of voters. The bill gave the vote to women thirty years of age or older who were eligible to vote in local government elections or who were married to men who were.

a man. In 1921, no doubt because she needed the money, Pankhurst wrote an article for the *Weekly Dispatch* under the promising title, 'Confessions of Christabel, "Why I Never Married": First of a Candid Series', but her answer to the question implied in the title was primarily that the Suffragette cause had required her undivided attention.[21] The journalist Alma Whitaker claimed that when Pankhurst came to California in the early 1920s she had arranged dinner parties for her in order to see if American men might take her fancy, but her only report on the results was that she 'proved as enticing a guest as any movie star, and gay and witty withal'.[22] In fact, it has long been fashionable to hint that Pankhurst was a lesbian. As for lesbianism in the W.S.P.U., Dangerfield was commenting upon that already in 1935:

> it was from some secret yearning to recover the wisdom of women that the homosexual movement first manifested itself, in 1912, among the suffragettes. . . . And this pre-war lesbianism – which, in any case, was more sensitive than sensual – was without any question a striving towards life.[23]

David Mitchell, in the only biography of Pankhurst, underlined this point, and went on to suggest that Pankhurst was herself a lesbian. Even if he was right, however, the paucity of evidence offered made his argument weak. Mitchell took a general comment that she had made about 'filthy' writing by 'young flappers' and assumed that Pankhurst had lesbian writers in mind and that this comment reflected something more emotive than her numerous other conservative comments on a wide variety of social and cultural issues, concluding that this betrayed evidence of a homosexual orientation: 'it is hard not to suspect that Christabel's exaggerated horror at any attempt to explore the "abnormal" was at least to some extent the rage of Caliban at seeing his reflection in the glass'.[24] Recently, Martin Pugh has hinted that Pankhurst was a sexually active lesbian. An article in the *Observer* summarizing his views states that some of the W.S.P.U. women were having sex with each other. Moreover, Pugh was reported to have claimed that Pankhurst herself was included:

> Pugh now believes she was briefly involved with Mary Blathwayt who, in her turn, was probably supplanted by Annie Kenney, a working-class activist from Oldham. . . . The two were sent to prison together that year after disrupting a public meeting and had an

---

[21] *Weekly Dispatch*, 3 April 1921, p. 1.
[22] 'Pankhurst Tradition Whets Christabel's Steel for Satan', *Los Angeles Times*, 13 July 1943.
[23] Dangerfield, *Strange Death*, pp. 148–9.
[24] Mitchell, *Queen Christabel*, p. 301.

intimate friendship for several years until Christabel became involved with another woman, Grace Roe.[25]

In his recent book, however, although lesbianism is a recurring theme, he is much more guarded in his judgments. Even for the strongest cases on the basis on his evidence, Pugh cautions, 'one should resist the temptation to project the late twentieth-century's perceptions back to the late Victorian era'.[26] His final verdict on Pankhurst is: 'As a result the evidence about Christabel is inconclusive, though the probability is that her need for companionship did not go as far as physical relationships.'[27] 'Absent' or 'nonexistent' would have been more apt than 'inconclusive' as all that he offers leading up to this statement is the speculation that Suffragettes who were interviewed many years after the W.S.P.U. had ceased to function might have withheld something that they knew.

It may well have been that Pankhurst had a lesbian sexual orientation: to make a judgment one way or the other is beyond the evidence thus far available and, in any event, irrelevant to the theme of this study. Even the (groundless) assumption that Pankhurst was sexually active before her religious conversion in 1918 in no way undermines the central theme of this book: her religious ideas and ministry during the 1920s and beyond. The issue of her sexual orientation is only raised here at all as it does have some bearing on how one views the book on venereal diseases that she wrote during the Suffragette campaign, *The Great Scourge and How to End It* (1913). Pugh's evidence for the suggestion that lesbianism was rife in the W.S.P.U. cannot simply be ignored, and there is no doubt that Pankhurst was the object of enormous devotion and affection from some of the Suffragettes. Moreover, there was even gossip about her mother, Emmeline Pankhurst, that has survived. The author Virginia Woolf confided in a letter in 1933: 'In strict confidence, Ethel [Smyth] used to love Emmeline [Pankhurst] – they shared a bed.'[28] On the other hand, it does seem a little odd that, if Christabel Pankhurst had been sexually active, no gossip about her affairs has survived. It seems likely that this would have been a particularly tempting piece of intelligence to bandy about after her conservative religious turn. One suspects that, should it have existed, Sylvia Pankhurst could hardly have missed such talk, and would have relished it, given the way that she felt judged by Christabel for her own move toward free love. Yet her son, Richard Pankhurst, asserts: 'In my mother's day, people did not talk of C[hristabel] being a lesbian.

---

[25] 'Diary reveals lesbian love trysts of suffragette leaders', *Observer*, 11 June 2000, p. 14.

[26] Pugh, *Pankhursts*, p. 93.

[27] Pugh, *Pankhursts*, p. 213.

[28] Virginia Woolf to Quentin Bell, 3 December 1933: Nigel Nicolson (ed.), *The Sickle Side of the Moon: the Letters of Virginia Woolf, Volume V: 1932–1935*, London: The Hogarth Press, 1979, p. 256.

I suspect the idea may have been thought of only by later historians.'[29] Moreover, Pugh's own evidence is a primary source that names some of the Suffragettes as sharing beds, but which fails to name Pankhurst. Finally, and most germane to the theme of this study, one has to ask how probable it is that a sexually active lesbian would have written *The Great Scourge*.

The Great Scourge is an exposé on the subject of venereal diseases. We are told on the very first page of the introduction that these diseases are due to 'sexual immorality'.[30] Pankhurst calls upon men to observe 'the same moral standard as is observed by women'. Venereal disease is proclaimed to be a punishment for 'sin'. For those who hope for a medical cure, she warns against a 'reliance upon remedies as a substitute for clean living'. One passage seems to contain a condemnation of oral sex:

> They want to resort to practices which a wife would not tolerate. Lewdness and obscenity is what these men crave, and what they get in houses of ill-fame. Marriage does not 'satisfy' them. They fly to women who will not resent foul words and acts, and will even permit unnatural abuse of the sex function.[31]

Even masturbation seems to be ruled out in Pankhurst's moral vision: the male desire for ejaculation, if not found in the sexual union of a husband and his wife, is to be experienced only in 'an involuntary emission during sleep'.[32] The whole book is a tirade against the 'double standard of morality' and the solution is certainly not free love for women, but rather 'the observance by men of the same moral standard as that accepted by virtuous women'.[33] Pankhurst roundly condemned the suggestion that sexual freedom for women was the way forward:

> 'You are asking for political freedom,' women are told. 'More important to you is sex freedom. Votes for women should be accompanied, if not preceded, by wild oats for women. The thing to be done is not to raise the moral standard of men, but to lower the moral standard of women.' . . . When women have the vote, they will be more and not less opposed than now to making a plaything of sex and of entering casually into the sex relationship.[34]

It is theoretically possible that Pankhurst was being hypocritical, or not entirely candid. It is theoretically possible that she did not view a physical lesbian affair as sex at all. Alternatively, and more convincingly, she might

---

[29] Richard Pankhurst to Timothy Larsen, e-mail dated 21 March 2001.
[30] Christabel Pankhurst, *The Great Scourge and How to End It*, London: E. Pankhurst, 1913, p. v.
[31] Pankhurst, *Great Scourge*, p. 46.
[32] Pankhurst, *Great Scourge*, p. 57.
[33] Pankhurst, *Great Scourge*, pp. 85–6.
[34] Pankhurst, *Great Scourge*, p. 130.

have viewed the lesbian affairs she knew of (or participated in) as an expression of a true spiritual union and therefore moral. Such a view might be reconcilable with a particular reading of *The Great Scourge*, but it does not seem reconcilable with Pugh's portrait of Suffragette lesbians seemingly making new sexual conquests at a nightly rate. Moreover, for a such a position not to be hypocritical by creating a new 'double standard', it ought to include unmarried men who open themselves up emotionally to a series of mistresses, but Pankhurst's strong disapproval of such a scenario is unequivocal. In fact, the most obvious reading of the book is that it is a sincere and candid work in a long line of campaigning for sexual purity that aimed at bolstering traditional Christian sexual morality. This tradition certainly had a place in the historic feminist movement, most notably through the widely admired work of the Christian social reformer, Josephine Butler (1828–1906), whose attack on the government's assumption that soldiers required prostitutes was argued from the perspective that the normative standard for British society ought to be sexual 'purity'.[35]

The Great Scourge was certainly *received* as a voice in favour of traditional Christian morality, and thus it provides an interesting point of continuity between Pankhurst's pre-conversion and post-conversion life. In the year of its publication, 1913, Rebecca West – who had just begun her famous love affair with H. G. Wells, which would produce a love-child the following year – claimed that the book expressed views 'that would be old-fashioned and uncharitable in the pastor of a Little Bethel'.[36] Sylvia Pankhurst noted:

> The propaganda for sexual purity made strong appeal to the clergy . . . Votes for Women had made great advances amongst the clergy during the years 1913–14, the period in which the W.S.P.U. had shrieked this propaganda of 'chastity for men' in every key of vehemence and excitement. A number of clergy were ardent supporters of the W.S.P.U., speaking from its platforms, contributing to its organ, hailing the militants as heroines and martyrs.[37]

Likewise Dangerfield remarked:

> VOTES FOR WOMEN AND PURITY FOR MEN was Christabel's new slogan. . . . Both the slogan and *The Great Scourge* became popular with evangelical clergymen, who took to distributing the pamphlet among the faithful; and many a Boys' Club and

[35] For a recent study of Butler and Christianity, see Helen Mathers, 'The Evangelical Spirituality of a Victorian Feminist: Josephine Butler, 1828–1906', *Journal of Ecclesiastical History*, 52, 2 (2001), pp. 282–312.
[36] Mitchell, *Queen Christabel*, p. 228.
[37] Sylvia Pankhurst, *Suffragette Movement*, p. 523.

Men's Bible Class must have sat and shivered at the thought of unguessed contamination as Miss Christabel's amazing pages were read aloud.[38]

It is certainly possible that Pankhurst's sexual orientation was same-sex, but it is entirely reasonable to assume that her sexual morality conformed to conservative Christian mores.

Religious Background

A study of Christabel Pankhurst and religion is long overdue. Pankhurst is a well-known figure in British history and her contribution to an intriguing section of the religious world of her day was extensive, high-profile and significant. Even leaving aside her religious work, Pankhurst has not been favoured with much attention by the scholarly community. Her sister, Sylvia, although less famous than Christabel, was the subject of no less than six scholarly biographies or monographs in the 1990s alone.[39] Christabel Pankhurst, however, has only ever been the central figure of one book, David Mitchell's *Queen Christabel*, a book written a quarter of a century ago. Moreover, Mitchell's lack of interest in the kind of questions that a religious historian would ask leaves one, after reading his biography from cover to cover, still uninformed about something as basic as her denominational identity. Pugh's recent study of the Pankhursts does not provide this rudimentary information either.[40] In fact, Pankhurst identified with the Church of England and its sister churches in North America. The ignorance and confusion that persists on even such an elementary point is illustrated by the fact that it has become standard for scholars to claim that she was a Seventh-Day Adventist.[41]

---

[38] Dangerfield, *Strange Death*, pp. 199–200.
[39] Ian Bullock, *Sylvia Pankhurst: From Artist to Anti-Fascist*, Basingstoke: Macmillan, 1992; Mary Davis, *Sylvia Pankhurst: A Life in Radical Politics*, Sterling, Va.: Pluto Press, 1999; Andrea M. Lindsay, *The Role of Sylvia Pankhurst in the Italo-Abyssinian Conflict*, Ottawa: National Library of Canada, 1990; Rosemary Taylor, *In Letters of Gold: The Story of Sylvia Pankhurst and the East London Federation of the Suffragettes in Bow*, London: Stepney Books, 1993; Patricia W. Romero, *E. Sylvia Pankhurst: Portrait of a Radical*, New Haven: Yale University Press, 1990; and Barbara Winslow, *Sylvia Pankhurst: Sexual Politics and Political Activism*, London: UCL Press, 1996.
[40] Pugh, *Pankhursts*.
[41] See, for example, Gail Malmgreen (ed.), *Religion in the Lives of English Women, 1760–1930*, Bloomington: Indiana University Press, 1986, p. 6; Marie Mulvey Roberts, 'Introduction', in Christabel Pankhurst, *The Militant* [a reprint of *Unshackled*] (eds Marie Mulvey Roberts and Tamae Mizuta), London: Routledge/ Thoemmes Press, 1995, p. xiv.

Pankhurst actually inhabited a religious milieu that considered Seventh-Day Adventists an heretical sect.[42] A book on the theme of Christ's return published in 1928 by Marshall, Morgan & Scott, the same conservative evangelical publishing company that published Pankhurst's books in Britain, listed 'Seventh Day Adventism' as one of the 'Modern Cults' that comprised part of 'The Religious Signs of His Coming'.[43] The *Advent Witness*, a newspaper that promoted Pankhurst's ministry, considered Seventh-Day Adventism one of the 'modern heresies'.[44] In short, scholars hitherto have demonstrated scant grasp of the contours of Pankhurst's religious world.

The religious background regarding Pankhurst's father has not been adequately understood either. Sylvia Pankhurst was an extraordinary woman who in recent years has benefited from extensive and often openly admiring attention from the scholarly community. Nevertheless, in order to understand Christabel Pankhurst and her background more accurately, one must break the spell of Sylvia's enchanting portrait of her family and the women's movement. When Winston Churchill published his history of the Great War, *The World Crisis*, in the 1920s, Samuel Hoare pronounced: 'Winston has written a huge book all about himself and called it "The World Crisis."'[45] In the same way, Sylvia Pankhurst wrote a magnificent book largely about herself and called it *The Suffragette Movement* (1931). We get the history of the W.S.P.U. through the decorations that Sylvia made to mark its great events. The book also offers a curious history of a women's movement in that the two great leaders who were at the head of the W.S.P.U. – Emmeline and Christabel Pankhurst – are repeatedly criticized, but two men are brought centre stage as irreproachable alternative heroes, Richard Pankhurst and Keir Hardie.

For the discussion at hand, it is most important to realize that Sylvia Pankhurst uses her account to settle old scores and justify her choices in life. Thus, at its most banal, we get a couple of paragraphs narrating how, when they were schoolgirls, Christabel received a better bicycle than her younger sister and would not cycle slower in order to allow Sylvia, who was labouring away on an inferior model, to keep up with her.[46]

---

[42] Pankhurst was an 'Adventist' – sometimes also termed 'Second Adventist' in the literature – in the generic sense of a Christian who is expecting the return of Christ, with the added implications that this point is particularly stressed as one of the most important messages that needs to be proclaimed and that Christ's return is considered imminent.

[43] Herbert W. Cox, *Epochs Connected with the Second Coming of Christ*, London: Marshall, Morgan & Scott, 1928, p. 24.

[44] *Advent Witness*, 1 May 1930, p. 80.

[45] In a similar vein, Arthur Balfour dubbed it, 'Winston's magnificent autobiography, disguised as a history of the universe'.

[46] Sylvia Pankhurst, *Suffragette Movement*, pp. 139–40.

An example of how Sylvia's account needs to be handled critically in the light of her own views is a little comment she makes about her mother's courtship with her father: 'She proposed that they should manifest both their independence of spirit and their solidarity with the suffering of unhappy wives, by dispensing with the legal formalities in their own marriage.'[47] This is an incongruous anecdote given the fact that the picture of Emmeline Pankhurst offered elsewhere in the book is of a fastidious Victorian lady, arguably a different kind of caricature arising from Sylvia's frustrations at her mother's restrictive conventions. On one occasion in Sylvia's account we are told how Emmeline left a political meeting rather too promptly: 'Outside she told us that she had found a bug on her glove, and therefore could not bear to remain any longer.'[48] We are told concerning Emmeline's later experiences in prison, which included the horrors of forcible feeding: 'she had been forcibly stripped and searched each time she was brought in, an indignity which wounded her more than physical suffering'.[49] The most likely reading is that Sylvia included the line about her mother's alleged offer to live with her father out of wedlock as a way of justifying her own decision to co-habit. Therefore, the question is: how much can we then presume to learn about Emmeline from this anecdote? After all, Emmeline and Richard did legally marry and we apparently only have Sylvia's word that any other possibility was ever even contemplated. Given her personal interest in the matter, is it not a strong possibility that she made more than was warranted of a passing comment made by her mother or father or someone who knew them at the time?

This leads on to the more germane question of the religious life of Christabel's and Sylvia's father. Sylvia was, according to her son, 'a life-long atheist'.[50] In *The Suffragette Movement*, the girls' father, Richard Pankhurst, is painted as a thorough-going agnostic and their childhood as more or less anti-Christian, but might not this have been over-played in order to add validity to Sylvia's adult choices? It is certainly true that Richard Pankhurst withdrew from organized religion and adopted scep-tical views, but an accurate picture might be more complex than the one that Sylvia painted. A dig at Christabel's post-W.S.P.U. path in life would certainly seem the most likely reason why we are informed that Richard Pankhurst told his children: 'If you ever go back into religion you will not have been worth the upbringing!'[51] In the presentation of her father that Sylvia offers, any commitment he might have had to organized religion is

---

[47] Sylvia Pankhurst, *Suffragette Movement*, p. 56.
[48] Sylvia Pankhurst, *Suffragette Movement*, p. 111.
[49] Sylvia Pankhurst, *Suffragette Movement*, p. 589.
[50] Introduction by Richard Pankhurst in Sylvia Pankhurst, *Suffragette Movement*, p. [iv].
[51] Sylvia Pankhurst, *Suffragette Movement*, p. 110.

relegated to days of immaturity and explained away as a product of his upbringing: 'As a youth he had been an earnest adherent of his father's faith, and had taught in the Baptist Sunday Schools.'[52] This has become the standard view. Pugh, for example, follows this lead: 'In his youth he taught in a Baptist Sunday School, though he became so disillusioned by the poverty of the children he saw there that he lost his faith and became an agnostic.'[53]

Richard Pankhurst may have actually been committed to organized Christianity for most of his adult life. He joined Union Chapel, Oxford Road, Manchester, where the prominent Baptist minister Alexander McLaren was the pastor, in July 1861 at the age of twenty-six. The church records do not appear to mention any other Pankhursts, so it is possible that this was a different congregation from that of his parents. This was certainly the choice of an adult, rather than a youth. Moreover, he maintained his membership there until July 1874, by which time he was thirty-nine years old.[54] Sylvia herself admits that her father was part of Paxton Hood's break-away congregation which met in Hulme town hall for a year beginning in mid-1880. She justifies this by saying that her father was showing solidarity with Hood who had been forced out of the congregation he had been serving, Cavendish Street Congregational Church, Manchester, owing to his vocal denunciation of Disraeli's foreign policy. But while there is no doubt that Richard Pankhurst would have been delighted to have a minister who was opposed to conservative politics, and perhaps he was unwilling to have any other kind of minister, it is highly improbable that he was an ardent unbeliever who was joining in corporate Christian worship as a way of endorsing another man's stand on a point of principle.[55] Union Chapel, was so named because it was comprised of a union between Baptists and Congregationalists. Thus a move to Cavendish Street Congregational Church would have been a perfectly natural one for him in terms of continuity of religious experience. The *Manchester Guardian* reported upon his death that Richard Pankhurst had 'gathered round the ministry of Mr Paxton Hood', which can be read as a longer-term commitment than merely the Hulme town hall ending.[56] It is possible that he had heard reports about Hood and, liking what he heard, had

---

[52] Sylvia Pankhurst, *Suffragette Movement*, p. 18.
[53] Pugh, *Pankhursts*, p. 16.
[54] 'Union Chapel Oxford Road and Union Chapel Fallowfield Church Register, 1842–February 1977': from notes taken by Professor Clyde Binfield of Sheffield when this source was in the care of the church at Fallowfield.
[55] The political element–which was a real enough component in the situation, albeit an insufficient one on its own to prompt a life of worship–would certainly have helped Sylvia to remember it and have made it more likely to be mentioned in later years.
[56] *Manchester Guardian*, 6 July 1898.

therefore begun attending Cavendish Street shortly after the new minister's arrival in 1877. It is even possible that he had moved straight from Union to Cavendish in 1874, or that he had attended another place of worship for the few years in between. In any event, it is indisputable that Richard Pankhurst – who died at the age of sixty-three – was habitually attending orthodox Christian worship at the age of forty-six.

Was Christabel Pankhurst ever baptized? Sylvia's son, Richard Keir Pethick Pankhurst, states unequivocally that Sylvia was not baptized as an infant (nor, of course, thereafter): 'It was, given Richard Marsden [Pankhurst]'s agnostic views (see the Suffragette Movement), unthinkable that my mother would have been baptized, and I know from her that she was not.'[57] However, given the assumption that *The Suffragette Movement* cannot be accepted uncritically, and the known fact that Christabel's father was sitting under Paxton Hood's ministry at the time of her birth, it cannot be taken for granted that Christabel was not baptized. Although one can take Sylvia's son's statement that his mother was never baptized as given, Sylvia was born after her father had ceased to attend corporate worship, while Christabel was born on 22 September 1880 when he was actively involved in congregational life. Moreover, although Richard Pankhurst is invariably put down as a lapsed 'Baptist', and thus infant baptism would not have come into it, it has already been demonstrated that he might well have been a Congregationalist, a form of Protestantism that does practise infant baptism. He had after all chosen a half-Congregationalist and then an all-Congregationalist congregation: these being the only two denominational choices he made that are on record. It is possible that Christabel was baptized as an infant.

If Christabel Pankhurst was *not* baptized as an infant, then we have to wonder whether or not she ever was. There is certainly something unexpected about the notion that she gave herself wholeheartedly to Christian thought and ministry for over thirty-five years and even declared herself to be 'a member of the Church of England' and yet was never baptized.[58] It seems much more probable that she either was baptized as an infant, that she *thought* she had been baptized as an infant, or that she chose to undergo baptism as an adult. Given her respect for Anglican teaching and her resolute acceptance of Christian orthodoxy, it is less probable that she would have known that she was not baptized and yet decided that it did not matter.

This raises the issue of more general limitations for scholars who wish to study Christabel Pankhurst. Firstly, very few private papers or letters

---

[57] Richard Pankhurst to Timothy Larsen, e-mail dated 21 March 2001.
[58] *Present and Future*, May 1934, p. 2. Baptism is a requirement for membership in the Church of England, although in practice this might be assumed and therefore overlooked.

from her religious period have apparently survived. Secondly, the numerous publications and printed records of her speeches all indicate that she was reticent to speak about her own experiences and feelings. This is perhaps one of the less obvious reasons why studying Sylvia has been so much more inviting for scholars than studying Christabel. Sylvia has left rich records of her emotional reactions and personal life. Sylvia's history of the Suffragette movement is a vibrant, engaging read, whilst Christabel's account of the same movement is a rather anaemic one that is largely saved by the excitement and interest inherent in the subject-matter. In their Suffragette days, for example, Christabel made it a matter of policy not to speak about her prison experiences, while Sylvia was all for narrating in great detail every inconvenience and petty deprivation. Sylvia recollected, 'Christabel, however, thought otherwise. She told me on her release that too much fuss had been made about the violence; she was ever a stoic in such matters.'[59] Thus it would have been just like Christabel Pankhurst, if she had accepted baptism as an adult, never to find a reason to mention this personal detail in her writings and speeches. This paucity of material hinders confident pronouncements on other subjects as well, notably, for this study, the contours of her conversion experience.

Having argued that Richard Pankhurst's commitment to Christianity lasted far longer than Sylvia indicated, it is nevertheless quite true that he withdrew from congregational life and became an agnostic. The implications of these facts for Christabel Pankhurst's life are that she received no formal religious education, she was not socialized into the Christian life through habitual acts of corporate worship or family religious devotions, and she was exposed to sceptical religious ideas during her childhood. Whatever knowledge she gained of orthodox Christian thought would have come primarily through private reading and informal conversations, probably supplemented by various special occasions that prompted attending a Christian service of worship such as rites of passage in the lives of people in their social world. Even as an adult, there is no evidence that Pankhurst habitually attended Christian worship prior to her conversion in 1918. On the other hand, it was very difficult to be an educated person at that time without imbibing a certain level of biblical and theological literacy. W.S.P.U. materials, for example, often contained biblical quotations.

It is tempting to speculate that Pankhurst's fascination with the Bible began when prison life made it one of the few diversions available. Even Sylvia, who proved to be permanently immune to religion, found that the Bible was better than nothing. Her son reports, 'My mother read the

---

[59] Sylvia Pankhurst, *Suffragette Movement*, p. 298.

Bible very extensively when she was in prison (there being no other literature), so she was very Bible-literate.'[60] Indeed, Sylvia's own account makes clear how large the Bible loomed in her imagination while in prison:

> I wrote verse as the most concentrated form of expression [given the need to conserve her small supply of paper], and the greater part of a play dealing with the Biblical story of David and Bathsheba. I hoped to complete it after release . . . Another time it was Ezekiel xxxiv., where it is told that the shepherds have eaten the fat and clothed themselves in the wool, but they have neither cared for the sick nor sought the lost. . . Reading the words I saw in my mind's eye a group of shepherds feasting together on the edge of a cliff beside a fire at which they had roasted a young lamb. . . . Here was another picture for my slate, but a slate is a dismal thing to draw on; one cannot long retain one's zeal in making drawings to rub out. . . . At night I scarcely slept . . . Passages from the Bible I had read during the day brought resplendent visions. 'How beautiful upon the mountains are the feet of him that bringeth good tidings that publisheth peace.' [Isaiah 52:7][61]

Christabel's narrative, as ever, is less revealing. Nevertheless, when recounting her own prison experience, she did recall: 'A Bible lay on the table, and for that much thanks! . . . Imprisonment was solitary, save for the time in chapel.'[62] In 1927, once her reputation as a Christian speaker was well-established, Pankhurst was asked to address the International Christian Police Association in London. In the course of her survey of the criminal justice system she remarked: 'Then the prisons. Let us be thankful that in every cell there is a Bible; there are chaplains, and ministers.'[63] Some scholars affect a knowing tone about her eventual move toward religion, pointing out her quasi-religious view of the Suffragette movement reflected in her promotion of Joan of Arc as a role model, and her increasingly moralistic and 'apocalyptic' tone. It is more accurate, however, to say simply that the new direction for her life that she first hit upon in 1918 was far from inevitable and could not have been predicted. The *Manchester Guardian* claimed in 1926: 'It would be almost impossible, I think, to cite a stranger conversion in our time than that of Christabel Pankhurst.'[64]

---

[60] Richard Pankhurst to Timothy Larsen, e-mail dated 21 March 2001.
[61] Sylvia Pankhurst, *Suffragette Movement*, p. 445.
[62] Pankhurst, *Unshackled*, p. 53.
[63] 'Christabel Pankhurst to the London Police: An Address by Miss Christabel Pankhurst at the Annual Meeting of the International Christian Police Association, London, Eng.' *Moody Bible Institute Monthly*, September 1927, pp. 10–14.
[64] 'Miss Christabel Pankhurst as Evangelist', *Manchester Guardian*, 20 August 1926.

Conversion Experience

As with most of her accounts of her personal experience, Pankhurst's narrative of her conversion leaves a lot to be desired. The principal source is the chapter, 'How I Learned of His Coming', in her first religious book, *'The Lord Cometh': The World Crisis Explained* (1923), and her comments on this matter elsewhere are basically recapitulations of it. It is therefore worth quoting at length:

> This faith, that Jesus will soon come again, first dawned upon me in 1918. When the acute danger of the earlier months of that year were over, with the Allied Armies on the way to victory, one could review the experience of the War, and, in the light of it, envisage the future. . . .
>
> Considering the issues, the events, and the currents and cross-currents of the War, and relating it, also, to the history of times past, and having regard to the way things go and ever have gone, even in times of peace, this is what I realised as I never had realised it before: – It is not laws, nor institutions, nor any national or international machinery that are at fault, but human nature itself. . . .
>
> Dark, dark was the future as I looked into a vista of new warfare, with intervals of strain, of stress, of international intrigue, of horrible preparations and inventions for slaughter . . .
>
> Just then, by what seemed a chance-discovery in a bookshop, I came across writings on Prophecy which pointed out that in the Bible there are oracles foretelling and diagnosing the world's ills, and promising that they shall be cured. Until that day I had taken the prophecies of the Bible no more seriously than a great many other people still do take them. I had simply ignored them . . . But now I eagerly followed up the clue which this bookshop discovery had given me. . . .
>
> 'Ah! That is the solution!' My heart stirred to it. My practical political eye saw that this Divine Programme is absolutely the only one that can solve the international, social, political or moral problems of the world. The only trouble was, that it seemed too good to be true. . . .
>
> For a long time, too, mine seemed too fragile a flower of belief to speak of, and expose to the cold wind of other people's possible scepticism.[65]

Although she retold it, the pattern was always the same: she was disillusioned about the possibility of human beings creating a good world, she came across a book on biblical prophecy (the book and its contents will

[65] Christabel Pankhurst, *'The Lord Cometh': The World Crisis Explained*, London: Morgan & Scott, 1923, pp. 8–13.

be discussed in the next chapter), and then she realized that Christ was coming again and that his return was the true answer to the world's problems. In one speech she did give a slightly more precise dating of this event: 'It was in the happier days, between Easter 1918 and the Armistice [11 November 1918].'[66]

The evangelical Christian world accepted her testimony with unquestioning gratitude. *Moody Bible Institute Monthly* ran an article in 1923 under the title 'Miss Pankhurst's Conversion', which proclaimed dramatically that 'her eyes have been opened, and that she has caught the true vision', but these were inferences made from the fact that a speech she gave was filled with sound doctrine and biblical truth, as conceived from a conservative evangelical perspective.[67] When her religious turn was announced in the *Christian* newspaper on the basis of some of her speeches and interviews – and before she had published the account quoted above – the final paragraph stated:

> A Canadian friend, when sending the above newspaper clipping, wrote: – 'Miss Pankhurst has most manifestly been soundly converted, and in addressing the students of the Toronto University, she spoke scripturally and powerfully of Sin, of the Blood of Christ, and of things to come.'[68]

This account is literally true in the sense that it was readily apparent that Pankhurst heartily believed evangelical Christian doctrine and therefore she must have come to believe in it at some point, a process one could call her 'conversion'. Nevertheless, Pankhurst's own account lacks virtually all the components of a standard evangelical testimony of personal salvation. So much so, in fact, that it could just as well be the story of how someone who was already a born-again Christian came to develop a new interest in or view of eschatology or biblical hermeneutics. There is no mention of repentance, no mention of asking Jesus to become her personal Saviour, no mention of prayer at all. Her personal emotions – a movement from utter despair and fear to great joy and peace on an individual, emotional level – are not nearly as much to the fore as they are in a typical evangelical conversion narrative. If one attempted to 'fill in the blanks', as it were, and reconstruct a traditional conversion narrative from her account, then the most promising clue for such a task is her mention of her new understanding of the inherent sinfulness of human nature: even that phrase, however, doctors up the language she actually used in order to add more content from a conservative theological perspective. Her aversion to speaking about her own experience together

---

[66] *Christian*, 23 September 1926, p. 5.
[67] *Moody Bible Institute Monthly*, September 1923, p. 14.
[68] *Christian*, 4 January 1923, p. 9.

with her irrepressible didactic instincts caused her habitually to express that point in general, collective terms, whereas a more conventional evangelical account would stress an awareness of one's personal sinfulness, and might well even make explicit that the person had become convinced that she was one of the worst sinners in all the world – despite the fact that her conscience was troubled by named violations of God's law that would appear to any outside observer as mere peccadilloes. The closest Pankhurst came to a more personal account on this point is the following, a confession still couched in the plural: 'Some of us have been in a fools' paradise and we thank God that our eyes are opened. Our experience educates us and we become acquainted with ourselves and we know that there is none that is good among us; no, not one.'[69] This does read as a true account of a new insight that she had that caused her to reconsider the basis for hope in the future in the light of the human condition. Therefore, once again, if one wished to transpose her song of salvation into a more standard key then it might sound something like this: she became aware that she was a sinner and that Jesus was the Saviour who could deal with her sin and she therefore put her faith in him. What Pankhurst actually offered, however, was primarily an account of her intellectual excitement at having made a connection between her interest in the world situation and its future and a newly appreciated biblical-theological timetable and overarching divine plan. A summary of one speech she gave claimed that she had 'spoken of the revelation by the Holy Spirit to herself, of her own sinful condition', but it is difficult to tell how much the reporter might have read between the lines of a more general statement.[70] Nevertheless, there is no doubt that she thought there had been a transition in her adult experience when she had moved from 'the unregenerated to the regenerated'. In one address she declared that she had 'come out of the world', and she reminisced about when she had been 'in the world' – classic evangelical language regarding the difference between a pre-conversion and post-conversion state.[71]

The Road to Ministry

The next stage was for her to make contact with like-minded believers. Her reading and thinking and, presumably, praying were moving her toward a stance that no one in her social world took. Pankhurst later recalled: 'At first I hardly liked to speak of this thing that I had realized then for the first time. I hid the book away, taking it out only when I was

---

[69] *New York Times*, 16 August 1923, p. 15.
[70] *Christian*, 14 October 1926, p. 37.
[71] *Moody Bible Institute Monthly*, March 1924, pp. 337–9.

alone, to comfort me.'[72] This period of private reflection, which was probably one marked by only intermittent interest in matters religious, apparently lasted for three years from around the summer of 1918 to the summer of 1921. In retrospect, one can see a glimpse of her private meditations in an article she wrote on her Suffragette work that was published in April 1921 in which she drew upon biblical language:

> A cloud no bigger than a woman's hand, the cloud of militancy, had appeared in the sky when his [Asquith's] party took office in 1906. Could they have read the signs of the times they would have made all haste to give women the vote . . .'[73]

Pankhurst dated her introduction to people from the religious subculture that her new reading matter reflected from shortly before her trip to North America in August 1921:

> When I first read about this great truth I longed to hear of sermons on the subject, but could not. At last, I saw in the personal columns of *The Times* about the monthly conference at Kingsway. I was, at that time, packing up to go to America and Canada, but I went to the Kingsway Hall, and got in just in time to hear Dr Meyer.[74]

Once again, her reading – this time of newspapers – led the way. What she saw in *The Times* was an advertisement for the monthly meeting of the Advent Testimony Movement, a conservative evangelical organization founded in 1917 in order to proclaim the imminent return of Christ. An evangelical, in the context of English-speaking Protestantism, is a person who lays particular stress on the authority of the Bible, the work of Christ on the cross as an act of atonement for human sin, the need for a conversion experience, and the obligation upon all Christians to share the gospel with unbelievers and to pursue good works with industry and dedication. A 'conservative' evangelical in the early twentieth century was an evangelical whose instinct was to reassert these distinctives defiantly in the face of contemporary challenges to them, in contrast to 'liberal' evangelicals, who sought to find new, more currently acceptable ways to articulate evangelical principles. 'Fundamentalists', during this period, were 'conservative evangelicals', though the latter term is slightly broader.[75] F. B. Meyer, a Baptist, and the most prominent and respected English conservative evangelical minister of the day, was an ideal person to serve as Pankhurst's sponsor.

---

[72] *Christian*, 21 October 1926, p. 24.
[73] *Weekly Dispatch*, 17 April 1921, p. 5. The first phrase of this quotation is a play on 1 Kings 18:44, and reading the signs of the times was central to the Christian ministry she would pursue for the rest of her working life.
[74] *Christian*, 16 September 1926, p. 5.
[75] See D. W. Bebbington, *Evangelicalism in Modern Britain: A History from the 1730s to the 1980s*, London: Unwin Hyman, 1989.

He was not only the chairman of the Advent Testimony Movement, and a director of the important evangelical newspaper, the *Christian* (and therefore also a man of influence at the solid evangelical publishing house Morgan & Scott), but also a well-known and well-respected figure on the North American evangelical scene. Meyer was a first-rate visa into the entire world of transatlantic conservative evangelicalism.

Once in North America, Pankhurst appealed to Meyer for information on how to connect with like-minded believers in her new context: 'She proceeded to record how, in America, she searched for a place where she might hear the Advent message proclaimed, and eventually got courage to write to Dr Meyer for help.'[76] Working her way into the network, she learned that A. C. Gaebelein was one of the leading speakers and writers on biblical prophecy and the return of Christ and the editor of an important newspaper on the subject, *Our Hope*, and that he was in California – where Pankhurst was living at that time – as a visiting preacher. Gaebelein recorded his first encounter with her in his autobiography, in a narrative that cleverly endeavoured to garner credit – undue, as this study makes clear – for Pankhurst's ministry while avoiding actually endorsing it:

> On one of my last visits, I think it was in 1922, a lady stepped to the front to greet me. She expressed herself enthusiastically over what she had heard. She said how very much it had helped her and opened her eyes to many things. She wanted *Our Hope* and later ordered my books for study. She handed me her card and it informed me the lady was Miss Christobel [sic] Pankhurst, living then in Hollywood. Since that time Miss Pankhurst has become an interesting lecturer and writer on prophetic truths.[77]

Mitchell has noted that while in California Pankhurst gave lectures to various 'women's clubs' that betrayed her religious turn: 'But her audiences were disconcerted when she ended a talk on the W.S.P.U. or a survey of world affairs with a tailpiece on biblical prophecy.'[78]

By the summer of 1923, Christabel Pankhurst had moved to Toronto in order to join her mother who was already living there. When A. B. Winchester, a leading Toronto minister and a well-known figure in the wider world of North American evangelicalism, visited the West Coast in May 1922 his contacts there were already buzzing with the intelligence that Pankhurst had adopted their cause:

> While ministering in one of our Pacific Coast cities last May, I was asked by a Christian brother if I had met Miss Christabel Pankhurst,

[76] *Christian*, 16 September 1926, p. 5.
[77] Arno Clemens Gaebelein, *Half a Century: The Autobiography of a Servant*, New York: Our Hope Offices, 1930, pp. 208–9.
[78] Mitchell, *Queen Christabel*, pp. 286–7.

who was then in that city. Or had I heard of the wonderful change that had come into her life? To both questions I had to reply in the negative. He assured me he had heard her give a remarkable address, in which she rang true to the great cardinal doctrines of our Christian faith.[79]

Winchester had been for the first couple of decades of the twentieth century the minister of Knox Presbyterian Church, Toronto, a large, powerful, flagship evangelical church. By this time he had an itinerant ministry, but one sponsored by Knox, where he carried the official title 'minister extra muros' (minister outside the walls), and where he still exerted considerable influence, not least over his young successor, J. G. Inkster.[80] Winchester wrote an account of the launch of Pankhurst's public Christian ministry:

> On my return in September to Toronto, and learning that Miss Pankhurst was residing here with her mother, I told my beloved colleague and successor, Rev J. G. Inkster, B.A., about her. After satisfying himself about the case, with the consent of the Kirk Session, he invited Miss Pankhurst to speak in Knox Church. She refused, on the ground that she desired more time for meditation in the Word of God, and more time for communing with the Lord before she would venture forth on public service again. Mr Inkster, being a man of God who had himself experienced a remarkable spiritual change many years after his ordination, was so impressed with her unique testimony – one so greatly needed in these 'last days', that he felt it was of the Lord that he should gently urge her to reconsider. She consented to speak on the following Sunday evening. Every available bit of space in the church auditorium was filled a good while before the time for service.[81]

The notion that Pankhurst was inclined to refuse is consistent with her own self-assessment of her desires. A summary of a sermon that she delivered in New York City in August 1923 stated: 'She had been in this country about a year she said at the close of the service. She went to Canada to rest and with a resolution never to make anything in the nature of a speech again in all her life.'[82] Nevertheless, her debut was so successful that Knox decided to ask her to deliver a series of seven Sunday evening addresses, an offer that she also accepted. The Kirk Session of Knox Presbyterian Church, Toronto, was able to look back on 1922 with satisfaction:

> During the Minister's vacation, Rev Dr Gaebelein occupied the pulpit on Sundays and conducted a week's special meetings, all of

[79] *Christian*, 29 March 1923, p. 20.
[80] William Fitch, *Knox Church Toronto*, Toronto: John Deyell, 1971, pp. 58–9.
[81] *Christian*, 29 March 1923, p. 20.
[82] *New York Times*, 16 August 1923, p. 15.

which were well attended. We also were privileged to hear that talented servant of our Master, Miss Christabel Pankhurst, who held a week's meetings last November. The freshness and earnestness of her wonderful testimony led many, we believe, to put their trust in the Saviour.[83]

After that, pulpits across North America were open to her and her ministry began in earnest.

Pankhurst's work as a Christian writer has also been neglected. Her entry in the *Dictionary of National Biography* fails even to mention that she wrote books on religious themes, let alone name a single title.[84] Nevertheless, her Christian writing career took off as quickly as her speaking one, and with the same good measure of success. In 1923, she published her first book on religion: *'The Lord Cometh': The World Crisis Explained*. For the North American market, it was published in New York by Book Stall, while in Britain it was published in London by Morgan & Scott. F. B. Meyer wrote the introduction. It sold very well: in the year after its publication reprints had already brought the print run up to 21,000.[85] The seventh edition was issued in 1928, and a 'popular' edition in 1934. In 1924, Morgan & Scott published her book *Pressing Problems of the Closing Age*. It was first published in October, and a second impression was already in print before the year was out. With only minor changes, this book appeared for the North American market with a different title, *Some Modern Problems in the Light of Bible Prophecy*. The publisher for this book was the Fleming H. Revell Company, a solidly evangelical New York firm. F. B. Meyer again wrote an introduction that appeared in both the British and the American versions. In 1926 came *The World's Unrest: Visions of the Dawn*. Morgan & Scott again published the British edition. The American edition was issued by another major evangelical operation, the Sunday School Times Company of Philadelphia, and the mainstream publishing house of Harper in New York apparently produced an edition of this book at some point as well. By February 1926, the *Christian* newspaper was referring to her as 'Miss Christabel Pankhurst, the well-known writer', but as it was also published by Morgan & Scott, this must be somewhat discounted as a piece of puffery, albeit not a risibly ill-fitting one.[86] In 1929, Harper & Brothers of New York published *Seeing the Future*.

---

[83] Knox Presbyterian Church Archives, Toronto: *Annual Report 1922 Knox Church Toronto* [1923], p. 10.

[84] Roger Fulford, 'Pankhurst, Dame Christabel Harriette (1880–1958)', *Dictionary of National Biography 1951–1960*, pp. 789–91. This oversight will be corrected in her entry in the *NewDNB*, written by Professor June Purvis.

[85] *Christian*, 6 November 1924, p. 24.

[86] *Christian*, 11 February 1926, p. 10. Likewise the *Sunday School Times* dubbed her 'the famous English writer': 30 October 1926, p. 636.

F. B. Meyer died that year and Pankhurst revealed in her tribute to him that he had read *Seeing the Future* and approved it 'in his last days'.[87] Finally, in 1940 the well-established London Christian publishing house of Hodder and Stoughton published *The Uncurtained Future*.

In addition to these books, Pankhurst contributed articles to periodicals. Most notably, she wrote a weekly column in the *Christian* newspaper from 25 November 1926 to 12 May 1927 – twenty-five articles in all – under the general title 'On the Watch Tower. Signs of the Lord's Return', and she wrote numerous contributions from 1925 to 1941 for the *Sunday School Times*, often in a series of four or five major articles that was heralded in advance and coupled with a special deal for new subscribers. For part of 1934 she issued her own journal, *Present and Future*. It was not intended as a commercial venture, but rather was given away free. It was primarily an attempt to shape the thinking of the influential in British society. The *Manchester Guardian* reported that 'the many leaders of public opinion who receive the first issue within the next few days will understand that Miss Pankhurst intends regularly to plead her case before them'.[88] Churchill's copy of the first issue, May 1934, along with a personal covering letter from Pankhurst, is in the Churchill Archives, Churchill College, Cambridge.[89]

Having drawn attention once again to her books, the next task is to explore their contents, an undertaking that requires a baptism by immersion into some rather advanced areas of theological speculation.

[87] *Christian*, 18 April 1929, p. 6.
[88] 'Miss Pankhurst's New Journal', *Manchester Guardian*, 14 May 1934.
[89] The cover letter for the second issue is also there, but not the issue itself. The British Library also has a copy of the May issue, along with the June and October issues. No other copies of this journal have been located.

Chapter Two

ESCHATOLOGY AND THEOLOGY

The Evangelical Movement

Evangelicalism is a movement arising out of English-speaking Protestantism in the 1730s. In Britain it was inaugurated with the revivals led by, most notably, John Wesley (1703–1791) and George Whitefield (1714–1770). Their ministries produced the Methodist movement, a cluster of churches and, eventually, denominations that were the primary expression of evangelicalism in the eighteenth century. David Bebbington has identified four characteristics of evangelicalism: conversionism (an experience of spiritual transformation that marks one's movement from spiritual death to spiritual life, from condemned to redeemed), activism (a sacrificial commitment to evangelism, missions and good works), biblicism (an emphasis on the authority of the Bible in the Christian faith), and crucicentrism (an emphasis on the work of Christ on the cross as achieving a substitutionary atonement that provides a way for the sins of human beings to be forgiven).[1] This definition has become standard for historians of religion.[2]

In America, in addition to George Whitefield, who spent much of his time ministering there, the Congregationalist Jonathan Edwards (1703–1758) was the most outstanding figure in that first generation of evangelicals. Evangelical doctrine, experience, and practice spread widely across the denominational spectrum on both sides of the Atlantic. In Britain, in addition to the large Methodist denominations that were added to the religious landscape, the largest of the older denominations outside the church establishment – the Congregationalists and

[1] D. W. Bebbington, *Evangelicalism in Modern Britain: A History from the 1730s to the 1980s*, London: Unwin Hyman, 1989, pp. 2–17.
[2] For example, it is the one used as a guide by the editor of a major reference work on evangelicalism: Donald M. Lewis (ed.), *The Blackwell Dictionary of Evangelical Biography, 1730–1860*, 2 volumes, Oxford: Blackwell, 1995, p. xix. It has become so standard that scholars have begun to use it without acknowledgment. See, for example, K. Theodore Hoppen, *The Mid-Victorian Generation, 1846–1886*, Oxford: Clarendon Press, 1998, p. 436.

Baptists – were thoroughly evangelical by the mid-nineteenth century. For example, two of the most famous religious figures of Victorian Britain were the Congregationalist missionary David Livingstone (1813–1873) and the Baptist preacher Charles Haddon Spurgeon (1834–1892), both of whom were evangelicals whose ministries were marked by a commitment to activism. Even the Society of Friends or Quakers, a body that had often been viewed as unorthodox by the other denominations, had a significant evangelical section in the Victorian era.[3] The prison reformer Elizabeth Fry (1780–1845) is a prominent example of an evangelical Quaker. The movement also spread into the establishment, and the evangelical party became a strong force in the Church of England. Already in the late eighteenth century, the movement was represented by notable evangelical Anglican laymen and women such as the anti-slavery campaigner William Wilberforce (1759–1833) and the 'Blue Stocking' and author Hannah More (1745–1833). As for the clergy, by 1848 an evangelical, John Bird Sumner, had secured the highest office in the church, the archbishopric of Canterbury. During the Victorian period, however, the Tractarian movement was also re-energizing the High Church party. In the late nineteenth century and into the twentieth century, Anglo-Catholicism became a major force in the established church. Broad Church was the name given in the nineteenth century to the more liberal school of Anglican theology. By the end of the nineteenth century, a theologically liberal movement that was open to abandoning or modifying traditional Christian beliefs in the light of contemporary thought and sensibilities was making notable inroads in most Protestant denominations. Theological liberals were a direct challenge to evangelicalism: notably, they often considered that modern scholarship made a traditional attitude toward the Bible untenable and that a traditional understanding of the atonement was morally offensive. In short, by the 1920s evangelicalism did not enjoy the measure of hegemony that it had experienced in the Victorian period.[4] Pankhurst had joined a movement that was no longer automatically assumed to be representative of the mainstream of Protestant Christian thought, especially from the perspective of many of the denominational leaders and theologians.

[3] For evangelical Quakers in Victorian Britain, see Elizabeth Isichei, *Victorian Quakers*, London: Oxford University Press, 1970.
[4] For British evangelicalism in the 1920s, see Ian M. Randall, *Evangelical Experiences: A Study in the Spirituality of English Evangelicalism, 1918–1939*, Carlisle: Paternoster, 1999. For evangelicalism's decreasing influence in British society as the twentieth century unfolded, see John Wolffe (ed.), *Evangelical Faith and Public Zeal: Evangelicals and Society in Britain, 1780–1980*, London: SPCK, 1995, chapters 7–9.

Eschatology in Credal Statements

In the historic creeds of the church, scant attention is paid to the subject of eschatology, that branch of theology that is concerned with the culmination of the divine plan for human history at the end of time.[5] The Nicene Creed of the early church merely affirms, in language similar to the Apostles' Creed, that Christ 'will come again with glory to judge the living and the dead. His Kingdom will have no end', and 'We look forward to the resurrection of the dead and the life of the world to come.' Despite its brevity, however, it is important to note that the historic, universal teaching of the Christian church is that there will come a day at the end of time when Jesus Christ will return to the earth, the so-called second coming or second advent of Christ. The Thirty-Nine Articles of the Church of England, although a much longer statement of faith than the early Christian creeds, do not expand the teaching of the ancient creeds on eschatology at all. The great Puritan, Reformed creed, The Westminster Confession (1646), is also a much longer document than the early creeds. It offers a notably larger account of the nature of the resurrection of the dead and the last judgment, and even ends with an eschatological prayer, 'Come, Lord Jesus, come quickly. Amen.' But it did not offer any guidance regarding the sequence of events that will culminate in what it refers to as 'the last day'. In short, historically the church has not considered a detailed discussion of the end times so important a matter of doctrine as to make it necessary to include it in its creeds.

By the early twentieth century, however, much of conservative evangelicalism had begun to invest significant import in doctrinal fullness, clarity, and purity in the area of eschatology. In terms of credal expression, this trend is reflected, for example, in the doctrinal statement officially adopted in 1925 by Dallas Theological Seminary, Dallas, Texas. Dallas, a large, fundamentalist stronghold and centre of theological reflection, was founded by three prominent conservative evangelical leaders, one of whom was A. B. Winchester, the Toronto minister who had arranged Pankhurst's first opportunity to speak in a church a couple years earlier. Although the creed as a whole is no longer than the Thirty-Nine Articles or the Westminster Confession, its section on eschatology is vastly more detailed. In addition to a paragraph-length article on the more traditional theme of 'The Eternal State' – the resurrection of the

---

[5] The quotations in this paragraph are taken from John H. Leith (ed.), *Creeds of the Churches: A Reader in Christian Doctrine from the Bible to the Present*, third edition, Atlanta: John Knox Press, 1982.

dead and the last judgment – the most relevant articles are as follows:

Article XVIII The Blessed Hope

We believe that, according to the Word of God, the next great event in the fulfillment of prophecy will be the coming of the Lord in the air to receive to Himself into heaven both His own who are alive and remain unto His coming, and also all who have fallen asleep in Jesus, and that this event is the blessed hope set before us in the Scripture, and for this we should be constantly looking (John 14:1–3; 1 Cor. 15:51–52; Phil. 3:20; 1 Thess. 4:13–18; Titus 2:11–14).

Article XIX The Tribulation

We believe that the translation of the church will be followed by the fulfillment of Israel's seventieth week (Dan. 9:27; Rev. 6:1–19:21) during which the church, the body of Christ, will be in heaven. The whole period of Israel's seventieth week will be a time of judgment on the whole earth, at the end of which the times of the Gentiles will be brought to a close. The latter half of this period will be the time of Jacob's trouble (Jer. 30:7), which our Lord called the great tribulation (Matt. 24:15–21). We believe that universal righteousness will not be realized previous to the second coming of Christ, but that the world is day by day ripening for judgment and that the age will end with a fearful apostasy.

Article XX The Second Coming of Christ

We believe that the period of great tribulation in the earth will be climaxed by the return of the Lord Jesus Christ to the earth as He went, in person on the clouds of heaven, and with power and great glory to introduce the millennial age, to bind Satan and place him in the abyss, to lift the curse which now rests upon the whole creation, to restore Israel to her own land and to give her the realization of God's covenant promises, and to bring the whole world to the knowledge of God (Deut. 30:1–10; Isa. 11:9; Ezek. 37:21–28; Matt. 24:15–25:46; Acts 15:16–17; Rom. 8:19–23; 11:25–27; 1 Tim. 4:1–3; 2 Tim. 3:1–5; Rev. 20:1–3).[6]

This is not only a statement of eschatology considerably longer than the whole of the Nicene Creed or the Apostles' Creed, but it is also a reflection of a long series of theological shifts and trends in the evangelical movement. It would take an entire book – and more patience than most are apt to have – to unpack the full theological import of the crucial words and phrases in this statement. Nevertheless, a working knowledge of the broad outline of eschatological views that it reflects is a prerequisite for grappling with Pankhurst's religious thought.

---

[6] *Dallas Theological Seminary 2000–2001 Catalogue*, pp. 154–7.

The Christian Millennium

In the early twentieth century, evangelicals often gave great weight to a right understanding of the Christian doctrine of 'the millennium' – the thousand-year reign of Christ and his followers on earth. The notion of the millennium is derived from a passage in the Revelation of St John the Divine:

> And I saw an angel coming down from heaven, having the key of the bottomless pit and a great chain in his hand. And he laid hold on the dragon, that old serpent, which is the Devil, and Satan, and bound him a thousand years. And cast him into the bottomless pit, and shut him up, and set a seal upon him, that he should deceive the nations no more, till the thousand years should be fulfilled: and after that he must be loosed a little season. And I saw thrones, and they sat upon them, and judgment was given unto them: and I saw the souls of them that were beheaded for the witness of Jesus, and for the word of God, and which had not worshipped the beast, neither his image, neither had received his mark upon their foreheads, or in their hands; and they lived and reigned with Christ a thousand years. And when the thousand years are expired, Satan shall be loosed out of his prison. (Revelation 20:1–7 Authorized Version)

The question that evangelicals debated among themselves was whether this period would take place before or after Christ's second coming.

In the late eighteenth century and the early and mid-nineteenth century, many leading evangelicals adhered to 'post-millennialism', the belief that Christ would return after the millennium and therefore that the millennium would arrive through the growth of the kingdom of God in the course of human history; a notion that gave those who pursued evangelism, missions and social reform immense optimism regarding the potential for success in their work. Jonathan Edwards, the dominant American in the first generation of evangelicalism and, arguably, the greatest theologian America has ever produced, was a post-millennialist. In 1743, he even went so far as to hope that the revival of religion that was then under way might be heralding an unfolding of God's purposes that would culminate in the millennium: 'It is not unlikely that this work of God's Spirit so extraordinary and wonderful, is the dawning, or, at least, a prelude of that glorious work of God, so often foretold in Scripture.'[7] Likewise, Charles Finney (1792–1875), the most prominent American revivalist and evangelist in the mid-nineteenth century, was also a post-millennialist. He even went so far as to argue that if 'the

---

[7] Iain H. Murray, *Jonathan Edwards: A New Biography*, Edinburgh: Banner of Truth Trust, 1987, p. 297.

church will do all her duty, the millennium may come in this country in three years'.[8] In Finney's mind, 'her duty' was both evangelism and social action – particularly securing the abolition of slavery – and he envisioned that such work would lead the course of human history toward a time when human affairs were in line with the sovereign will of Christ.

During the course of the nineteenth century, however, a fresh wave of interest in 'pre-millennialism' began to grow, the belief that Christ would return to establish the thousand-year reign, a position that undercut any notion that current efforts at improving the world might be part of a path of continuous improvement leading to the coming age. This perspective initially had to live down the disgrace created by the teachings of the American William Miller (1782–1849), who had convinced a significant number of people that the second coming of Christ would take place in 1843 or 1844. Nevertheless, the pre-millennialist view became more and more convincing to conservative evangelicals during the late nineteenth century, until by the early twentieth century there was a complete consensus among the leaders in this camp that pre-millennialism was the true teaching of the Bible. Moreover, this doctrine was now so important that it was often included in credal statements. For example, a denomination founded in twentieth-century Britain, the Elim Pentecostal Church, was merely in keeping with standard practice among conservative evangelicals at that time when it included the word 'pre-millennial' in its own succinct little creed that it adopted in 1934.[9] The transition from eminent evangelical post-millennialists to credally prescribed pre-millennialism, is illustrated by the history of Wheaton College in Illinois, a major evangelical institution. It was founded by Jonathan Blanchard (1811–1892), a post-millennialist and social reformer similar in kind to Charles Finney. He gave the institution the motto, 'For Christ and His Kingdom', a slogan that was tinged with the notion that the college's graduates would go out and transform the world and thereby help to usher in the kingdom of God, the millennial age. In 1926, however, the college – its veneration for its founder notwithstanding – adopted a nine-sentence long statement of faith. It was so minimalist that, for example, it made no mention of the church at all, yet it still affirmed: 'We believe in "that blessed hope", the personal, pre-millennial, and imminent return of our Lord and Saviour, Jesus Christ.' A historian of the college and its Director of Evangelism, writing in 1950, after presenting this creed assured his readers that on 'minor questions of doctrine, however, there are many different viewpoints in the faculty and staff', thereby underlining the fact that

---

[8] Keith J. Hardman, *Charles Grandison Finney, 1792–1875*, Syracuse, New York: Syracuse University Press, 1987, p. 152.
[9] *The Constitution of the Elim Pentecostal Church (Elim Foursquare Gospel Alliance): Deed Poll and General Rules*, Cheltenham: Elim Pentecostal Church, 1975, p. 2.

pre-millennialism was now considered a major point of doctrine to which evangelicals across the denominational spectrum were expected to adhere.[10]

To complicate the matter yet further, there were two camps within pre-millennialism, and Pankhurst's religious life cannot be adequately situated without outlining that distinction as well. Members of the one group were called 'historicists', and the other, 'futurists'. Historicists interpreted the prophecies about the future that lead up to the end of the world (especially those in the Book of Daniel), as unfolding over the whole course of Christian history. Futurists, on the other hand, believed that the fulfilment of all these prophecies was still yet to come, and that therefore they would all happen in a kind of burst of prophetic activity at the very end of age.[11] Historicists, for example, were apt to identify the anti-Christ with the institution of the papacy, and therefore to view the fulfilment of those texts that contain this term as having already been inaugurated many centuries ago. Futurists, in contrast, believed that the anti-Christ would be an individual leader and that only the last generation would witness the manifestation of this figure and thus he had either not yet arisen or he was a leader in the world today whose career had yet to enter its most dramatic phase.

The triumph of pre-millennialism in the evangelical world in the early twentieth century was due in large measure to the increasing attractiveness of a scheme of biblical interpretation called 'dispensationalism' that was developed by the Anglo-Irish Plymouth Brethren leader, John Nelson Darby (1800–1882).[12] It derived its name from the attention that it gave to the different 'dispensations' of the Almighty's working in human history that a particular reading of the Bible identified. Darby's dispensationalism – which came to dominate so much of evangelicalism in the first half of the twentieth century – was a futurist form of pre-millennialism. Darby had toured America teaching doctrine and many evangelical leaders had been convinced by the views on eschatology he had presented. The historicist view was therefore rapidly going out of fashion in the early twentieth century. Nevertheless, historicism had more support amongst

---

[10] W. Wyeth Willard, *Fire on the Prairie: The Story of Wheaton College*, Wheaton, IL: Van Kampen Press, 1950, pp. 191–3. For a general history of the modern pre-millennial movement, see Timothy P. Weber, *Living in the Shadow of the Second Coming*, enlarged edition, Grand Rapids: Academie Books (Zondervan), 1983.

[11] For a contemporary account of the nature of these two schools (albeit one written by a futurist), see F. W. Pitt, 'Historicist and Futurist', *Advent Witness*, 1 Feburary 1934, pp. 27–38.

[12] For this development, and a wider discussion of trends within evangelicalism, especially those related to eschatology, see Ernest R. Sandeen, *The Roots of Fundamentalism: British and American Millenarianism, 1800–1930*, Chicago: University of Chicago Press, 1970.

English evangelicals than it did with American ones, not least because the most influential champion of the historicist view had carried out much of his ministry in England, the Irishman Henry Grattan Guinness (1835–1910).

A Book on Prophecy

All this brings us back once again to the book that Christabel Pankhurst read in 1918 that so altered the course of her life. As has already been shown, in her own classic account of her change of direction in life she does not name the book in question. Mitchell (erroneously, as will be shown) claimed that it was 'a book by the Rev F. B. Meyer – a prolific scribbler'.[13] Pugh echoes this, referring to it as a volume 'written by the Reverend F. B. Meyer, a prolific writer on Biblical prophecy'.[14] Mitchell was guessing, and his description of Meyer indicates that he was unable to hit upon a likely title in his œuvre. In fairness to him though, Pankhurst was deliberately concealing the matter. Apparently, it is not only scholars who would like to know the name of the book; Pankhurst herself acknowledged that there was curiosity on this matter – without satisfying it – in a speech she gave in October 1926 to a large crowd in the great Free Trade Hall in Manchester, her old home town: 'In the time of my despair I providentially found a book on prophecy. What was the book? you ask. That doesn't matter. There are many such books.'[15] When she went to speak in Ireland, however, Pankhurst could not resist playing to her audience by revealing that the book was written by one of their own: 'In my darkest moment I came across a book by the late Dr Grattan Guinness, which taught me that God has expected and prepared against human failure.'[16] Finally, the book itself is revealed by W. Y. Fullerton, in a biography of F. B. Meyer, written shortly after his death:

> Miss Christabel Pankhurst, to the surprise of those who only knew her as a militant Suffragist, has also become an eloquent exponent of the need, and the hope, of Christ's Return to the world for which He died, all other hope being in vain. First aroused to the thought of it by the title of Dr Grattan Guinness's great book, 'The Approaching End of the Age,' she has studied and written and spoken much on the subject. Early in her advocacy she came into touch with Dr Meyer and joined him in meetings in various parts of the country – meetings, which it is hardly necessary to say, were very crowded. The combination of two

[13] Mitchell, *Queen Christabel*, pp. 284–5.
[14] Pugh, *Pankhursts*, p. 378.
[15] *Christian*, 21 October 1926, p. 24.
[16] *Christian*, 4 November 1926, p. 15.

such personalities, apart altogether from the subject, made a strong appeal.[17]

Although Grattan Guinness' *The Approaching End of the Age Viewed in the Light of History, Prophecy, and Science* was first published in 1879, it is less surprising than it might seem that it came to Pankhurst's attention in 1918, for Morgan & Scott – who would become her own publisher – issued a new edition of Guinness' book in that year. Moreover, in addition to the fact that an apocalyptic title would have had fresh resonance in the context of the Great War, the content itself also had renewed relevance. In the last preface Guinness had written for the volume, and therefore the first thing one reads when starting the book, he discussed how, according to his interpretation, biblical prophecy predicted that the Turkish empire would lose control of the land of Palestine, and that the Jewish Diaspora would begin to return there, followed by 'the restoration of Israel to a national existence in Palestine', and the second coming of Christ.[18] Pankhurst, a compulsive student of current events and reader of newspapers, had undoubtedly noted, just a year earlier (2 November 1917), the Balfour Declaration, in which the British foreign secretary had announced that 'His Majesty's Government view with favour the establishment in Palestine of a national home for the Jewish people, and will use their best endeavours to facilitate the achievement of this object'. This was followed in December 1917 by General Sir Edmund Allenby's triumphal entry into Jerusalem as the leader of a conquering British army.

Grattan Guinness, although he was in full-time Christian ministry, pursued his own theories with such dedication and rigour that he was elected a Fellow of the Royal College of Astronomers and of the Royal Geological Society. His book is a 700-page *tour de force* in which he unfolded an elaborate scheme that ostensibly demonstrated a quantifiable pattern running throughout the unfolding of biblical prophecy, the course of human history – especially the rise and fall of great empires – and astrological time. He had had his calculations checked by no less a figure than John Couch Adams (1819–1892), the director of the Cambridge Observatory and the discoverer by mathematical calculation of the planet Neptune. Guinness' scheme is so complex and detailed as to defy summarization, but a quotation from his own 'Concluding Remarks' may serve to provide a flavour of what had gone before:

> We have traced, very imperfectly, but still sufficiently to demonstrate its existence, *a system* of times and seasons running through

[17] W. Y. Fullerton, *F. B. Meyer: A Biography*, London: Marshall, Morgan & Scott, [1930], p. 159.
[18] H. Grattan Guinness, *The Approaching End of the Age Viewed in the Light of History, Prophecy, and Science*, twelfth edition, London: Hodder and Stoughton, 1894, p. iv.

nature – organic and inorganic, – and through Scripture – historic and prophetic: – a system which consequently we have ventured to call, *a Divine system* of times and seasons. We have shown that this system is characterized by soli-lunar dominion causal and chronological, and by a marked and peculiar septiformity; that a law of completion in weeks can be traced alike in Scripture, in physiology (normal and abnormal), in history, and in astronomy.[19]

From his historicist stance of interpretation, Guinness was convinced that biblical prophecies had told of:

> the reception of Christianity by Constantine and the Roman empire, of the gradual growth of corruption in the church, of the irruptions of the Goths and Vandals, and the break up of the old Roman empire into ten kingdoms, of the rise and development of the papacy, of the rise and rapid conquests of Mohammedanism, of the long continued and tremendous sufferings of the church under papal persecutions, of the fifty millions of martyrs slain by the Romish Church, of the enormous political power of the popes, of their Satanic craft and wickedness, of the Reformation, of the gradual decay of the papal system and the extinction of the temporal power of the popes . . . [20]

Therefore, according to Guinness, if one projects the scheme forward it is possible to discern when prophetic time (and therefore human history) will run out. After all, he argued:

> Is it not most natural and suitable, that great events, deemed worthy of prediction by the Spirit of God ages before they occurred, should have had their fore-ordained duration marked off by the occult movements and coincidences of those orbs, which together constitute God's glorious chronometer?[21]

All of his calculations prompted Guinness to conclude that 'the Times of the Gentiles' – the period of history, in a standard theory of biblical interpretation, which contains the whole Christian era hitherto and also all of human history henceforth save the prophetic endgame – were scheduled to run out in 'about forty-five years from the present time (1879 A.D.)'.[22] Indeed, his calculations were even more precise than that. Imagine how the following passage must have read in 1918, when Pankhurst first stumbled upon it:

> But dated 145 years later, from the era of Seleucidae, this period measured in *lunar* years expires, *seventy five years later*, in A.D. 1919. . . . when the nations of Europe, actuated it may be merely by

---

[19] Guinness, *Approaching*, p. 461.
[20] Guinness, *Approaching*, pp. 124–5.
[21] Guinness, *Approaching*, p. 464.
[22] Guinness, *Approaching*, p. 472.

mutual distrust and political jealousy, or it may be by higher motives, shall conspire to reinstate the Jews in the land of their forefathers, *then* the last warning bell will have rung; then the last of the unful-filled predictions of Scripture as to events prior to the great crisis, will have received its accomplishment, then the second advent of Israel's rejected Messiah to reign in conjunction with his risen and glorified saints as King over all the earth, will be *close* at hand, then the mystery of God will be all but finished, and the manifestation of Christ immediate.[23]

Guinness' main calculation, however, was that the last grains in the prophetic hour glass would find their resting place in the year 1923. In *The Approaching End of the Age*, therefore, Christabel Pankhurst found a scheme which, firstly, validated her sense – engendered by the Great War – that she was living in momentous times and that the world would never be the same again; which, secondly, seemed to have predicted accur-ately the trend of current events some forty years in advance; and which, thirdly, seemed to be based on a pile of objective knowledge and calcula-tions that would have appeared to her legal mind and natural intellectual curiosity as a satisfying brief to explore.

It is most likely that Pankhurst did not mention the title of the book in her writings and speeches because she quickly became aware that the funda-mentalist circuit she was joining was largely and resolutely committed to a futurist view.[24] Guinness, conversely, was not only an historicist, but also one who had attacked futurists and their ideas repeatedly in his book, and even had added an appendix to later editions 'Containing Answers to Futurist Objections'. Pankhurst's own teaching on biblical prophecy was never explicitly historicist, and was on some points explicitly futurist. Indeed, it would be fair to label her a futurist. She was very committed, for example, to the idea that the anti-Christ was a dictator who was either currently on the world scene or who would be manifest there shortly, a view that Guinness ridiculed as:

> wild and unauthorized speculations, about some coming man, who is, in three years and a half, to exhaust these divinely given predictions, which the church has for eighteen centuries been studying. . . . Was it to warn the church of the nineteenth century against some short-lived Napoleon, that the Holy Ghost unveiled the future to the prophet Daniel, and that the Lord Jesus gave the Apocalypse to the saintly John?[25]

---

[23] Guinness, *Approaching*, pp. 473–4.
[24] It is telling that the one person who named the book, W. Y. Fullerton, gave the impression that she had been inspired merely by its title. This is certainly inaccurate, and was probably a conscious attempt to be tactful: Fullerton, *F. B. Meyer*, p. 159.
[25] Guinness, *Approaching*, p. 226.

Pankhurst also advised her hearers to 'buy a Scofield Reference Bible', a book that played a crucial role in the widespread dissemination of Darby's views and became ubiquitous in circles influenced by his scheme and which was therefore literally the Bible of dispensational (futurist) pre-millennialists.[26] Nevertheless, she could not resist keeping one eye on Guinness' scheme. In a published letter to F. B. Meyer written at the start of 1924, she remarked tellingly, and somewhat pathetically, that the events of 1923 'fully entitle it to the outstanding place given to it according to the interpretations of prophetic chronology of Grattan Guinness'.[27] This judgment would have looked less and less tenable as the years unfolded, and therefore undoubtedly have moved her more and more squarely into the futurist camp.

Such cross-party dabbling was possible at this time in the context of English evangelicalism because a historicist-futurist coalition had developed in 1917 and been institutionalized in the work of the Advent Testimony Movement, an organization that was founded in that year. Just below the masthead of its journal, the *Advent Witness*, always appeared a notice that made this point explicit:

> The Editor equally welcomes to these pages articles dealing with the Historicist and Futurist interpretation of Prophecy, in conformity with the principle adopted as the basis of the Advent Testimony Movement – viz., the necessity of Preparedness for the near advent of our Lord, which is the cherished hope equally of both schools of Prophetic Interpretation.

One can infer that historicists were still significant enough in England that an organization such as this did not wish to snub or exclude them. Pankhurst noted this alliance in *'The Lord Cometh'* when she (without using any party labels) outlined the two views, and then remarked: 'At the present day all exponents of prophecy, be it noticed, whether they trust to chronology [historicists], or only to the signs of the times [futurists], are united in believing that the return of our Lord is now very near.'[28] It is tempting to speculate that F. B. Meyer himself was never quite ready to write off completely the historicist view. It is certainly true that Meyer had been friends with Grattan Guinness, and had been the person who had kept his missionary training college running when Guinness had once needed a break to recover from an illness, and Meyer had again been the one to step in to facilitate the institution's transition when Guinness died.[29]

[26] *Christian*, 29 March 1923, p. 24.
[27] *Christian*, 24 January 1924, p. 19.
[28] Pankhurst, *'The Lord Cometh'*, p. 97.
[29] A. Chester Mann, *F. B. Meyer: Preacher, Teacher, Man of God*, London: George Allen & Unwin, 1929, pp. 97–8.

In any event, Meyer was a bridge-builder who was not trying to secure Pankhurst's aid for any internecine battles among pre-millennialists.

The Basic Eschatological Scheme

This irenic approach – albeit within the context of what was already a tightly prescribed subgroup – seemed to suit Pankhurst well. The *New York Times* learned from one of her addresses in 1923 that 'Miss Pankhurst will not classify herself with any body of Adventists.'[30] In an energetic commitment to the promotional side of the book trade that would be the envy of any author, Morgan & Scott ensured that their well-circulated newspaper, the *Christian*, reviewed Pankhurst's *The World's Unrest* no less than seven times, three of the reviews being cover stories. Moreover, the reviewers were invariably leading figures in the evangelical world. These reviews indicated that Pankhurst was viewed as having managed, in a welcome and refreshing way, to circumnavigate the issues that divided the community while still offering an original, stimulating read. For example, A. Douglas Brown, a Baptist minister and a star of the platform at the influential annual holiness convention at Keswick, wrote:

> First of all, I would like to state very frankly, that a great deal of recent writing upon the all-important subject of the Lord's Return has been disappointing, in that it has obviously been the expression of the views of a particular section of Advent believers, rather than the straightforward and independent exposition of Holy Scripture. . . . [a book that can 'claim the attention' of everyone is needed] . . . Miss Pankhurst has met that need, and met it magnificently.[31]

In Pankhurst, the movement had found not a divisive controversialist, but rather an effective popularizer.

The Advent Testimony Movement had formed its alliance around the fact that both historicists and futurists (for different reasons) agreed that the return of Christ was patently imminent. They expressed this convergence of opinion in a joint statement, the first four points of which were the most telling:

> 1. That the present Crisis points towards the close of the Times of the Gentiles.
>
> 2. That the Revelation of our Lord may be expected at any moment, when He will be manifested as evidently as to His disciples on the evening of His Resurrection.

---

[30] *New York Times*, 19 August 1923, p. 19.
[31] *Christian*, 22 July 1926, p. 5.

3. That the completed Church will be translated to be 'for ever with the Lord.'

4. That Israel will be restored to its own land in [un]belief, and be afterwards converted by the appearance of Christ on its behalf.[32]

These points became the long-term platform of the Advent Testimony Movement, although the word 'belief' rather than 'unbelief' in point four was simply a copying error and 'the present Crisis' in point one was later changed to 'the signs of the times'.[33]

The biblical clues that were amassed to create the kind of involved prophetic patterns such as the one Pankhurst adopted and championed were many and scattered. One passage from Luke's Gospel, however, may serve to illuminate some of the most prominent contours of the basic scheme Pankhurst was using:

> And they asked him, saying, Master, but when shall these things be? And what sign will there be when these things shall come to pass? And he said, Take heed that ye be not deceived: for many shall come in my name, saying, I am Christ; and the time draweth near: go ye not therefore after them. But when ye shall hear of wars and commotions, be not terrified: for these things must first come to pass; but the end is not by and by. Then said he unto them, Nation shall rise against nation, and kingdom against kingdom: And great earthquakes shall be in divers places, and famines, and pestilences; and fearful sights and great signs shall there be from heaven. . . . and Jerusalem shall be trodden down of the Gentiles, until the times of the Gentiles be fulfilled. . . . And then shall they see the Son of man coming in a cloud with power and great glory. And when these things begin to come to pass, then look up, and lift up your heads; for your redemption draweth nigh. . . . So likewise ye, when ye see these things come to pass, know ye that the kingdom of God is nigh at hand. (Luke 21:7–31 Authorized Version)

The 'Times of the Gentiles' were said to have begun before the time of Christ at the captivity of Judah during the reign of Nebuchadnezzar, king of Babylon. This passage from Luke, amongst others, was interpreted as teaching that at the very end of human history Jerusalem would revert to Jewish control once again. Therefore, a major preoccupation of Pankhurst and her ilk was the restoration of the Jews to Palestine. Pankhurst's primary contribution to prophetic studies was in the area of the 'Signs of the Times'. She would watch current events and endeavour to demonstrate that they demonstrated the 'signs' that Christ and other

---

[32] *Christian*, 8 November 1917, p. 14.

[33] See F. A. Tatford, *The Midnight Cry: The Story of Fifty Years of Witness*, Eastbourne: Bible and Advent Testimony Movement, [c. 1967], pp. 17–18. There were also several other subtle changes.

biblical characters or authors apparently predicted would mark the end times. Alternatively, she would predict how the world situation would develop on the basis of areas of prophecy deemed to be still unfulfilled. From the passage above, in addition to the 'Jewish' sign, Pankhurst's main preoccupations were with 'wars and rumours of wars' (as parallel passages in Matthew's and Mark's Gospels expressed it), and with earthquakes and other such natural phenomena.

The Advent Testimony coalition agreed that 'the Revelation of our Lord may be expected at any moment'. This was Pankhurst's view as well. She could conclude an address to the faithful with the words: 'Do let Him come to hearts that are full and overflowing with love and longing for Himself. Oh, that it might be tonight!'[34] Such a view had significant advantages: it allowed preachers to maximize the potential comfort of their message (for those longing for Christ to intervene), as well as offering motivational potential for encouraging unbelievers to accept Christ and misbehaving believers to reform their ways in preparation for the possible return of Christ before the day was out. Nevertheless, there was a *prima facie* contradiction between this teaching and the assumption that the signs of the times were indicators of the return of Christ which in turn implied that second advent would not occur until all the signs had been fulfilled and all the relevant prophecies had come to pass – and they clearly had not. John Nelson Darby had developed the teaching of the 'rapture', a view that solved this difficulty and that appears to have been attractive even to many historicists by the early decades of the twentieth century. Darby argued that Christ would first gather his people 'in the air', but that the final stage of his second coming would happen later, and that world and prophetic history would continue between these two events. This teaching is often referred to as 'the Blessed Hope' in evangelical literature. This blessed hope – Christ gathering true believers from the earth – was independent of any prophetic timetable and therefore could happen at any moment. Nevertheless, as it obviously needed to happen before the second stage could take place, if the signs of the times were revealing that that later event was fast approaching, then the likelihood of the rapture happening shortly was greatly increased.

Pankhurst herself believed in the notion of the rapture. For example, she remarked in 1924, 'I do not think there are many who look for the Lord's Coming who have one shadow of doubt that they will be delivered from the Great Tribulation.'[35] In other words, the rapture would take place before this item on the final prophetic checklist at the end of the age was ticked off. This stance is known in the parlance of the movement as 'pre-trib', and it was the view adopted by the powerful dispensationalist camp.

[34] *King's Business*, September 1924, p. 598.
[35] *King's Business*, September 1924, p. 597.

The alternatives were 'post-trib' and 'mid-trib'. The whole discussion presupposes a rapture.[36] Pankhurst's teaching and preaching did not focus on the rapture though, and far from highlighting the rapture/final stage of the second coming distinction, tended to ignore it, or even to conflate it, as will be shown in chapter four. The simple expectation that 'The Lord Cometh' was her great message.

Orthodox Doctrine and the Evangelical Gospel

Pankhurst's speeches and writings are littered with statements conveying her adherence to traditional evangelical views on other doctrinal issues in addition to eschatology, particularly those related to the person and work of Jesus Christ. Although there might have been people who became so engrossed in the minutiae of the visions of Daniel and Revelation that their teaching lost all sense of perspective and proportion, Pankhurst's message – its own quirky obsessions notwithstanding – was remarkably christocentric. She never lost sight of the notion that, as she told a BBC radio audience in 1926: 'The main theme of Bible prophecy is, of course, the history of the Lord Jesus Christ.'[37] In a letter of hers published in the *Advent Witness*, she explained in advance what she hoped to achieve with her first religious book:

> While emphasizing the prophetic truth in the book, I want to make it a fully sounded out declaration of faith in the whole Gospel, including the atoning death and the resurrection of our Saviour, the Son of God in whom dwells all the fulness of the Godhead bodily. There would be no profit spiritually in expatiating upon the prophecies and their progressive fulfilment if we did not use them as a finger-post to salvation through the Blood of Jesus Christ.[38]

As fundamentalists were wont to do, Pankhurst occasionally paused in order to berate modernists or theologically liberal ministers or theologians for not holding their ground on traditional Christian views of the work and person of Christ. For example, she warned in *The World's Unrest* of: 'sceptical elements in Christendom itself . . . who profess themselves

---

[36] A stray bit of teaching that clearly betrays a dispensational orientation (although in a way too complicated to elucidate here) came in her last book: 'The course of the seventy years was interrupted, and the interruption has lasted now for some two thousand years. The final week of the seventy has yet to begin.' Dame Christabel Pankhurst, *The Uncurtained Future*, London: Hodder and Stoughton, 1940, p. 167. The same teaching was given even more attention in an article of hers published in the following year: *Sunday School Times*, 17 May 1941, pp. 399–400, 413.
[37] *Christian*, 4 November 1926, p. 12.
[38] *Advent Witness*, March 1923, p. 36.

unable to accept what has, since the first days of the Christian Church, been taught of Jesus as to His deity, His atoning death, His resurrection and return'.[39] Commenting on a report that Bible reading was declining, she blamed the trend on modernist theology: 'Why should it receive the old attention—as the Living Word—if it tells of One who died a martyr's death, and not as a propitiation for man's sin? Setting aside the doctrine of the Fall, men speak of Christ as One who set a moral example.'[40] Therefore, in her view, people often were not hearing the true gospel: 'They hear only of a form of godliness without the power thereof, which power is the Lord Jesus Christ in His Deity, His Incarnation, His Death and real Resurrection.'[41] In a little article in the first issue of her journal, *Present and Future*, entitled 'Reason and Theology', she breezily pronounced that orthodox views of the latter had the support of the former, working her way through the Trinity ('it is logical to believe in "God in three persons, blessed Trinity"'), the resurrection of Christ ('self-evidently true'), and Christ's ascension and second coming ('also quite scientifically and rationally credible'), in short order.[42]

Pankhurst once remarked that her favourite passage of Scripture was the very christocentric second chapter of the Epistle to the Philippians: 'for it tells me of the One who came down from heaven the first time, and died for my sins, and who is coming again that He may be glorified and obeyed throughout the world'.[43] In fact, this thought seems to have grown in her mind, making the message of the first coming more important in her ministry. By 1943, she was claiming that her message was 'the Cross of Christ for redemption of sin and His second coming to deliver the world from war and unrighteousness'.[44] Pankhurst also emphasized a conservative evangelical doctrine of the Bible and, in the shibboleth language of fundamentalism, was quite willing to pronounce it 'unerring'.[45] In 1926 she complained, 'The Church is not proclaiming the message of the Bible to-day. Instead, it is denying the essentials.'[46] In a risible specimen of a fundamentalist preoccupation with the doctrine of Scripture, she even declared once regarding Christ's second advent: 'He is coming to establish finally the authority of the Bible, and to prove it actually written by the inspiration of God the Holy Spirit.'[47]

---

[39] Christabel Pankhurst, *The World's Unrest: Visions of the Dawn*, London: Morgan & Scott, 1926, p. 73.
[40] *Christian*, 23 December 1926, pp. 20–1.
[41] *Christian*, 30 December 1926, p. 5.
[42] *Present and Future*, May 1934, p. 4.
[43] *Christian*, 14 October 1926, p. 38.
[44] 'British Suffrage Leader Here for Religion Talks', *Los Angeles Times*, 9 July 1943.
[45] *New York Times*, 5 January 1925, p. 9.
[46] *Christian*, 14 October 1926, p. 37.
[47] Pankhurst, *'The Lord Cometh'*, p. 7.

Still, some orthodox theologians might argue that her efforts at theodicy were tinged with dualism. Her apologetic for the current evil and suffering in the world was one in which the sovereignty of God was minimized and the work of Satan magnified. In a typical statement, she observed:

> When men have asked how a God of love could allow a great war, involving the death of numberless men, only too frequently answer has been attempted by those who disregard the larger and deeper and more far-reaching purpose of God. While the work of the great enemy is overlooked . . . [48]

The following passage from her first religious book is perhaps the crudest expression of this view:

> The kingdoms of this world are not yet the Kingdom of Jesus Christ. Whatever some may say, He does not yet rule over the earth: His reign as foredestined Prince of this world has not yet begun, just as David's reign, after he was anointed as king, did not at once begin. . . . When both human and supernatural resistance to His reign is overcome, as it will be in the Age-end crisis, the Millennium, the new and golden Age, so long foreseen, can begin.[49]

On the other hand, it would probably have required someone from outside the dispensational pre-millennialist camp to offer such a critique. Within her own evangelical subculture, Pankhurst's soundness on basic doctrinal issues appears to have been beyond all cavil.

The Modernity of Fundamentalism

Fundamentalists have often been painted as people bewildered by the modern world and nostalgic for a golden age that seemed to be slipping away; a time when divorce rates and hem lines were low and biblical literacy and church-attendance were high. Although this stereotype has probably been overplayed, there is certainly truth in it. The fundamentalist camp has even sometimes self-consciously fostered this perception. After all, one of their central preoccupations has been attacking (theological) 'modernism'. A leading fundamentalist radio evangelist of the 1930s and 1940s, Charles E. Fuller, tellingly called his extremely popular programme 'The Old-Fashioned Revival Hour'. Jerry Falwell, one of the best known fundamentalists from the second half of the twentieth century, titled his radio and television programme the 'Old-Time Gospel Hour'. Even this can be easily misconstrued though. This language was, after all, rooted in

[48] *Christian*, 23 December 1926, pp. 20–1.
[49] Pankhurst, *'The Lord Cometh'*, p. 123.

a belief that timeless doctrinal truths had been revealed in the Bible that ought not to be jettisoned, and therefore it would be unfair to assume that these fundamentalists were against modernity in all its forms or in favour of all 'old-fashioned' ways. 'The Old-Fashioned Revival Hour' and the 'Old-Time Gospel Hour' are themselves both examples of the savvy way that fundamentalists have been quicker than most to discern the potential of new technologies and media.

Nevertheless, Pankhurst stood out from the fundamentalist pack in her determined effort to switch the tags so that fundamentalism, if she was to be believed, was strikingly bolstered by 'modern' thought, while what was called 'modernism' was actually shown to be old-fashioned. For example, she handled modern biblical criticism briskly in the introduction to *'The Lord Cometh'*:

> Throughout this book I have ignored destructive criticism of the Bible, because that criticism is now old-fashioned, super-annuated, based on an exploded materialism which could no longer claim to be scientific, had no foundation in historic fact, was wholly unphilosophical, was false to real experience of life.[50]

This was a recurring gambit of hers. She pronounced in a speech in 1926: 'The anti-Christian scientific notions of the nineteenth century are being discredited, and the new science is much less materialistic in its outlook.'[51] In the following year she made the reversal even more explicit, reassuring the faithful and any potential seekers with her wonderfully confident air 'that unenlightened incredulity of the nineteenth century, which, in some quarters, still passes as *"modern scholarship"* is effectually swept away'.[52] On the celebrated Victorian scientist and original 'agnostic', T. H. Huxley, she commented in 1929:

> The advance of knowledge since Huxley's day has slain the old-fashioned scientific dogmaticism of last century. . . .
>
> Nevertheless, Huxley, – for all his scepticism born of the very limited science of his time, a science so dangerously limited that it ensnared men in the illusion of knowing far more than they did, – nevertheless, Huxley, in spite of this very illusion to which so many gifted men of his time fell victim, said some sage things, that may even to-day be recommended to the consideration of those now living, who are tempted to hark back to the defunct, sceptical fallacies of the 1860s.[53]

---

[50] Pankhurst, *'The Lord Cometh'*, pp. vii–viii.
[51] *Christian*, 7 October 1926, pp. 20–1.
[52] *Christian*, 10 March 1927, p. 12.
[53] Christabel Pankhurst, *Seeing the Future*, New York: Harper & Brothers, 1929, pp. 82–3.

This rhetoric was surely the right tack to take if one truly had the genuine interests of the movement in mind. Pankhurst was clear-sighted enough to see that one must appeal to the young rather than merely the old, and not having grown up in a sheltered Christian subculture and never having restricted her social world to believers, she knew how a still unpersuaded generation thought in a way that few other fundamentalist leaders did. It is also tempting to read into her words an apologetic for her father's sceptical turn: he lived at a time when it was hard to know any better.

Fundamentalists everywhere trumpeted the latest findings of archaeology as confirming the veracity of scriptural accounts and overturning more sceptical views regarding biblical history that had been championed in the past, and Pankhurst made the most of the latest scientific finds of archaeology in this way as well.[54] She also moved beyond this, however, to create her own heady blend, combining contemporary technological and scientific advances and thought with traditional Christian doctrines. The *Los Angeles Times* aptly summed up the approach she often took with the headline it gave for its report of a speech of hers in 1943: 'Bible Conference Told Science Aid. Dame Pankhurst Declares Prophecies Easier to Understand Through Work of Learned Men.'[55] Again and again she would expound the latest scientific ideas and then go on to argue, for example, that the logistical problems of the second coming could therefore no longer be viewed as insurmountable:

> A sudden, visible second advent is 'a thought form' which is 'not really compatible with modern knowledge' protests one clergyman, but the reason he gives is far from modern! He actually argues that 'if Christ were to appear to-night in the clouds over England, the people in Australia would not see him, because Australia is beneath our feet.' Extraordinary idea in these days, with television already a fact and only needing to be perfected to make the people of London visible in Australia! Sound and sight girdling the earth is a modern possibility which helps us to understand that Christ, as Lord of all the marvellous powers of the universe, can, when He returns, make Himself visible by world-circling rays which will act direct upon the human eye.[56]

One could compile numerous such quotations from Pankhurst's writings and speeches. While it is hardly necessary to remark that they would sound quaint, if not downright laughable, to many today, it is worth noting that an embarrassed reaction was possible even within the evangelical orbit of her

[54] Pankhurst, *'The Lord Cometh'*, p. 115.
[55] 'Bible Conference Told Science Aid', *Los Angeles Times*, 15 July 1943.
[56] Pankhurst, *Seeing the Future*, pp. 165–6.

own day. Dr Webb Anderson, notwithstanding the fact that he was reviewing *The World's Unrest* in the *Christian*, could not resist adding pointedly: 'Personally, I would wish that in the next edition the references to "radio-activity" in relation to the opposition of the Evil One to CHRIST's Return – or our seeing Him who is yet invisible (*vide* Cap. 20) might be cut out.'[57] Pankhurst was determined to claim modernity for Christ and his word.

[57] *Christian*, 5 August 1926, pp. 1–3.

Chapter Three

CURRENT EVENTS

The Signs of the Times

The signs of the times formed a rather elastic and expansive category. Adventist Fundamentalists, at their most excitable, were tempted to find significance and meaning in almost anything and everything happening in the world. Even Pankhurst herself could make the prophetic news rather than just report it: the Revd H. Tydeman Chilvers, the Baptist minister at Spurgeon's Metropolitan Tabernacle in London, once remarked about her in a burst of enthusiasm, 'Surely she herself is a "sign" for this day and generation', although he did not bother to elucidate what biblical prophecy regarding the end times found its partial fulfilment in the redeemed Suffragette.[1] Moreover, even when the field is narrowed to a strict correlation between an event and a specific biblical text, there is such a dizzying array of obscure verses that might suddenly come to the fore in the light of contemporary events that members of the faithful who had not made prophetic study a special hobby might not have even been aware that such a 'sign' had been foretold in the Bible until its apparent fulfilment had been announced to them. Familiar imagery could continually take on new meanings in the light of current events. As Communist Russia became more of a concern, the *Advent Witness* could write knowingly of the prophecy in Revelation that speaks of the so-called four horses of the apocalypse under the proof-texting title: 'Another Horse that was Red'.[2] On the other hand, there is no doubt that, if asked what the signs of the times were, almost any member of the movement could have listed the major themes that were perennially emphasized by prophetic teachers.

Pankhurst, in particular, largely limited her teaching to a few major themes, finding ample room for variation and expansion in the hunt for their fulfilment. At one point, she expounded a three-fold scheme of the signs of the times that encapsulates well her preoccupations in this area

---

[1] *Christian*, 26 August 1926, p. 14.
[2] *Advent Witness*, 1 May 1931, p. 69 (Revelation 6:4 is the biblical text).

throughout the whole of her ministry:

> The signs of Christ's coming are of three classes. Firstly, there is the general disturbance of the nations and of nature, expressing itself in warfare and the rumour thereof, in social unrest, in earthquake, storm, and flood. Secondly, there is the Jewish return to Zion, for the first time since the tragic dispersion of A.D. 70. Thirdly, there is the restoration of the Roman empire, which is becoming a dominant feature of present day international politics.[3]

The first point is probably best separated for consideration into two distinct ones. Thus her sets of signs were four-fold: (1) national and political unrest, especially wars and rumours thereof, (2) natural disasters and remarkable natural events, especially meteorological, seismological or astronomical, (3) Jewish developments in Palestine, (4) political developments and alignments reminiscent of the Roman empire.

Contemporary Thought and Literature

Pankhurst's particular gift – undoubtedly partially the fruit of her legal training – was a capacity to imbibe impressive amounts of contemporary expert opinion and employ it as evidence for the claim that these signs were now being fulfilled. In 1926 she described her own methodology, having just recounted (to the extent that she ever did) her conversion:

> And I kept silent until I saw the signs of the times were fulfilling the Scripture promises. For eight years now this thing has been my constant study. I read the world's newspapers, I read the new books, and I tear the heart out of them in my search for the ever-multiplying proofs of the truth of the prophetic utterances in the Bible.[4]

One clear advantage that she had over most of the other fundamentalist writers and speakers in the English-speaking world was that she had lived in continental Europe. When she was seventeen years old she went to Geneva to round off her education and she lived in Paris for a couple of years as a Suffragette leader in exile. After that, she went back to France periodically. In 1925–26 she spent another period living in France, and it was there that she wrote *The World's Unrest*.[5] Pankhurst enthused in 1929 about the edifying time that she had enjoyed at an evangelical

---

[3] *Christian*, 5 May 1927, p. 12.
[4] *Christian*, 21 October 1926, p. 24.
[5] Parts of *The World's Unrest* were serialized in the *Sunday School Times* and these articles were marked as from Paris at the end. See, for example: 23 October 1926, pp. 615–16; cf. Mitchell, *Queen Christabel*, p. 292.

holiday and retreat centre, Maison Evangélique, Houlgate, on the Normandy coast.[6] She was both fluent in French and conversant with and interested in French politics, as well as in politics elsewhere in Europe. Her writings are littered with references to books and articles that she read in French. This reading was far from light or intellectually dubious. In the field of historiography, for example, there was arguably no more important book published in the 1920s than Oswald Spengler's *The Decline of the West*, which was written in German. Pankhurst was already discussing this book in her volume, *The World's Unrest*, which was issued in July 1926 and, therefore, perhaps before the English translation of Spengler's work, which also came out in 1926, had even been released. Pankhurst had become familiar with Spengler's argument from Maurice Muret's *Le Crépuscule des nations blanches*, which had also been issued that year, in Paris. Although she was living in England at the time, she was discussing Henri Massis' *Défense de l'Occident* in an article she published on 12 May 1927, even though that book had been published in Paris that same year and thus had only been in circulation for, at most, a handful of months.[7] It is not clear whether or not she could also read some other European languages, or if her references to newspapers from elsewhere were dependent on translations reprinted in the French or English press. Nevertheless, her references to items in a wide variety of newspapers were extensive. For example, in one two-page article published in January 1927 in a weekly column she had at that time, she cited *L'Avenir*, *Figaro*, *Lokalanzeiger*, *Ere Nouvelle*, and *Gaulois*, as well as the *Morning Post*, the *Times*, and the *Daily News*.[8] Pankhurst was a fundamentalist who was conversant with many of the latest ideas and developments in Europe.

Pankhurst also made an impressive effort to keep up with current scientific thought. In the 1920s she often referred to Einstein, Sir Ernest Rutherford, atomic theory, relativity, and the like. One source of knowledge of this material was a work by the astronomer of the Paris Observatory, Charles Nordmann's *Einstein et l'univers* (Paris, 1921). She read F. J. M. Stratton's *Astronomical Physics* in the year that it was issued (1925). The cumulative impact of her reading and references was something truly extraordinary in the subculture she was serving. Illustrating this adequately necessitates a rather lengthy example. Here is a list of references to persons and writings from just one of her books,

---

[6] *Sunday School Times*, 30 November 1929, p. 689. She spoke at worship services there and dubbed the place 'one of the "Keswicks" of France', a reference to the extremely popular holiness convention in the Lake District of England that had also inspired the founding of 'Keswick' conventions in America and Canada.

[7] *Christian*, 12 May 1927, p. 5.

[8] *Christian*, 13 January 1927, pp. 19–20.

The World's Unrest, in her own words:

> Mr Bonar Law; the present prime minister [Mr Stanley Baldwin];
> Mr T. C. Cramp, Industrial Secretary, National Union of Railway-
> men; Mahaffy; Mr George Trevelyan's *History of England*; the
> *Times*; Sir Isaac Newton; Alexander the Great; The Paris *Temps*;
> Signor Mussolini; Hegel's *Philosophy of History*; Mr Frank Simonds;
> *La Vie Latine*; the *New York Times*; Julius Caesar; *Le Petit Parisien*;
> Count Volpi, Italian Minister of Finance; the *Morning Post*;
> M. Briand; Lord Salisbury; the French Deputy, M. Andre Fribourg;
> the *English Review*; M. Gustave le Bon; the winner of the American
> Bok Peace Award, Dr Charles Levermore; M. Paul Boncour; Gibbon;
> anon., *Manuel de Politique Musulmane*; the *Jewish Chronicle*; Lord
> Balfour; M. Paul Cambon, the French diplomat; Lord Bertie of
> Thame; Professor Bertram Windle, *The Romans in Britain*;
> W. R. Halliday, *The Pagan Background of Early Christianity*; M. E. de
> Pressense, *Early Years of Christianity*; *The Legacy of Rome*; *Martyrs
> and Apologists*; Mr James Beck, former Solicitor-General of
> the United States; Sir Sidney Low, *The Governance of England*;
> Sarfatti, *Life of Mussolini*; Dr Andre Reversz; Paul Fontana de
> Vico, *The Saviour of France*; M. Ernest Seilliere; Bishop Butler's
> *Analogy*; Merivale's *Conversion of the Roman Empire*; Professor
> A. S. Eddington's *Space, Time, and Gravitation*; Francis Bacon's
> *Advancement of Learning*; Pascal; Lord Shaftesbury; W. E. Gladstone;
> Professor Frederick Soddy, *The Interpretation of Radium and the
> Structure of the Atom*; Professor J. Y. Simpson; A. S. Eddington's
> *Stellar Movements and the Structure of the Universe*; F. J. T. Stratton's
> *Astronomical Physics*; Mr William J. Leyton of Harvard University;
> Abbe Moreux's *Astronomy To-day*; Jeans' *The Nebular Hypothesis
> and Modern Cosmogony*; A. S. Peake's *The People and the Book*;
> Dr Klausner; Professor J. Arthur Thomson's *Science and Religion*;
> Schlegel's *Philosophy of History*; J. C. Wordsworth's *Adventures in
> Philosophy*; Professor Leon Brunschweig; Plato; Aristotle; *Journal of
> Philosophical Studies*; Einstein; Rutherford; John C. Foley's *Sources of
> Volcanic Energy*; M. Louis de Launay's *La Science Geologique*; the
> *Daily Express*; Professor Robert Flint's *Philosophy of History*; and
> M. Muret's *Crepuscule des Nations Blanches*.

There are many observations that could be made about such a list – not least the absence of much theological literature – but the point in hand is that it represents a disciplined commitment to exploring the latest scientific, political, philosophical, and historiographical thought.[9] The fundamentalist world had few people beside her who could have an eye for how

---

[9] Those curious about Pankhurst's biography more generally may be interested in the fact that she once remarked in one of her religious speeches that she had gone through a phase of studying philosophy when she was fourteen years old: *New York Times*, 4 May 1925, p. 14.

a volume with such an unpromising title as *Sources of Volcanic Energy* or *The Interpretation of Radium and the Structure of the Atom* might be put to work for the cause, and the will and intellectual curiosity to do it. F. B. Meyer himself declared that she was 'a rare gift to the movement', citing 'her intellectual grasp of modern philosophy and its outlook'.[10] The Revd G. H. Lunn noted appreciatively, 'Miss Pankhurst has drawn largely from current literature of a very wide range, including history, prophecy, psychology, philosophy, science, and poetry, as well as theology.'[11] The response of the Revd D. M. McIntyre, principal of the Bible Training Institute, Glasgow, however, was somewhat cool; and it seems right, by way of balance, to allow him to have the last word. In his review of *The World's Unrest*, McIntyre observed at one point: 'In this Section there are many references to philosophic and scientific considerations. These no doubt add piquancy to the book, and will interest many of its readers, but they do not seem to advance the argument to any extent.'[12]

A standard argumentative technique of Pankhurst's was to push forward an expert to make her point for her. She pursued this course in *The Great Scourge*, and thus carried into her new commitment to religion established habits. During the course of the twentieth century, fundamentalist teaching and argument regarding the end times was often marred by conspiracy theories and, in general, political and technological developments were often presented in a distorted or inaccurate manner to the faithful. One thinks of the discussions in the 1970s and beyond regarding computers named 'the Beast' or systems supposedly being structured around the biblically portentous number 666 that were said to be on their way to controlling the lives of ordinary people. Timothy P. Weber has summarized the ideas of one fundamentalist end-times teacher, Mary Stewart Relfe, who published a popular book, *When Your Money Fails* (1981), as follows:

> She asserted that the '666 System' is already well established in the world's economic system. She based her conclusion on the widespread use of the numbers 666 in computer programs, credit-card systems, and the 'universal product code,' which appears on virtually all products and is 'read' by electronic scanners at supermarket checkout counters. She found what she believed was irrefutable evidence for the 666 system in the production codes of Olivetti business machines, NCR computer systems, Boss work gloves, Scotty fertilizer, McGregor clothing, Italian shoes, and parts for Caterpillar tractors. She found evidence that Sears, J. C. Penney, Montgomery

[10] *Christian*, 28 October 1926, p. 21.
[11] *Christian*, 19 August 1926, pp. 1–2.
[12] *Christian*, 29 July 1926, pp. 1–2.

Ward, Visa, and MasterCard had all used 666 as a prefix in account numbers.[13]

However, projecting what we know about fundamentalism in the second half of the twentieth century back on to the fundamentalism of the 1920s produces significant misconceptions. It is worth underlining that no evidence has been found that Pankhurst ever distorted the ideas contained in her sources, as Relfe did. There is never a blurring between what the sources themselves argue (which she faithfully presents) and her assertion that these facts or ideas make a Christian teaching seem more plausible or are in line with the prophesied signs of the times. Of course, as has already been intimated, the gears could grind in a way that would make many uncomfortable when she made the shift. Here is a typical specimen:

> Sir Ernest Rutherford said the other day to the Royal Society: 'During this year E. A. Milne has shown how certain atoms of matter ejected from the sun, notably those of calcium, may in consequence of absorption and emission of radiation, acquire sufficiently high velocities to penetrate deeply into our atmosphere. It may be that brilliant aurorae and magnetic storms which so often accompany sunspot activity, are a consequence of the projection into our atmosphere, not only of electrons as has long been supposed, *but of swiftly-moving atoms of matter.*' Tremendously important is the implication of such a theory! No less than this – that the Lord Jesus 'by whom all things were made', He who has made the atoms that are able to travel from Sun to Earth, is himself much more able to travel from Heaven to Earth![14]

It does not seem likely that an erstwhile sceptic would have had his or her doubts regarding the second coming of Christ alleviated by a discourse on solar calcium particles, although perhaps many more would have found endearing a fundamentalist Bible teacher who consistently paid serious attention to such things.

Whenever scholars discuss the teaching of popular thinkers there is a natural temptation to gravitate to the more risible statements in their writings or speeches and highlight them. In actuality, Pankhurst spent most of her time on the sign 'wars and rumours of wars', offering her audiences and readers detailed accounts of geo-political and diplomatic developments that needed no fanciful eye in order to illustrate her point that there was much well-informed speculation that real tensions between various nations might well be signalling the possibility of another war. Her vigilant and voracious reading, moreover, was rewarded occasionally

---

[13] Weber, *Living in the Shadow*, p. 224.
[14] *Christian*, 9 December 1926, p. 6.

by a true gift in which her expert really did make her point for her without her having to shift the gears at all. The richest of such boons was undoubtedly General Sir Ian Hamilton's article on war in the then recent edition (13th) of the *Encyclopedia Britannica* in which he helpfully asserted, 'Nothing will stop war save a Second Advent of Jesus Christ.'[15] Slightly less sharply defined, but still quite serviceable was a *New York Times* article that pronounced: 'Universal peace could come only by a miracle.'[16] A decent prize was when Signor Farinacci, in his farewell address as general secretary of the Fascist party, said of Mussolini that 'the only one who can replace him is Jesus Christ'.[17] On the other hand, some of her sources disdainfully anticipated her efforts. Pankhurst had the intellectual honesty, when reporting a story in the *Daily Mail* that offered data demonstrating that the frequency of earthquakes was on the increase, also to quote the writer's pejorative aside: 'Will some of the weird societies and sects see in these statistics some further proof of their theories?'[18] And so her dance between expertise and eschatology went on.

False Predictions

It is hardly necessary to labour the point that Pankhurst, despite having the Bible in one hand and a pile of contemporary thought and reportage in the other, did not prove to be an infallible guide to how current events would unfold. Perhaps most of all, the world has gone on its rhythmic way for several generations more, an eventuality she clearly did not anticipate. The Adventist movement had thoroughly learned the lesson from William Miller's error and was utterly committed to avoiding announcing a supposed date for Christ's return. Pankhurst wrote in *'The Lord Cometh'*: 'The learned writers who have helped so many of us to our present supreme interest in prophecy as found in the Bible, have never tried to fix the precise day and hour of their Lord's return.'[19] This is a point she made again and again. On the other hand, she was influenced by Grattan Guinness' historicist scheme that *did* attempt to calculate when prophetic time would run out (c. 1923, for example); this unquestionably underlined her suspicion that hers was the last generation. Moreover, the whole thrust of her teaching scheme was that her generation was watching the end before their very eyes. When she was being most careful, she would say that what was being witnessed in contemporary events were developments of

---

[15] *Christian*, 12 April 1927, p. 23.
[16] *Present and Future*, May 1934, p. 6.
[17] *Present and Future*, June 1934, p. 4.
[18] *Christian*, 24 March 1927, p. 22.
[19] Pankhurst, *'The Lord Cometh'*, p. 96.

the same ilk as the signs of the times and therefore, if the end was not imminent, then it meant that the world was destined to live through an even more intense period of war and earthquakes and the like:

> Are these signs the same in degree, as well as in kind? That is the one open question now! We must hope that they are, and that the Lord's coming is indeed near. God grant that the grievous signs now present will not have to recur at some future time with still more intensity![20]

She mellowed over time, as Grattan Guinness' key dates came and went, and became more reconciled to the possibility that the end might take more time to unfold than a handful more years or so. Nevertheless, it was not always so. Most tellingly, Pankhurst told an audience at the Bible Institute of Los Angeles (Biola) in 1924 that the anti-Christ (a term she does not actually use in her speech, but her description of this final world ruler would have been instantly recognizable to her prophetically literate hearers) 'we may be sure is living in the world at this present time'.[21] We may be quite sure, therefore, that in 1924 she did not think that the twentieth century would pass into history with the anti-Christ still having failed to make his bid for world power.[22]

Beside the timetable, the biggest red herring in her reading of the world situation was her obsession, typical of the movement in general, with the restoration of the Roman empire. It would be tedious to expound the various biblical passages (most notably in the book of Daniel) that were interpreted as indicating that the Roman empire was not confined to the past and would never be totally destroyed in the course of human history, but rather in a newly revived form would play a central part in the end times. It might suffice, however, to evoke this view by quoting the note in the enormously popular and influential dispensational handbook, *The Scofield Reference Bible*, on Revelation 13:3 ('And I saw one of his heads as it were wounded to death; and his deadly wound was healed: and all the world wondered after the beast'):

> Fragments of the ancient Roman empire have never ceased to exist as separated kingdoms. It was the imperial form of government which ceased; the one head wounded to death. What we have prophetically in Rev. 13.3 is the restoration of the imperial form as such, though over a federated empire of ten kingdoms; the 'head' is 'healed,' i.e. restored; there is an emperor again – the Beast.[23]

[20] *Christian*, 9 June 1932, p. 22.
[21] *King's Business*, September 1924, p. 553.
[22] In 1925, she referred to the anti-Christ as 'the Roman Caesar of the Twentieth Century': *Sunday School Times*, 31 October 1925, p. 684.
[23] C. I. Scofield (ed.), *The Scofield Reference Bible*, New York: Oxford University Press, 1917, p. 1342 (n. 1).

Pankhurst was utterly convinced that there would be a federation of nations more or less in line with the boundaries of the historic Roman empire that would soon emerge, offering a platform to a great dictator. This was one of her four major signs and therefore a theme to which she devoted a sizeable portion of her teaching. A good source for her thinking on this point is several chapters dedicated to it in *Pressing Problems of the Closing Age* (1924). She began by giving evidence for the notion that the Roman empire had, in some sense, continued to exist down through the centuries of the common era, Lord Bryce's *Holy Roman Empire* providing some useful ammunition, before speculating on possible contemporary activities that might lead on to the end-time federation. The Adventist movement in general was keenly interested in the rise of Mussolini. In a delicious anecdote, it has even been hinted that the movement might have given the fledgling dictator a little pep talk in order to help buck up his sense of ambition:

> Prophecy journals carried a story about an interview between *Il Duce* and Mr and Mrs Ralph Norton, Belgian premillennialists who were well known in American prophetic circles. During their meeting with Mussolini, they asked him if he intended to rebuild the Roman empire. He answered that it would be impossible. 'We can only revive its spirit, and be governed by the same discipline.' Evidently the Nortons were not satisfied with his answer, so they informed him of the biblical prophecy and the new Roman empire of the last days. According to the Nortons' report, 'Mussolini leaned back in his chair and listened fascinated, and asked, "Is that really described in the Bible? Where is it found?"'[24]

Presumably they neglected to tell him that the leader of the revived Roman empire was the anti-Christ.[25]

It would appear that Pankhurst's scheme, at its loosest, could accommodate a revival of the Roman empire under a German dictator, as had happened before (in her theory that the empire had waxed and waned throughout the centuries) under, for example, the rule of Otto the Great.[26]

---

[24] Weber, *Living in the Shadow*, p. 179.

[25] Pugh thinks the evidence indicates that Pankhurst was 'on the high road that leads to fascism', claiming that she 'expressed great admiration for Mussolini and his efforts to resurrect the Roman empire': Pugh, *Pankhursts*, p. 342, see also p. 431. This is to confuse political views with eschatological exuberance. She was enthusiastic that biblical prophecy might be coming to fulfilment, and as a commentator she was interested in explaining the attractive qualities and arguments Mussolini might possess or employ that could lead to his success, but the whole point of her scheme was that the restored Roman empire and the great dictator (the anti-Christ) were not a true solution to the world's problems but rather a counterfeit and ultimately doomed one.

[26] Christabel Pankhurst, *Pressing Problems of the Closing Age*, London: Morgan & Scott, 1924, p. 96.

Nevertheless, her repeated prediction was that there would come a Franco-Italian entente, that Italy would gravitate toward an alliance with France rather than Germany, and thus students of prophecy purportedly knew in which direction European diplomacy was heading in the 1920s. One article of hers, for example, began by offering a detailed survey of the current mood as expressed in French newspapers regarding an alliance with Italy. It is worth quoting a few phrases of this background in order to keep in mind the way that she arrayed detailed bits of concrete evidence behind her grand assertions and speculations:

> A big step toward entente was the Italian leader's denunciation of the anti-French disturbances, attributed to *agents provocateurs* and persons hostile to Fascism . . . When, soon after, came the narrow escape at Bologna and the 'incidents' which were its sequel, the editor of *L'Avenir* was unshaken in his policy . . . Other advocates of entente with Italy are 'Pertinax' of the *Echo de Paris*, and M. Auguste Gauvain of the *Journal des Debats*, both these being careful to stipulate that the dignity of France must be closely safe-guarded. . . .
> A Swiss exhortation to Franco-Italian entente is provided in the *Journal de Geneve*, where we read . . .

And that is but a small fraction of it, all leading up to the conclusion: 'As the centre and basis of the larger Latin Union, a Franco-Italian entente was bound to come. It will come: it is coming and coming swiftly.'[27] In short, in this respect, her scheme was a hindrance to prescience in the inter-war period as the real coming alliance was the one between Germany and Italy, Hitler and Mussolini. As events developed, she defaulted back to the more generic view, declaring already in 1934, for example, that 'The very name, Third Reich' was an acknowledgment that the empire the Nazis planned to build was in the succession of manifestations of the Roman empire, a revival of the Holy Roman Empire.[28] If Pankhurst had found the key for discovering how world events would play out, she did not always manage to use it in a way that successfully unlocked major unfolding developments.

Pankhurst the Pundit

Nevertheless, the coincidence between Pankhurst's predictions and the actual course of current events in the 1930s and 1940s was rather uncanny. It would be clearest to elucidate this convergence in categories.

---

[27] *Christian*, 25 November 1926, p. 6.
[28] *Present and Future*, May 1934, p. 7.

War

Pankhurst was utterly convinced from the very beginning of her ministry that, far from the Great War having been 'the war to end all wars', another world war was inevitable and imminent. In 1923 she claimed that she had realized already in 1918 that the 'German thrust for world-power, though thwarted in the late War, would be resumed, if not by German, then by some other power.'[29] In a typical statement, she remarked in 1926 that 'nothing is more likely than that another war will happen'.[30] More than that, her reading of military and technological advances made her keenly aware that the next world war would be far worse, especially for civilians. In a 1924 speech that was reported under the title 'Peace or War?' she remarked:

> I was in Paris during its bombardment by 'Big Bertha' that gun which from an incredible distance used to throw shells into the French capital. But even in Paris the damage was not so great as it will be in the next war for, according to the scientists, much worse things are in store for us. They make no secret that it will be practically a war of extermination – armed forces and non-combatants alike.[31]

While not many people in the 1920s would have been so naïve as to consider war a thing of the past, few would have had the notion and contours of 'the next war' so clearly fixed in their minds. In her book of that same year she quoted a military specialist who had tipped her off to the fact that a central strategy for prosecuting the next war would be 'direct action from the air against the civil population of crowded industrial centres'.[32] In other words, London devotees of Pankhurst's ministry had been warned the blitz was coming fifteen years in advance. Winston Churchill's views on India and the abdication crisis proved that he was no infallible guide in the inter-war period either. It is also true, however, that his nation came to believe that he had been right when few others agreed or were listening about the most vital issue of the period for the British people, the German threat. Keith Robbins encapsulated this view: 'He was a prophet without honour in his own country.'[33] There is a certain logic, therefore, in the fact that Pankhurst and Churchill had time for each other in the early and mid-1930s, all the rancour of their past fights by then gone. According to Churchill's pocket diary, he met Pankhurst at the Carlton Club on 27 July 1931.[34] One cannot help but wonder if either

---

[29] Pankhurst, *'The Lord Cometh'*, p. 10.
[30] *Sunday School Times*, 23 October 1926, p. 615.
[31] *King's Business*, September 1924, p. 553.
[32] Pankhurst, *Pressing Problems*, p. 16.
[33] Keith Robbins, *Churchill*, London: Longman, 1992, p. 133.
[34] Information provided by Louise King of the Churchill Archives Centre, Churchill College, Cambridge, in an e-mail dated 23 May 2001.

commented on the fact that its windows had once been smashed on her orders![35] Mitchell also records that Pankhurst visited Churchill at his home, Chartwell, several times, beginning in September 1931.[36] Moreover, they swapped at least a handful of letters in the period 1930–40. For example, Pankhurst wrote to Churchill the day before Christmas eve, 1937:

> Unhappily, Christmas 1914 was followed by nearly four years of bitter fighting, the use of poison gas & other breaches of the laws of warfare. This was bad enough but worse still, nearly quarter of a century later, the world, as you truly say is arming on a scale never before imagined & forging itself weapons more ever deadly to be used not only against armies, but whole populations.[37]

As has been shown, it did not take the promptings of Churchill or developments in Germany to the point of 1937 for Pankhurst to adopt this view. Her views were informed by the latest expertise in the field. In an article in December 1926 she told her readers that 'we learn of such devastating means of war now in preparation as wireless-controlled aircraft. The highest award in the United States engineering profession has just been given to the inventor of an aerial torpedo.'[38] In an article published on 31 March 1927 she was making use of a book on the nature of the latest in modern warfare that was published that same year (and was therefore not more than three months old), Major-General Sir George Aston's *The Study of War for Statesmen and Citizens*.[39] (One wonders in which of those two categories she classified herself.) Pankhurst's watchful eye upon international relations in Europe was not in vain either. For example, in a prescient prediction of how the next world war would start, she elucidated in 1927 that it 'should be emphasized again that the peace of Europe is a chain whose distressingly weak link is Germano-Polish relations, and, as we know by cruel experience, that is a matter not too small to kindle a very big fire!'[40] Pankhurst's instincts about the coming of a war, and the nature of that conflict once it came, were exceptionally sound and accurate.

Dictatorships

Christabel Pankhurst claimed that students of biblical prophecy were not surprised by the decline of democracy and the rise of dictatorship.

---

[35] Sylvia Pankhurst, *Suffragette Movement*, p. 434.
[36] Mitchell, *Queen Christabel*, p. 300.
[37] Churchill Archives Centre, Churchill College, Cambridge: Christabel Pankhurst to Winston Churchill, 23 December 1937.
[38] *Christian*, 16 December 1926, p. 6.
[39] *Christian*, 31 March 1927, p. 12.
[40] *Christian*, 24 February 1927, p. 5.

Pressing Problems of the Closing Age contained an entire chapter on 'The Challenge to Democracy'.[41] While she was more observing than predicting this change, she did highlight it, and was watching vigilantly for its spread. Already in 1926 she wrote when discussing this theme, 'From Germany come recurrent reports of threatened political change,' and she stated clearly that she would not be surprised to see that nation embrace a strong man as its political saviour.[42] Mitchell reports that Pankhurst predicted that Franco would win the Spanish Civil War.[43] Christabel Pankhurst peered into the Bible and saw an end-time world in which dictatorship would have more and more allure for people. This instinct was quite serviceable for an inter-war pundit.

Zionism

As was the wider Adventist movement as a whole, Pankhurst was pre-occupied with Zionism. Already in her first religious book, she was predicting a much more substantial emigration of Jews to Palestine, although she did not know what circumstances would prompt it: 'The immediate occasion of that larger regathering, who can tell!'[44] With her typical research habits, this led her into reading contemporary Jewish literature. One of her weekly columns in 1926, for example, quoted both the *Zionist Review* and the *Zionist Record* and endeavoured to elucidate this world with more than a broad stroke: 'That body of Zionists known as the Revisionists . . . Their leader M. Vladimir Jabotinsky . . .'[45] Once again, the basic prediction was unequivocal: 'After all, the Jews must and will return thither. More and more the Jews, from desire and from necessity, will be drawn to Zion.'[46] She quickly found, read, and praised Sophie Irene Loeb's *Palestine Awake: the Rebirth of a Nation* (1926). In *Seeing the Future*, Pankhurst declared that her political instincts, honed by the Suffragette cause, told her that Zionism would succeed:

> The writer of these pages is better qualified by experience, than some, to judge the significance and the prospects of Zionism, having been concerned in another movement, which began as a weak and small thing and eventuated in the enfranchisement of millions of women who, from being politically non-existent, became numerically predominant, with a corresponding change in their whole social influence. As great a transformation in human institutions as the

---

[41] Pankhurst, *Pressing Problems*, chapter 4.
[42] Pankhurst, *World's Unrest*, p. 80.
[43] Mitchell, *Queen Christabel*, p. 368 (ch. 16, n. 22).
[44] Pankhurst, *'The Lord Cometh'*, p. 98.
[45] *Christian*, 2 December 1926, p. 6.
[46] *Christian*, 2 December 1926, p. 6.

world has ever known! Zionism, to an eye thus trained in the school of practical experience, has, and had from the beginning, all the mark and promise of a practical success.[47]

This is the opening of a chapter surveying the Zionist movement that refers to (amongst others) Herzl, the Zionist Congress, Dr Weizmann, the *Jewish Chronicle*, Feisal of Iraq, Herzl's *The Jewish State*, Dr Oscar Wasserman, Sir Alfred Mond (Lord Melchett), Nahum Sokolow, Pierre la Mazière's *Israël sur la Terre des Ancêtres*, M. J. Kessel's *Beloved Land of Palestine*, Sokolow's *History of Zionism*, and the London *Jewish World*. Such reading indicates more than a mere vague gesturing toward the subject. *The Evangelical Christian and Missionary Witness*, a Toronto-based evangelical newspaper, reported an entire address that Pankhurst had given at Knox Presbyterian Church, Toronto, under the title 'Miss Christabel Pankhurst on Zionism'. In a neat convergence of some of the themes of her bedtime reading, she informed her audience that Einstein was a supporter of Zionism.[48] Already in the summer of 1941 – when the Second World War was far from being won – she was instructing her hearers at a major Bible conference on how Zionism would fare in the post-war situation:

> A resettlement of the Jewish question will undoubtedly form part of the peace terms at the close of this war, as was the case in a minor degree at the close of the last war. . . . [The Jews] will no doubt ask the United States to take part in this new deal for Jewry in the hope, for one thing, that joint British and American action or influence will more easily overcome the difficulties which the Balfour policy and League of Nations mandate encountered in Palestine, between the two world wars.[49]

Pankhurst and the other voices of fundamentalism were not merely spouting a general truism of the inter-war period when they argued that Zionism was a movement that would grow in significance and be crowned with success.

Anti-Semitism

A related theme is Pankhurst's awareness of the rise of anti-Semitism. Her speaking out against anti-Semitism contrasts with the widespread acceptance of this sentiment in inter-war England, not least amongst the educated elite. A report of a speech she gave in 1926 noted: 'Reference

---

[47] Pankhurst, *Seeing the Future*, p. 269.
[48] *Evangelical Christian and Missionary Witness*, January 1930, pp. 61–2.
[49] Dame Christabel Pankhurst, 'After the Second World War – What?' in *Winona Echoes 1941*, Grand Rapids: Zondervan, 1941, p. 125.

was made to the way of anti-Semitism in the world to-day, such as has not been in recent centuries. The Jew is being made the scapegoat of the world.'[50] This seems to have been the position of Pankhurst's conservative evangelical milieu in England as a whole. The *Quarterly Paper of the Bible Testimony Fellowship* regularly ran advertisements from a conservative Christian organization, the British Jews Society, that had the headline 'Anti-Semitism is anti-Christian'.[51] The *Advent Witness* persistently spoke out against anti-Semitism. An article in 1928 on this subject declared that 'it is a noticeable fact that nations that have ill-treated the Jews, such as Russia, have suffered whereas those that have treated them with kindness, have prospered'.[52] Pankhurst's status as a friend of the Jewish community was such that she was even invited to address Jewish groups. In April 1931 she spoke to the twelve sections of the Women's League for Palestine at the community house of Temple Emanu-El in New York, and she also delivered an address 'from the pulpit of Congregation Rodeph Sholom', also in New York.[53] Pankhurst the pundit, already in the 1920s, was paying attention to and denouncing the rise of anti-Semitism.

Possible Explanations

In short, one could do far worse for a guide to developments that mattered in the inter-war period than to follow the lead of someone who was emphasizing the fact that another world war was coming, that it would be marked by massive bombing of civilian populations, that dictatorships were on the rise, that anti-Semitism was increasing, and that the Zionist movement was a strategic one that would ultimately triumph.

What is one to make of the degree of success that Pankhurst achieved as a forecaster? First, it would seem – to whatever extent it might be appropriate to generalize from this case study – that it is a safer bet to expect the human condition to continue to be vexing and troublesome rather than to anticipate great leaps forward that will vastly improve the fortunes of humankind. This can be illustrated by a quirky story from the *New York Times* that reported an exchange that Pankhurst had with the celebrated scientist and inventor, Dr Charles Proteus Steinmetz (1865–1923). Enthralled with the benefits that his discipline could bestow, 'Dr Steinmetz contended that with the aid of electricity and the full development and utilization of the sciences, life could be made a great deal

---

[50] *Christian*, 23 September 1926, p. 5.
[51] See, for example, *Quarterly Paper of the Bible Testimony Fellowship*, 8, 1 (January–March 1935), p. 6.
[52] *Advent Witness*, September 1928, p. 142.
[53] *New York Times*, 16 April 1931, p. 23; 20 April 1931, p. 20.

easier for both the laborer and the scholar, and the maximum working day reduced to four hours.' To this Pankhurst retorted, 'I am not a scientist, but I believe Dr Steinmetz's statement greatly over-estimated.'[54] It would seem that a realist disposition when it came to the nature of human life in the future may have been a better asset when it came to such punditry than technical expertise. Or to come at the same point from the other direction, Pankhurst seemed a bit at a loss as to what to do with the biblical prediction – inconveniently in the same text as wars and rumours of wars – of famine as a sign of the end times. She half-heartedly did what she could with this, suggesting 'though there are nowadays very abundant food supplies, yet the economic depression has brought artificial famine to millions'.[55] It would appear that even Pankhurst, realist though she was, could not have envisioned that the twentieth century would indeed unleash a series of famines that no one could deny were worthy of the name. Famines of biblical proportions were awaiting, just as her text and scheme ought to have led her to predict, yet she apparently found this hard to conceive. A bolder stance on this issue would have paid off for her in the prediction stakes. Realist instincts have proved pretty sound thus far.

Second, one cannot dismiss the fact that the contents of the Bible did set an agenda that happened to be apt in some very specific ways for life in the twentieth century. War might be a perennial fact of human life, but it is clearly there as a predicted sign of the end times, and it was not fanciful for Pankhurst to insist that if war was a sign it was being fulfilled in an unprecedented way in the two world wars. In 1934 she argued: 'Truly we have, as the critics of prophecy observe, "always had war and rumours of war" – but never so terrible as now.'[56] In 1941 she wrote, 'War is, in fact, assuming apocalyptic size and violence. Formerly the anticipations of St John seemed to critics beyond all possibility, but facts have undeceived them.'[57] Even more tellingly, evangelical interpreters of biblical prophecy had been predicting already in the mid-Victorian period (and even earlier) that the establishment of a modern state of Israel would come. This was not therefore a reading of contemporary events into the biblical text, but rather a convergence of current developments with long-held expectations based on a particular reading of the scriptures.

Third, Pankhurst's degree of accuracy as a forecaster is attributable to her political experience, her disciplined efforts to keep up with current affairs and thought, and her considerable ability to work out what it all meant and where it was all heading. Like all pundits, her 'predictions'

---

[54] *New York Times*, 21 August 1923, p. 12.
[55] *Present and Future*, May 1934, p. 5.
[56] *Present and Future*, May 1934, p. 5
[57] *Sunday School Times*, 24 May 1941, p. 419.

were largely a dissemination to a wider audience of the existence of present realities that they had not yet noticed or the full import of which they had not yet grasped. This, of course, is no small skill. One of her more incidental bits of futurology was to observe in 1926 that 'Radio-vision [i.e. television] . . . soon will enable spectators all around the globe to watch . . . lawn tennis at Wimbledon'.[58] Once again, Churchill was no prophet in the biblical sense, but he was able to add the score up quickly on the Nazi menace in a way that many others did not. Pankhurst was no Churchill, but she was astute enough for him to take her seriously. An example of her talents for reading the road ahead can be seen in a speech she gave in Los Angeles in 1943 in which she several times declared that 'material prosperity will increase'.[59] This prediction arguably did not fit well with her reflex realism about the human situation, and she did not even attempt to claim that it was found in the Bible, but nevertheless her talent for gathering and evaluating relevant clues had already tipped her off (two years before the end of the war) as to the post-war era of American prosperity that was coming and she wished to help the faithful readjust their thinking and planning to fit that coming climate.

Christabel Pankhurst was a great gift to the fundamentalist movement. Many of the first generation of fundamentalist leaders were well-educated people who cross-pollinated with the intellectual and cultural forces of the larger society in a way that would not always be true for the leaders of subsequent generations. Later fundamentalist leaders too often viewed the wider culture from the outside and made judgments about it without ever really comprehending it. It will be a continuing theme in what follows, however, that it is a mistake to view 'fundamentalism' as a static phenom-enon and therefore project back on to past generations of fundamental-ists what one knows (or thinks one knows) about contemporary fundamentalists. Pankhurst serves as a reminder of the kind of funda-mentalist leader who kept up with the latest learning in a wide variety of fields, and who did not handle it with fear or suspicion. Moreover, although many of the first generation of fundamentalist leaders were well-read and trained (indeed, much more so than Pankhurst in the field of theology), she did bring unique assets all her own. The situation in continental Europe, after all, was arguably the most vital one to watch in inter-war Britain and North America, and it would not be easy to name other fundamentalist leaders who were regularly reading continental newspapers. Furthermore, her personal political experience was hard to rival, and this did bear fruit in a real capacity to judge how politicians would behave and political events develop. For more than one British

[58] *Sunday School Times*, 11 December 1926, p. 755.
[59] 'British Suffrage Leader Here for Religion Talks', *Los Angeles Times*, 9 July 1943.

prime minister she could pontificate on what they were or were not likely to do based on her private knowledge of them. She herself claimed, 'My political training and experience have helped me to estimate and to discern the signs of these present times, and for that I am thankful.'[60] Pankhurst could effortlessly score double points as a political insider – if not name-dropper – while illustrating her teaching: 'The poignant words of a former British Prime Minister, Mr Bonar Law, as transmitted to us by the present Prime Minister [Stanley Baldwin] . . .'[61] The *Sunday School Times* was thrilled to report that 'Mr Lloyd George presided at one of her meetings, on this subject [biblical prophecy], in England not long ago.'[62] Fundamentalism did well to gain her services.

On the other hand, the movement had a lot to offer her as well. Votes for women had been a glorious cause – the cause of a lifetime for most of her co-workers – and she had risen to international fame on it and the whole thing had been wrapped up victoriously while she was still in her thirties. Other causes, however worthy, would be likely to seem mundane and anti-climactic. Whatever else one may say about it, the return of Christ and the sudden end of the age can hardly be called mundane or anti-climactic. It was also a field that she could blaze ahead in as a leader as soon as she joined it, a criterion in keeping with her reputation, fame, and temperament. She had her law degree, but there would have been something incongruous about her slogging away with a lot of rookies to climb the first rungs of the ladder in law. A parliamentary career would probably have suited, but she had contested a seat unsuccessfully in 1918 and one cannot simply sit around being a parliamentarian-in-waiting. Not only did proclaiming the second coming of Christ give her a vast cause and a chance to start where she had left off in her last movement (at the top),[63] it also provided an outlet for her enormous intellectual curiosity, her legal skills for marshalling evidence and making a case, her political acumen, and her speaking and writing skills, as well as her general powers of persuasion and inspiration. Nevertheless, it would be unfair to paint too calculating a picture. Whatever weight one may or may not give to a more spiritual interpretation of her motivations, it is

---

[60] *Sunday School Times*, 31 October 1925, p. 684.
[61] *Sunday School Times*, 23 October 1926, p. 615.
[62] *Sunday School Times*, 14 July 1934, p. 453. Mitchell also mentions what is apparently a different, earlier occasion: 'In July 1931 she and Lloyd George spoke at the same service in a Welsh Baptist Chapel in London.' Mitchell, *Queen Christabel*, p. 299.
[63] Fundamentalism at this time was a fluid world that was not yet very institutionalized. The fundamentalist community was ready to give the limelight and leadership to those who demonstrated that they were gifted or who brought with them an aura of success. These traits were far more important than formal training and could substitute for it.

possible to catch her genuine enthusiasm for her new cause. As she wrote in the preface to her first religious book: 'It is awe-inspiring to watch current history fitting into the very mould of prophecy. Once you have the clue to the meaning of the existing world crisis you marvel that everybody else does not also see how prophecy is fulfilling itself in the world-events of the passing days.'[64] Christabel Pankhurst had found her new life's work.

---

[64] Pankhurst, *The Lord Cometh*, p. vii.

Chapter Four

DOOM AND HOPE

The Great War and the Charge of Pessimism

Pankhurst invariably attributed her general openness in 1918 to the
message of Christ's return to the disillusioning effect that the Great War
had had on her. In 1923 she said of the war: 'many of us believed when it
began that it was the war that would end all war. How could any one have
lived in that fool's paradise?'[1] In 1926 a report summarized a portion of a
speech of hers as follows: 'The War shattered her ideals, and she found
herself without a philosophy of life.' A direct quotation from the same
account has her declaring that 'the War brought us face to face with the
"changelessness of human nature".'[2] In other words, she had been
assuming gradual, unceasing human progress, but the war disabused her of
that assumption. Pankhurst made this point explicitly in her journal,
Present and Future:

> In all this, the inconvenient fact is not perhaps remembered, as it
> should be, that humanity cannot lift itself by its own boot straps, and
> also that the brightest dawns and noon of human civilisation have
> ever been followed by twilight and night. . . . 'Progress' and 'evolu-
> tion' are disappearing from current philosophies of the future. The
> world-war and after-war experience have convinced many that
> progress is not sure and continual, and recent archaeological research
> has taught more plainly than ever that ancient, now-dead civilisations
> were remarkably progressive, and in many ways rivalled our own . . .[3]

In *The Uncurtained Future*, she gave a simple, clear account of the impact
of the war: 'The outburst of war in 1914 shattered my illusions. Till then,
a better world had seemed near . . . Life would never again be the same.
The world as we knew it was finished.'[4]

---

[1] *Moody Bible Institute Monthly*, September 1923, p. 14.
[2] *Christian*, 11 November 1926, p. 6.
[3] *Present and Future*, May 1934, p. 1.
[4] Pankhurst, *Uncurtained Future*, pp. 22–3.

Her message, of course, was literally apocalyptic, and the overtones of that word were sometimes warranted. She warned in 1923: 'Human methods of abolishing war will end in the Battle of Armageddon!'[5] As will be shown in chapter six, Pankhurst is often portrayed as having thrown in the towel and given up on feminism and social reform when she ought to have continued faithfully to give her time and energy to such causes. Therefore, it is important to be reminded that her new-found realism about the limits of human achievement was an entirely typical response to the Great War. Indeed, this reaction is often regarded as the only thoughtful one possible in discussions of its presence in the lives and work of authors and artists. So much so, in fact, that the disillusioning effect of the war is a truism in the relevant literature. To take a random example to hand, Paul Johnson comments on the impact of the war:

> The war had demonstrated human frailty but otherwise would resolve nothing, generate nothing. Giant plans of reform, panaceas, all 'solutions', were illusory. . . . [The novelist Joseph] Conrad insisted: 'I have never been able to find in any man's book or any man's talk anything convincing enough to stand up for a moment against my deep-seated sense of fatality governing this man-inhabited world . . . The only remedy for Chinamen and for the rest of us is the change of hearts. But looking at the history of the last 2,000 years there is not much reason to expect that thing, even if man has taken to flying . . .' . . . In 1920, the great classical scholar J. B. Bury published a volume, *The Idea of Progress*, proclaiming its demise.[6]

Johnson is summing up the entire period, but that passage could work rather well as a summation of Pankhurst's views on the possibilities of human achievement.

To come at it from a different angle, those who proclaim the imminent end of the age have routinely been labelled pessimists and doom-mongers. Betty A. DeBerg, for example, has written that there 'seems no doubt that the characterization of premillennial fundamentalism as pessimistic is accurate'.[7] As to Pankhurst herself, Pugh confidently speaks of 'her role as prophet of doom' and 'her pessimism'.[8] It is perhaps even more likely

---

[5] Pankhurst, *'The Lord Cometh'*, p. 125.
[6] Paul Johnson, *Modern Times: The World from the Twenties to the Eighties*, New York: Harper & Row, 1983, pp. 12–13. For a general account of the interplay between literature and the Great War, see Paul Fussell, *The Great War and Modern Memory*, London: Oxford University Press, 1975. For a recent review of the historiography of the Great War and a fresh engagement with some of the themes it has raised, see Jay Winter, Geoffrey Parker, and Mary R. Habeck (eds), *The Great War and the Twentieth Century*, New Haven: Yale University Press, 2000.
[7] Betty A. DeBerg, *Ungodly Women: Gender and the First Wave of American Fundamentalism*, Minneapolis: Fortress Press, 1990, p. 122.
[8] Pugh, *Pankhursts*, p. 832.

for this assumption to be made in retrospect, but it was certainly a charge with which Pankhurst had to deal in her own lifetime. A speech she made in 1926 was reported thus: 'Believers in and proclaimers of the Second Coming of Christ are sometimes stigmatized as "prophets of doom." On the contrary, declares Miss Pankhurst, "we are prophets of salvation and sunshine."'[9] In an article in the *Sunday School Times* Pankhurst averred:

> Pessimists, we others have been called, who believe in and are looking for the literal fulfillment of that blessed hope and the glorious appearing of the great God and our Saviour. . . . The real pessimists are not we, but they who cannot believe this Gospel of the kingdom. We are the true optimists, because we believe in the best – and our optimism has a sure, because a divine, foundation. How greatly our heavenly optimism excels the optimism of the world![10]

She endeavoured to defuse this charge again in *The Uncurtained Future*:

> 'The voice of the Prophets,' I read the other day, 'is of judgment and doom: they are harbingers of woe.' A mistaken view! The prophets bring, above all, good tidings, the very same good tidings of great joy brought on the night of the Nativity to the Shepherds and to all people.[11]

Nevertheless, despite this categorical denial and the apologetic that followed it, a reviewer of this very same book in a 'religious weekly' (presumably one that served the mainline, liberal-leaning Christian world) dismissed it as teaching a 'Gospel of Despair'.[12]

What is to be made of this charge? First, as has already been intimated, assuming the charge is true (which, as will be shown, cannot be assumed), it would still be strange to judge Pankhurst harshly for succumbing to pessimism and despair in the wake of the Great War when this was in fact a widespread and typical response, perhaps especially among the more analytical sort. Second, if the pre-millennialist pundits are viewed (incorrectly) as a kind of lunatic fringe, nevertheless it is worth recalling that mainline Protestant thought in the English-speaking world had been developing a theology of progress and innate human goodness that did not offer adequate resources for understanding the war. William R. Hutchison has written a sympathetic account of theological liberalism or modernism in America that shows with great clarity that this school of

---

[9] *Christian*, 21 October 1926, p. 23.
[10] *Sunday School Times*, 21 December 1929, p. 739.
[11] Pankhurst, *Uncurtained Future*, p. 120.
[12] 'The Rationale of Advent Teaching. A Critic and "The Uncurtained Future"', *Advent Witness*, December 1940, pp. 167–8. (The name of the publication that contained the hostile review and that of the reviewer is not mentioned.)

Christian thought was sorely shaken by the war.[13] Hutchison cites the confessions of various liberals, such as a leading theologian, Shailer Matthews, who admitted 'we were incredibly optimistic, which is another way of saying we were incredibly blind'. Another liberal, George Gordon, conceded in the midst of the war:

> during the last three light-hearted decades, we have been smoking the opium pipe of evolution, telling the world how far it has risen, chiefly by its own force, from the depths in which it began, describing the speed by which it has mounted under our sage and dreamy eyes, and prophesying of its complete ascension in the near and sweet bye and bye. Recent events have broken the opium pipe and dispelled the delusion.

The war so exposed the naïveté and false optimism of theological liberalism that it could no longer go on as before: 'publishers cannot issue the same books, magazines cannot print the same articles, lecturers cannot give the same courses'.[14] That, of course, could not be said of the kind of conservative theology Pankhurst came to embrace. It, conversely, found its views confirmed by the war and pre-millennialists delighted in reprinting material they had published before the war as it so clearly illuminated current events. It is odd to condemn Pankhurst for giving in to pessimism when abandoning optimism was the only real option in the light of the ghastly realities of the times.

Pankhurst the Messenger of Hope

The more germane response, however, is to observe that it is a gross distortion of her ministry to claim that Pankhurst offered a 'Gospel of Despair'. In fact, she was extraordinarily upbeat. Far from spreading pessimism, she assumed that people were already pessimistic and that what they needed was a ray of hope that was credible, that is to say, that took into account the full weight of the realities of war, evil, cruelty, suffering, and human sinfulness. She announced confidently in 1927: 'Pessimism is the keynote of the world's thinking at this time. Optimism now belongs only to those who have discovered in the Bible prophecy and the present signs the assurance that this present age is hastening to its close, to be followed by the reign of the Lord Jesus Christ.'[15] Likewise, in

---

[13] He acknowledges in the preface that he has 'a greater personal sympathy for liberal than for conservative forms of religious expression'. William R. Hutchison, *The Modernist Impulse in American Protestantism*, Cambridge, MA: Harvard University Press, 1976, p. viii.

[14] Quotations all from Hutchison, *Modernist Impulse*, chapter 7.

[15] *Christian*, 10 March 1927, p. 10.

Present and Future, she endeavoured to explain how the message of the second coming could keep away despair at the worst of times: 'Tell us the signs of Thy coming, asked the disciples, and Jesus answered them in words that give good news to us because they show that when world conditions are darkest and human hopes faintest, then He will come again.'[16] She gladly received testimonials that her efforts were bearing fruit:

> Typical also was the word of a distinguished old Frenchman wearing the emblem of the Legion of Honor in his buttonhole, who said at the close of the meeting in Paris: 'Mademoiselle, you have given us new hope; you have put a radiant cross in our sky.'[17]

A discussion of her teaching in the *Christian* newspaper asserted that it presented 'a philosophy of hope, and in a time when hope seems to be dying down on all hands, Miss Pankhurst is setting herself to re-state the case for the Lord's Return.'[18] Pankhurst endeavoured to offer a steadying voice – a voice of realism – that navigated between what she called 'thin and brittle optimism' and despair.[19] When she began her newspaper column, 'On the Watch Tower', she explained: 'The watchmen are neither depressed nor elated by those present world-conditions which by some who ignore Biblical Prophecy, are hailed as promising world-recovery, and by others are viewed as presaging the reverse . . . our hearts are not to fear.'[20] In *The Uncurtained Future* she pronounced: 'Prophecy prevents false optimism – but it also prevents false pessimism.'[21] In a speech she gave in Los Angeles in 1943 she pleaded simply, 'Don't make me out a pessimist.'[22] Finally, in an article in 1934 entitled 'Why Preach Prophecy?' she offered an apologetic to all those bewildered by the turn her life had taken that had at its core the belief that this message was a realistic antidote to the despondency the times were apt to induce:

> Why preach prophecy, do they still ask? Because the hope it gives endures and brightens, while other hopes fade into darkness; because bread and butter policies collapse beneath overabundance, or wither in drought . . . because peace panaceas and pacts are scorched by the hot breath of oncoming war and finally are consumed in its blaze; because, as novels reflect and newspapers report, man, even in time of peace, and now as before the Flood, 'corrupts his way upon the earth.'

---

[16] *Present and Future*, May 1934, p. 5.
[17] *Sunday School Times*, 3 January 1931, p. 5.
[18] *Christian*, 25 February 1926, p. 4.
[19] *Sunday School Times*, 23 October 1926, p. 615.
[20] *Christian*, 25 November 1926, p. 6.
[21] Pankhurst, *Uncurtained Future*, p. 151.
[22] 'British Suffrage Leader Here for Religion Talks', *Los Angeles Times*, 9 July 1943.

Why preach prophecy? The question, asked whether in wonder or complaint, is answered. Let those, and there are many, who choose other forms of service, act as they are moved. We, on our part, aspire to no more useful role, or greater privilege than that of sharing the faith, and the plain reasons thereof, which gives to us, amid world-crisis, a confident and joyful anticipation of the future, as it will be shaped by the direct and divine intervention of the 'great God and our Saviour, Jesus Christ.'[23]

Christ's Return: the Great Panacea

Pankhurst filled volumes of print discussing everything from the Locarno treaties to the westernization of Turkey – everything from a terrific cyclone in Madagascar to Romania's claim to Bessarabia – but the facts, theories, opinions, and intelligence she so industriously amassed were all employed to make a very simple point. The message that she spent much of her adult life endeavouring to communicate to the world may be summed up as follows: the world's problems are humanly insoluble, but Christ is coming again soon to solve them all. In her teaching, the second advent was truly the great, universal panacea for all the world's problems. She wrote F. B. Meyer a letter in 1924 in which she articulated this view: 'Over and over again in a day my cry to Him is, "Come!" That seems the one and only answer, and remedy, for everything in these days.'[24] In her column in the *Christian* in 1927 she again summed up the core message of her teaching with admirable brevity: 'For each and all the many world evils of our time there is but one cure – His Coming!'[25]

Innumerable current events could serve to illustrate this message. Thus one of Pankhurst's standard didactic techniques was to take an issue of current concern, to argue (or pronounce) that it was insoluble by human efforts, and then to point to the second coming of Jesus Christ as the true solution. For example, on the problem of divisiveness in the Christian community she commented:

> But how I wish and hope and pray that the Lord will come and cut short our service here below and call us to new lessons and new service in His presence. The divisions and subdivisions of belief in the visible Church are, if possible, on the increase; and what can ever put an end to them save the Lord's return?[26]

[23] *Present and Future*, June 1934, p. 6.
[24] *Advent Witness*, November 1924, p. 131.
[25] *Christian*, 13 January 1927, pp. 19–20.
[26] *Advent Witness*, November 1924, p. 131.

On the issue of war, she wrote to Winston Churchill in 1934:

> Theocracy is the only real remedy for war as it is the only real remedy for the evils whether of Democracy or dictatorship. . . . The outcome of the fifteen years of postwar efforts toward peace proves the limitations of the human agent. Some recovery from, some abatement of the present world-crisis & national peril may be possible – but only as a respite & perhaps a very short one, for history moves with a new rapidity now. The public have at least learned to look beyond temporary calm to the inevitable next storm in human affairs & the only thing that can restore their hope of the future & their faith in the ultimate victory of *right* is the belief in an ultimate, if not imminent, personal & direct intervention by God in human affairs.[27]

Lest there should be any doubt as to what kind of divine intervention she had envisioned, in 1937, in another letter to Churchill, she pontificated, after some remarks on the Great War:

> The Christ must Himself return, before His Kingdom of peace & justice & goodness can exist on the earth. . . . Clemenceau, according to his 'Boswell', Jean Martet, pronounced the failure of all human regimes to be inevitable, & declared that only one can be successful, namely *Theocracy* – provided, as he said, that there *is* a God, a Theos. We who differ from Clemenceau in our belief, that God *is*, must agree with him in believing that nothing less than Theocracy can avail as the ultimate if not imminent cure for war & all the other evils that abound on the earth.[28]

This vision arguably had a certain perspective and grandeur to it: it was a reminder of the difference between the ideal that human beings can conceive and the reality of what they can actually achieve, and it held out the promise that the ideal was attainable through the divine. Nevertheless, this stance could start to look rather comic when wheeled out too quickly in the face of the details of that day's news. Thus, at her most embarrassing, Pankhurst could breezily launch into an article with the words: 'The sheer necessity of the Second Advent of "the great God and our Saviour Jesus Christ" – that is the one great fact brought into clear relief by current events in China.'[29] Humanity's problems were innumerable and ever shifting but, according to Christabel Pankhurst, the return of Christ was the answer to them all.

---

[27] The Churchill Archives Centre, Churchill College, Cambridge: Christabel Pankhurst to Winston Churchill, 14 May 1934.
[28] The Churchill Archives Centre, Churchill College, Cambridge: Christabel Pankhurst to Winston Churchill, 23 December 1937.
[29] *Christian*, 9 December 1926, p. 6.

Hell, Judgment, and Satan

High up on the list of general perceptions of fundamentalists are words such as 'judgmental', 'condemnatory', and 'intolerant'. George Marsden has defined a fundamentalist vividly as 'an evangelical who is angry about something'.[30] Fundamentalist preachers are routinely viewed as 'hell-fire' preachers. They are, so the perception goes, obsessed with dividing people into the 'saved' and the 'unsaved' and promising the former eternal life while informing the latter that their lot is unquestionably everlasting torment. This is particularly true of evangelists (and, as will be shown in chapter seven, Pankhurst was an evangelist), who used the threat of hell as a motivation to prompt conversions. The theme of hell, moreover, is presumably unavoidable when discussing the second coming of Christ and the end of the age, as that is when the final destinies of all mortals will be declared and commenced. Therefore, it is particularly striking that Christabel Pankhurst does not mention hell once in all her religious writings. She wrote five books on biblical prophecy, the end times, and Christ's return, without once mentioning hell. The reality of hell is nowhere to be found in all her newspaper articles and reported speech. In short, she spent several decades devoting her life to speaking and writing about the end of the age and offering evangelistic appeals, and yet ignored hell altogether. Heaven, of course, was another matter. A report of an address she gave in 1923 revealed that 'Miss Pankhurst said that she was looking forward to eternal life, and would be willing to sing praises all day if she but be permitted to enter the gates of Heaven.'[31] Although it is hard to know what exactly he had in mind, it is very suggestive that when the conservative evangelical Dr Webb Anderson reviewed *The World's Unrest* he observed that it 'is not what the writer says, so much as what she left unsaid, which will provoke thought and possibly some retort'.[32] More specifically, in a fascinating chapter in *The Uncurtained Future* entitled 'How to Preach Prophecy', Pankhurst took to task those who preached 'more wrathily than winningly' arguing, in an arresting phrase: 'A terroristic preaching of prophecy is not true to the note of the Bible.'[33] Certainly, no one could accuse her of using terror tactics in her preaching. The *Advent Witness*, on the other hand, ran an article in 1937 entitled 'Shall we give up Doctrine?' in which it attacked the liberal tendency to abandon teaching on hell. The article revived, in order to

---

[30] George M. Marsden, *Understanding Fundamentalism and Evangelicalism*, Grand Rapids: William B. Eerdmans, 1991, p. 1.
[31] *New York Times*, 19 August 1923, p. 13.
[32] *Christian*, 5 August 1926, pp. 1–3.
[33] Pankhurst, *Uncurtained Future*, pp. 120, 122.

fume at, the Victorian quip regarding a court case that demonstrated that Anglican clergymen could not be disciplined for rejecting a traditional view of eternal punishment, 'Hell dismissed with costs'. It called the jettisoning of teaching on hell 'one of the snares of the present day'.[34]

From this, it would be easy to leap to the conclusion that perhaps Pankhurst was not a fundamentalist at all. It will be demonstrated in detail in chapter five, however, that she *was* a fundamentalist. Moreover, sufficient evidence has already been given in this volume in order to make that reasonably clear. Certainly theologically liberal Christians did not go about 'heralding the personal, visible, and powerful Second Coming of the Lord Jesus Christ as foreshown by the present signs of the times'.[35] Even more tellingly, the absence of hell notwithstanding, Satan loomed large in Pankhurst's teaching. In *'The Lord Cometh'* she viewed her own new-found belief in a personal devil as part of a wider trend in society toward a more accurate apprehension of reality: 'many are now regaining, or acquiring, a belief in Satan as a supernatural person'.[36] Addressing an evangelistic meeting in New York City in 1923 she declared, 'Do you believe in Satan? My friend I do.'[37] Reflecting her penchant for getting close to the world of politics, Pankhurst had attended, in the press gallery, an assembly of the League of Nations in Geneva, and she informed her hearers in Knox Presbyterian Church, Toronto, that the problem with the deliberations of the delegates at the League of Nations was that they were unaware of 'the Satanic'.[38] In *The Uncurtained Future* she argued that reformers were disillusioned because they had been overly optimistic: 'their disbelief in the devil' had made them naïve about what it was possible to achieve.[39] Therefore, Alma Whitaker did not need much journalistic licence in order to come up with a suitably dramatic title for her article on the old Suffragette leader in 1943: 'Pankhurst Tradition Whets Christabel's Steel for Satan'.[40] This, of course, did put her back in line with stereotypical fundamentalism. She was now singing from the same hymn sheet as the *Advent Witness* which also took exception to some remarks by the Congregationalist, W. B. Selbie, Principal of Mansfield College, Oxford, who had offered an anecdote about how 'when he told a devout woman some years ago that

---

[34] *Advent Witness*, July 1937, p. 130.
[35] This description of her work – which has the ring of having been written by herself – was for many years in her *Who's Who* entry. See, for example, *Who's Who 1938*, London: A. & C. Black, p. 2591.
[36] Pankhurst, *'The Lord Cometh'*, p. 105.
[37] *New York Times*, 16 August 1923, p. 15.
[38] *Evangelical Christian and Missionary Witness*, January 1930, pp. 61–2.
[39] Pankhurst, *Uncurtained Future*, p. 148.
[40] Alma Whitaker, 'Pankhurst Tradition Whets Christabel's Steel for Satan', *Los Angeles Times*, 13 July 1943.

he did not believe in a personal Devil she complained that he had taken away her religion'.[41] Pankhurst, however, had her own exchange to report that was almost a precise inversion of that one:

> An American friend, a woman of great intelligence and education with a long lifetime of wide experience, wrote to me the other day: 'I am still an agnostic, but although I am not sure about God, I am quite certain of this – that there is a Devil and that he rules at the present time. Such a world!'[42]

Pankhurst was not embarrassed to talk about Satan as a real, living, spiritual being.

So how does one account for her unabashed teaching on Satan being combined with her sense that mentioning hell would be counter-productive? The answer is that she really did see herself as a thorough-going messenger of hope. Belief in Satan was an indirect message of hope because it was a way of explaining what people already knew (that there is a lot of unpleasantness in the world) while also being able to point to its resolution (Christ will soon return and sort out both the devil and the world). On the other hand, one could hardly threaten people with hell – which, arguably, might be an indirectly hopeful thing to do if it prompted them to take the steps to secure eternal life for them-selves – without at least tacitly acknowledging that the fate of some people who had died already is unquestionably eternal damnation. It was a message therefore that, at the very least, implicitly revealed the hopeless situation of those souls. Pankhurst appears to have taken the attitude 'let the dead worry about the fate of the dead', and concentrated on offering a positive message to the living. Her principle continually seemed to be to maximize hope, albeit never in a way that failed to take into account what people already knew from their own experience about the evil, suffering, and sin that was in the world. Her gospel was thoroughly good news.

The Destiny of Living Unbelievers at the End of the Age

This point is made even more apparent when one examines the question of the eternal destiny of people at the end of the age. Evangelicals had always taught that believing in and 'accepting' Jesus Christ as Lord and Saviour was a necessary condition of salvation. The question there-fore arose: what is the fate of those people who have not accepted Jesus Christ at the end of the final dispensation of human history? This consid-eration could be subdivided on the basis of three distinct categories of

---

[41] *Advent Witness*, September 1925, p. 100.
[42] *Sunday School Times*, 3 January 1931, p. 5.

people: (1) Gentiles who had heard the gospel, but rejected it, (2) Gentiles who had never heard the gospel, (3) the Jews. The fundamentalist-evangelical consensus was that Gentiles who had heard the gospel but rejected it would be destined for hell at the second coming. Even more soberingly, the *Advent Witness* consistently taught that those who rejected Christ had no hope of salvation once the rapture had taken place. Thus they would enter the time of tribulation leading up to Christ's second coming, but there was no hope of them gaining salvation during that period. The fact that this issue was repeatedly raised (often in letters) indicates that the faithful wondered if this was not unduly harsh, but the paper held its ground on this point.[43] In fact, the *Advent Witness* eventually reduced this teaching to the blunt slogan: 'Which will it be? Caught up or Cut off. There is no third choice.'[44] In other words, if you are not raptured – deemed by Christ to be one of his own and so taken up to meet him in the air – then you are excluded from the possibility of salvation forever thereafter. Pankhurst, on the other hand, was so positive that salvation at the price of enduring the great tribulation was still too negative a message for her.[45] The *Advent Witness* noticed a booklet in 1923 with the title, 'Shall I Be Left Behind?' (the author, one assumes, never imagined that he had the kernel of a best-seller on his hands). Another speaker even addressed this same question when sharing a platform with Pankhurst, but such 'terroristic' tactics are not to be found in her teaching.[46]

This leads on to the peculiar notion that developed in fundamentalist circles regarding the fate of the Jews. Ian Randall has summarized this teaching as 'that Israel would be territorially restored and converted by Christ's appearing'.[47] This idea was even taught in the pared down, coalition-building, seven-point creed made at the founding of the Advent Testimony Movement: 'Israel will be . . . converted by the appearance of

[43] See, for example, *Advent Witness*, January 1927, pp. 13–14; August 1928, p. 128.
[44] *Advent Witness*, July–August 1947, p. 244.
[45] Hence her tendency to ignore the rapture and just speak about 'the second coming'. She once offered a telling apologetic for this habit: 'The hope of the Church came to me later, and just added to what had seemed to me already perfect. Thus I inclined to think that to present first and to give chief emphasis to, the glorious and all-visible, powerful appearing has most effect in its appeal to non-Christians and is most glorifying to our Lord, for it speaks of his own ultimate victory and complete pre-eminence over all things and peoples.' *Sunday School Times*, 28 May 1932, p. 287.
[46] *Advent Witness*, July 1923, p. 84; *Christian*, 21 October 1926, p. 24.
[47] I. M. Randall, 'The Career of F. B. Meyer (1847–1929)', CNAA M.Phil thesis, 1992. I had not realized the true import of what was being said about the Jews until reading Randall's work. I am also grateful to Dr Randall for supplying me with a copy of the relevant chapter from his thesis, and for faithfully answering various questions I put to him periodically by e-mail.

Christ on its behalf.'[48] Zechariah 12:10 was thought to be germane: 'And I will pour upon the house of David, and upon the inhabitants of Jerusalem, the spirit of grace and of supplications: and they shall look upon me whom they have pierced, and they shall mourn for him, as one mourneth for his only son' (Authorized Version). This is taken to mean that at his return the Jews will see Jesus and recognize him as their Messiah, 'And so all Israel shall be saved'.[49] According to many fundamentalists, Jews who have rejected Christ hitherto could still gain eternal salvation at the time of the second advent.

Although she had a genius for not making her precise views on these kinds of issues explicit, it seems probable that Pankhurst developed a theological innovation all of her own in which she at least nurtured the hope that it might be possible for Christ-rejecting Gentiles to gain salvation at the moment of Christ's appearing as well. Part of the ambiguity of this terrain is that all evangelicals taught that, in the words of the Bible: 'For it is written, As I live, saith the Lord, every knee shall bow to me, and every tongue shall confess to God.'[50] This was taken to mean, however, that unbelievers would be forced to acknowledge that Jesus was Lord at the end of the age by his unequivocal appearing in power, but by then it would be too late for them to be saved. Pankhurst, however, put this teaching forward optimistically, implying that they might be redeemed. For example, in 'The Lord Cometh' she expounded: 'The world, like Thomas, will not, until it sees, hail Him, as we who know Him by faith already hail Him: MY LORD AND MY GOD.'[51] Thomas, of course, was (from an evangelical point of view) saved and converted by this encounter, and so that analogy is a rather intriguing one for her to have used. After mentioning a minister who had denied Christ's divinity, she declared in 1923: 'There is nothing that will convince people of this sort but the visible appearing in power and glory of our Lord.'[52] Now it was patently true from a fundamentalist perspective that Christ's return would convince him, but the remark is nevertheless odd because the issue of how to 'convince' various groups of people was central to evangelistic strategy in this subculture and therefore the comment leaves the impression that the modernist clergyman might be redeemed by this encounter with Christ. This connection was made even more explicit in a passage in her newspaper column in 1927 regarding the situation in China:

> What a Missionary is coming, in the Person of the living, visible Lord Himself! When He shall reward His missionaries with His 'Well done,

---

[48] *Christian*, 8 November 1917, p. 14.
[49] Romans 11:26 (Authorized Version).
[50] Romans 14:11 (Authorized Version).
[51] Pankhurst, *'The Lord Cometh'*, p. 15.
[52] *Moody Bible Institute Monthly*, September 1923, p. 14.

thou good and faithful servant,' and shall cause all peoples, in China and throughout the world, to fall down and worship Him, great will be the victory![53]

Again, although this can be read as strictly true from an evangelical mindset, it is nevertheless an extraordinary statement. It is probable that no other fundamentalist teacher or preacher ever referred to Christ at his return as a missionary. The impression is clearly left that he will gain converts on his appearing and that they will receive salvation. Even more overtly, Pankhurst discussed Chinese developments again a few weeks later, remarking: 'the missionary situation there may be one of the most important of all the signs of this moment. If His ambassadors be denied opportunity to speak in His Name, will not the King Himself return to speak in person!'[54] This is a bizarre conflation if one assumes (as standard fundamentalist teaching would lead one to) that missionaries who are gaining souls for eternal life are to be replaced by Christ returning to pronounce everlasting damnation on those who have not yet converted. The only natural reading is that Jesus will also be offering salvation, only far more effectively than the missionaries are able to do in the face of current opposition. The traditional view led some members of the faithful to have mixed feelings about the return of Christ owing to a fear that an unregenerate loved one would thereby be damned. Pankhurst sought to reassure them, but in a way that leaves the impression that she suspected something that most fundamentalists did not:

> I have the conviction that when he comes he will bring all good things with him. When he comes and takes us away he is not going to leave our dear ones behind. We can trust him for that.[55]

Pankhurst, at the very least, thus teased her hearers and readers with the possibility of unbelievers receiving salvation at Christ's return.

The reason for her apparent departure from evangelical thought on this point is simple: for Pankhurst, Christ's coming again was the great panacea – the solution to all human problems – and it did not fit that grand theme of hers to highlight the possibility that the second advent might be bad news for anyone. She told an audience in 1927: 'He will come and so order things on this earth when every man and woman shall sit under their vine and fig tree and none shall make them afraid.'[56] This statement was largely a biblical quotation, and therefore unimpeachable, and yet, once again, it carried the connotation that Christ's coming was pure good news for everyone: a normative fundamentalist presentation

---

[53] *Christian*, 13 January 1927, pp. 19–20.
[54] *Christian*, 3 February 1927, p. 12.
[55] *Sunday School Times*, 31 October 1925, p. 684.
[56] *Moody Bible Institute Monthly*, September 1927, pp. 10–14.

would have stressed that this idyllic situation was reserved for the faithful alone. Pankhurst may have been unusually pessimistic about what human effort could achieve in this age (a question that will be discussed more fully in chapter six), but she was exceedingly bright and upbeat for a fundamentalist when it came to what the world might expect from Christ's return.

Avertible Doom

Equally distinctive was Pankhurst's willingness to apply a doctrine of avertible doom to the end times. Prophecies that forebode unpleasant occurrences are apt to arouse the question of whether or not they might be somehow avoided. Such a reaction is immortalized in Dickens' character, Ebenezer Scrooge, who, having been shown the unsavoury end that awaited him, inquired of the Last of the Spirits: 'Are these the shadows of the things that Will be, or are they shadows of things that May be, only?'[57] Pankhurst's teaching on this point developed over time. Her clearest statement on the contingent nature of negative predictions was in her last book, *The Uncurtained Future*. In her first religious book, however, she actually denied it: 'What is the lesson of it all? Not that we can avert these great world-happenings!'[58] Already by the following year (1924), however, she had begun to see an alternative, albeit a rather improbable one: 'If the whole world were to be converted, then its doom might be averted as was the doom of Nineveh when they repented at the preaching of Jonah.'[59] By 1934, she was teaching it as more a general principle than a remote possibility in *Present and Future*: 'but here we meet the paradox of prophecy as it applies to mankind – a merciful paradox, for by a mystery of mercy, divine foretelling to man is forewarning, rather than foredooming'.[60] She was even willing to teach that it was not a foregone conclusion that an anti-Christ would arise who would fight against Christ: 'But that resistance is not inevitable: as witness the second Psalm with its appeal . . . It would suffice to respond to this appeal, to make the closing phase of this Age reflect the dawn of the new Age, when, Christ the Sun of Righteousness, will reign in His own person and presence.'[61] She published in 1934 a revised edition of *'The Lord Cometh'*,

---

[57] Charles Dickens, *A Christmas Carol and Other Christmas Stories*, New York: Signet Classic (Penguin), 1984 [originally 1843], pp. 127–8.
[58] Pankhurst, *'The Lord Cometh'*, p. 55.
[59] *King's Business*, September 1924, p. 597.
[60] *Present and Future*, May 1934, p. 6.
[61] *Present and Future*, June 1934, p. 4.

when it had already gone through seven editions plus a 'popular' edition. It contained a new introduction that made her change of mind explicit:

> But the past years of study and meditation have caused me to see more and more clearly that the solemn prophecies of events preceding His coming are forewarnings rather than foredoomings. They do not foredoom the nations and their leaders to rebel against our God and against His Christ: they forewarn them not to do so. Indeed they plead with them not to do so . . .[62]

In *The Uncurtained Future* her doctrine of avertible doom became a major theme.[63] She averred that the 'prophets say nothing of unconditional and inevitable judgment and doom. Their message forewarns: it does not foredoom.'[64] This principle was even applied to the great final battle of Armageddon which she declared we are told about in order to make sure it never happens.[65] She then went on to outline various biblical supports for this view such as (again) the judgment prophesied against Ninevah being avoided by their repentance, and Moses pleading with God not to punish the Israelites despite the divine intention to do so having already been made known. This led her on to jettison cheerfully all the lesser things she had thought she knew about the future for the one big thing she knew for sure: 'The one good and glorious Absolute and certainty of prophecy, we must note again, is that Jesus, Lord and King, will come in His glory. All else in prophecy is relative and contingent upon the will of human beings and their response to the divine warnings and appeals.'[66] In the end, therefore, the desire to have a message that was unqualified good news trumped her desire to have a blueprint for the future. Hope was truly the keynote of her message. There was no inevitable doom. The great, inevitable event was the divine panacea for the world's woes: 'The brightness of prophecy is unconditional: the Lord will come and will reign.'[67]

[62] Christabel Pankhurst, *'The Lord Cometh': The World Crisis Explained*, revised edition, London: Marshall, Morgan, & Scott, 1934, p. ix.
[63] David Mitchell was apparently unaware of this volume as he never referred to it and it does not appear in the list of Pankhurst's works in his bibliography. Martin Pugh is aware of it, but he does not interact much with its contents and offers the odd judgment that it was largely 'a réchauffé of the earlier books', dismissing it as 'this rather stale volume': Pugh, *Pankhursts*, p. 454. *The Uncurtained Future* actually reveals some substantial and intriguing theological and thematic developments in Pankhurst's thought. Moreover, even for those not particularly interested in theology, this is the only one of her books published during her lifetime in which she reminisces at length about her parents and the Suffragette movement.
[64] Pankhurst, *Uncurtained Future*, p. 120.
[65] Pankhurst, *Uncurtained Future*, p. 113.
[66] Pankhurst, *Uncurtained Future*, pp. 253–4.
[67] Pankhurst, *Uncurtained Future*, p. 122.

Darwinism, Bible Translations, and Theologians

Not only did Pankhurst preach an exceptionally positive message in terms of the fate of unbelievers at Christ's return and the possibility of averting unpleasant events predicted in the Bible, but she also sidestepped a lot of the fights that fundamentalists were prone to pick. For example, she managed to avoid a head-on struggle with Darwinism. It is well known that many fundamentalists made combating Darwinism into a major preoccupation. *The Fundamentals* series of edited volumes of articles (1910–15), which arguably marked the inauguration of the movement, contained several articles on evolution, including one entitled with evocative alliteration, 'The Decadence of Darwinism'.[68] The fundamentalist battle with evolution by natural selection reached a peak in 1925 – during the most active period of Pankhurst's ministry – with the Scopes Trial, the so-called 'Monkey Trial', in Dayton, Tennessee. The American nation read the reports avidly, as the great fundamentalist champion, William Jennings Bryan, was grilled by an urbane, scoffing lawyer regarding his anti-Darwinian views. By that time, anti-Darwinism had virtually become a shibboleth in the fundamentalist camp. Pankhurst did take pot-shots at Darwinism occasionally, but she was far too astute to allow herself to fall into the trap of pitting old-fashioned Christianity against the latest scientific thought. Instead, she cleverly employed her technique of endeavouring to capture the modern ground for the Bible and Christianity. She only addressed the issue at length once, and it was in an article in the *Sunday School Times* tellingly entitled 'Science's Attack on the Evolutionary Theory' in which she employed her cagey tactic of wheeling out a parade of experts to make all the points.[69] When William Jennings Bryan had written an article on this theme for the same paper, its title reflected his far more unequivocal and confrontational approach, 'Why Evolution is anti-Christian'.[70] Pankhurst noted in passing in *Seeing the Future* that, for the younger generation, Darwinism is '*vieux jeu*'.[71] In *Present and Future* she suggested that Einstein might be the undoing of Darwin: 'the theory of relativity may require evolution to be relegated to the realm of "mere appearance."'[72] This incidental line of thought was

---

[68] Henry H. Beach, 'The Decadence of Darwinism', in R. A. Torrey and A. C. Dixon (eds), *The Fundamentals: A Testimony to the Truth*, Los Angeles: the Bible Institute of Los Angeles, 1917 (reprinted Grand Rapids: Baker Book House, 1988), volume IV, chapter V.
[69] *Sunday School Times*, 15 February 1930, p. 91.
[70] *Sunday School Times*, 1 March 1924, p. 143.
[71] Pankhurst, *Seeing the Future*, p. 52.
[72] *Present and Future*, May 1934, p. 3.

elucidated a bit more in a subsequent issue: 'Time is not creative. Time, we learn, does not even really exist.'[73] Again, it is doubtful that any other fundamentalist teacher would have made such a suggestion. Pankhurst was not about to be manœuvred into denouncing scientists and educators.

A similar issue involved English translations of the Bible. Fundamentalists, at their most conservative, were (and are) apt to trust only the Authorized Version (which is often referred to in America as the King James Version), and to view all others as liberal distortions. One of the most prominent Canadian fundamentalist leaders during the time of Pankhurst's ministry was William 'Bible Bill' Aberhart. He went so far as to claim that the Authorized Version was inerrant.[74] D. A. Carson, himself a conservative evangelical though not a King-James-only man, noted in 1979 that:

> There has arisen a sizable and vocal body of opinion that defends the King James Version (KJV) as the best English version now extant. Some of these defenders merely argue strongly; but others have gone so far as to make the adoption of this view a criterion of orthodoxy. They dismiss those who dissent from them as modernists, compromisers, or dupes.[75]

A very recent new translation during Pankhurst's ministry was the one made by James Moffat (New Testament, 1913; Old Testament, 1924; whole Bible published in one volume, 1928).[76] It has not generally met the approval of fundamentalists. Carson dismissed it peremptorily on the grounds that its 'liberal propensities are well-known'.[77] F. F. Bruce, who was also an evangelical, was gracious in his assessment, as was his temperament, but he nonetheless faulted Moffat on the crucial point of Christology. Bruce commented on Moffat's use of the phrase 'the Logos was divine' ('the Word was God' in the Authorized Version) in John's Gospel chapter one:

> In that last clause he falls short of the ideal of equivalent effect; considering the wide use of the adjective 'divine' in modern English, we must observe that 'the Logos was divine' says something rather less than the Evangelist himself says.[78]

[73] *Present and Future*, October 1934, p. 6.
[74] John G. Stackhouse, Jr, *Canadian Evangelicalism in the Twentieth Century: An Introduction to Its Character*, Vancouver: Regent College, 1999, p. 38.
[75] D. A. Carson, *The King James Version Debate: A Plea for Realism*, Grand Rapids: Baker Book House, 1979, pp. 9–10.
[76] F. F. Bruce, *The English Bible: A History of Translations*, London: Lutterworth Press, 1961, p. 167.
[77] Carson, *King James Version*, p. 64.
[78] Bruce, *English Bible*, p. 169.

Moreover, these are not later assessments that are unreflective of Pankhurst's own time. The *Advent Witness* pronounced in 1933 that '"Moffat's Translation" is less a translation than a modernist para-phrase.'[79] Yet Pankhurst was delighted with Moffat's work. In *Seeing the Future* she betrayed her belief that, at least on one text, Moffat's wording was better than the Authorized Version's, extolling 'Moffatt's very modern translation'.[80] Once again, 'very modern' was a compliment in her parlance, whereas 'modernist' was a pejorative term in the argot of the *Advent Witness*. Pankhurst again followed what she believed to be the superior rendering of relevant biblical passages by 'so modern a trans-lator as Moffat' in an article in *Present and Future*, and in *The Uncurtained Future*.[81] If appealing to the Bible was old-fashioned, the Bible that Pankhurst appealed to could be the very latest rendition.

Finally, Pankhurst was not given to denouncing specific liberals, a favourite pastime for many fundamentalist leaders. Her advice was: 'Let us take no notice of apostate Christianity, but let us go forth with the Bible.'[82] It is true that she was not above criticizing the views of liberal clergymen or theologians whom she had heard or read, but she always did this in vague terms, without revealing their identity. She was even willing to handle respectfully the theological pronouncements of leading contempor-ary non-evangelicals. In her column in the *Christian*, Pankhurst gave considerable attention to 'a very recent address on the Kingdom of God' by 'Bishop Gore'. Gore was a leading Anglo-Catholic, who was open to making some accommodations to liberal trains of thought. Nevertheless, Pankhurst's tack was to seize upon statements that Gore had made with which she agreed. Essentially, Gore was enlisted as one of her expert witnesses in order to advance points regarding theology and biblical inter-pretation that she wished to be made. Pankhurst led into one quotation with the words 'it is impressive to hear from Bishop Gore that . . .', and followed another with the words, 'That being the truth about the Kingdom of God, let us pray that . . .'[83] Conservative evangelicals in Britain were not apt to quote Gore as a reliable, authoritative source.

Another instance of Pankhurst's open approach is the sympathetic treatment she gave to Reinhold Niebuhr in *The Uncurtained Future*. Although Niebuhr was arguably America's greatest theologian in the middle decades of the twentieth century, fundamentalists were apt either to ignore or criticize him. He was part of the Protestant mainline establishment from which they had been excluded (or had excluded

[79] *Advent Witness*, 1 November 1933, p. 179.
[80] Pankhurst, *Seeing the Future*, p. 104.
[81] *Present and Future*, May 1934, p. 2; Pankhurst, *Uncurtained Future*, p. 79.
[82] *Moody Bible Institute Monthly*, March 1924, pp. 337–9.
[83] *Christian*, 27 January 1927, p. 12.

themselves). He accepted the kind of biblical criticism that they found anathema.[84] He taught at Union Theological Seminary in New York, one of the suspect mainline bastions that fundamentalists were establishing their own institutions in order to avoid. In fact, it had been an outcry regarding the perceived unorthodoxy of Union students that had ignited the conservative backlash which resulted in the writing of the famous five-point fundamentalist statement of faith.[85] The source that prompted her comments was Niebuhr's *Europe's Catastrophe and the Christian Faith*, published in 1940, the same year as Pankhurst's book was, showing once again that she was reading the newest literature as soon as it appeared. As with Gore, she enlisted Niebuhr as a witness on behalf of the truth as she was expounding it: 'There is one modern theologian, Dr Reinhold Niebuhr, of Union Theological Seminary, in New York, who recognises the fact that . . .', 'Dr Niebuhr very truly points out that . . .', 'Dr Niebuhr makes these highly interesting observations', 'Dr Niebuhr draws this important conclusion . . .' It was clear to her that he was not even an evangelical – let alone a fundamentalist – but Pankhurst chose to see him as a fellow-traveller who had already grasped much truth and who just needed to continue a bit further down the same road:

> We may hope that Dr Niebuhr will eventually agree that literalism is needed for the understanding of the promises of God in Christ. . . . if, as Dr Niebuhr seems to say, the prophecy of wars and perilous times is being literally fulfilled at this present day, why should not the prophecy of our Lord's second coming be just as literally fulfilled by His actual and visible appearance?[86]

It is striking that she could concede that he did not believe in a personal second coming – the great doctrine she had given her life to expounding – and yet she could still treat his thought with such deference. Pankhurst surpassed most, if not all, of her fellow fundamentalist teachers in how positive the content of her ministry was. She did not preach a message of hell-fire, inevitable doom, damnation and denunciation, but rather sought to maximize those themes that would foster hope in troubling times.

---

[84] For example, he would refer incidentally to 'The second Isaiah', reflecting the view that the book of Isaiah was not the unified work of a single prophet: Reinhold Niebuhr, *The Nature and Destiny of Man: A Christian Interpretation*, volume 1, London: Nisbet & Co., 1941, p. 148. For a study of his life, see Richard Wightman Fox, *Reinhold Niebuhr: A Biography*, San Francisco: Harper & Row, 1985.
[85] George M. Marsden, *Fundamentalism and American Culture: The Shaping of Twentieth-Century Evangelicalism, 1870–1925*, New York: Oxford University Press, 1980, p. 117.
[86] Pankhurst, *Uncurtained Future*, pp. 109–11.

Chapter Five

THE FUNDAMENTALIST CIRCUIT

Defining Fundamentalism

Throughout history, new Christian groups have recurrently taken pejorative labels applied to them by outsiders and appropriated them as badges of honour: one thinks, for example, of the 'Quakers' and the 'Methodists'. It has been the peculiar fate of the fundamentalists, however, to have had their own self-chosen designation transmuted by outsiders into a general term of abuse. Perhaps the closest parallel is the Jesuits, who did have to endure the passing of 'jesuitical' into general circulation as a pejorative adjective but, even in their case, no one ever dreamed of talking about 'Jesuit' Moslems, 'Jesuit' Sikhs or the like, in the way in which 'fundamentalist' Moslems and 'fundamentalist' Sikhs are routinely discussed today. Indeed, in a world in which almost all groups – whether distinguished by race, culture, gender or sexual orientation – have been afforded the right to be referred to by only their own self-chosen designations, somehow the right to impose the word 'fundamentalist' on groups who do not so identify themselves has been retained. This is not merely a media phenomenon. Numerous scholarly projects have been created that subsume a dizzying array of religious groups – varieties of Jews, Moslems, Hindus, Sikhs and Roman Catholic Christians as well as Protestant ones, just to name the most prominent examples – under a discussion of 'fundamentalism'.[1] While scholars usually ensure that a pejorative tone is kept to a minimum, the media have popularized the negative connotations of the word so effectively that those meanings easily creep into any learned discussion that is not careful about excluding them. In short, it is the

---

[1] Most notably, the massive The Fundamentalist Project at the University of Chicago. The first volume of this project's output was a sizeable tome that ranged widely across the world's religions and regions: Martin E. Marty and R. Scott Appleby (eds), *Fundamentalisms Observed*, Chicago: University of Chicago Press, 1991. (Admittedly, the plural 'fundamentalisms', and the introduction, reflected an awareness of this criticism.) Another example would be Lionel Caplan (ed.), *Studies in Religious Fundamentalism*, Albany: State University of New York Press, 1987, which contains chapters on Jews, Moslems, and Sikhs, as well as Christians.

intention of this study to use the word 'fundamentalism' in its specific, original meaning, but that cannot be done as effectively as it ought to be unless what we think we know about 'fundamentalism' from the term's more general use in contemporary discourse is set aside.

Fundamentalism is a movement within conservative evangelical Protestantism in the English-speaking world, especially America. In the years 1910–15 twelve edited volumes containing numerous chapters by a notable collection of conservative evangelicals were published under the title *The Fundamentals: A Testimony to the Truth*. George Marsden has confirmed that this series is 'usually regarded as a signal of the beginning of the organized fundamentalist movement' and as 'one of the sources for the movement's name'.[2] *The Fundamentals* was preoccupied with defending the Bible (the most dominant theme), the atonement, personal evangelism, and other core beliefs and practices of conservative evangelicals against modern(ist) attacks, and with attacking groups, trends, and modern(ist) lines of thought that were deemed unorthodox or destructive. Although some of the articles were learned treatises by well-respected scholars, perhaps the most delightful title contributed to the series was the anonymous compilation, 'Tributes to Christ and the Bible by Brainy Men Not Known as Active Christians'.[3] In 1919, the World's Christian Fundamentals Association was founded as an umbrella group for concerned conservative evangelicals. The W.C.F.A. may be seen as the official organizational centre of this emerging movement in America, although it must be borne in mind that it was merely connecting the true source of the movement's strength, its regional strongholds. Curtis Lee Laws, the conservative evangelical editor of the Baptist newspaper, the *Watchman-Examiner*, coined the word 'fundamentalist' in 1920, defining fundamentalists as those 'who still cling to the great fundamentals and who mean to do battle royal for the faith'.[4] The 1920s are seen as the great decade of the 'fundamentalist-modernist controversy', when the churches and Christian leaders increasingly polarized into two warring camps. In other words, strictly speaking, it is anachronistic to speak of 'fundamentalists' and 'fundamentalism' prior to the twentieth century, and the stars of the movement in the 1920s ought to be considered the first generation of fundamentalist leaders.

Such a movement, however, is not created *ex nihilo*, and historians have given it a pre-history of varying lengths, highlighting various sources. In a study of 'the roots of fundamentalism', Ernest R. Sandeen began as far

[2] G. M. Marsden, 'The Fundamentals', in Daniel G. Reid (ed.), *Dictionary of Christianity in America*, Downers Grove, IL: IVP, 1990, p. 468.
[3] *The Fundamentals: A Testimony to the Truth*, Chicago: Testimony Publishing Company, volume II, chapter 7.
[4] W. H. Brackney, 'Curtis Lee Laws', in Reid (ed.), *Dictionary of Christianity*, p. 634.

back as 1800.[5] The subtitle of Sandeen's book is 'British and American Millenarianism, 1800–1930'; what is particularly interesting about his work from the perspective of this study is that he included aspects of the British scene as part of the fundamentalist movement (a theme that will be further addressed below), and that he placed 'the millenarian tradition' and the 'Prophecy and Bible Conference Movement' at the centre of fundamentalist identity. Sandeen's argument thus positions Pankhurst's preoccupations and the scenes of much of her work at the heart of fundamentalism.[6] A decade after Sandeen's work came George Marsden's *Fundamentalism and American Culture: The Shaping of Twentieth-Century Evangelicalism, 1870–1925* (1980).[7] Marsden accepted Sandeen's emphasis on millenarianism as an important key for understanding fundamentalism, but he also argued that other factors (such as the holiness movement) were equally strong when it came to forming the identity of the movement. In terms of chronology, although his study begins in 1870, Marsden squarely locates fundamentalism itself as a twentieth-century movement.

Fundamentalism and Britain

It has long been fashionable to minimize the applicability of the word 'fundamentalism' in Britain. This policy has been followed both by British evangelical leaders defining their own community and by scholars. The noted English evangelical Anglican author and theologian, J. I. Packer, might serve to represent the former. In a book that was quite influential in evangelical circles, *'Fundamentalism' and the Word of God: Some Evangelical Principles* (1958), Packer spent the bulk of a chapter discussing '"Fundamentalism" An Objectionable Term', a section structured around explaining why British evangelicals should resist the label 'fundamentalist'. He argued numerous points, including that to 'persons ignorant of the American debate about "the fundamentals" (as most Englishmen are) the word can convey no obvious meaning'.[8] Scholars on both sides of the Atlantic have adopted a similar approach. Marsden offered an entire section in his book entitled 'Fundamentalism as an

[5] Ernest R. Sandeen, *The Roots of Fundamentalism: British and American Millenarianism, 1800–1930*, Chicago: University of Chicago Press, 1970.
[6] Sandeen offered, as a second root, the development of the doctrine of biblical inerrancy, a movement that was led by Presbyterian theologians at Princeton.
[7] George M. Marsden, *Fundamentalism and American Culture: The Shaping of Twentieth-Century Evangelicalism, 1870–1925*, New York: Oxford University Press, 1980.
[8] J. I. Packer, *'Fundamentalism' and the Word of God: Some Evangelical Principles*, Leicester: Inter-Varsity Press, 1996 [originally 1958], p. 29.

American Phenomenon'. This is a nuanced discussion that, none the less, is built upon contrasting 'American fundamentalism' with 'English evangelicalism'.[9] It is important to recall, however (as Marsden himself pointed out), that many of the articles in *The Fundamentals* were written by British figures: James Orr, of the United Free Church College, Glasgow; G. Campbell Morgan, Westminster Chapel, London; Sir Robert Anderson; H. C. G. Moule, the bishop of Durham; Thomas Whitelaw of Kilmarnock; W. H. Webb-Peploe, a vicar in London; Thomas Spurgeon of London; W. C. Procter of Croydon, and others.

From the British perspective, the most substantial contribution to this area of study has been made by David Bebbington, who has written two important articles on fundamentalism in Britain.[10] He acknowledges that there was a British fundamentalist community. Nevertheless, Bebbington seems preoccupied with quarantining them as a fringe group distinct from 'conservative evangelicalism'.[11] While this distinction is a valid and useful one, Bebbington's use of it is problematic. Firstly, he is so concerned to reserve the word 'fundamentalist' as a label of last resort that conservative Christian organizations where fundamentalists felt well at home were deprived of the label because some figures deemed to be 'conservative evangelicals' also felt at home there. Moreover, Bebbington seems to issue temporary passes into the fundamentalist world so that figures who are clearly talking and behaving like fundamentalists are deemed 'conservative evangelicals' who had a bout of fundamentalism. Secondly, Bebbington's definition of fundamentalism is problematic. He delineates the difference in terms of temperament: 'The disagreement was essentially about method: conservative Evangelicals wished to avoid *ad hominem* denunciations; Fundamentalists were eager to engage in vigorous polemic.'[12] This is reminiscent of Marsden's quip, noted earlier, that 'a fundamentalist is an evangelical who is angry about something'.[13] The difficulty with these

---

[9] Marsden, *Fundamentalism*, pp. 221–8.

[10] D. W. Bebbington, 'Baptists and Fundamentalism in Inter-War Britain', in Keith Robbins (ed.), *Protestant Evangelicalism: Britain, Ireland, Germany and America, c. 1750–c. 1950*, Oxford: Basil Blackwell for the Ecclesiastical History Society, 1990, pp. 297–326; and D. W. Bebbington, 'Martyrs for the Truth: Fundamentalists in Britain', in Diana Wood (ed.), *Martyrs and Martyrologies*, Oxford: Blackwell for the Ecclesiastical History Society, 1993, pp. 417–51. See also the references to fundamentalism in his *Evangelicalism in Modern Britain: A History from the 1730s to the 1980s*, London: Unwin Hyman, 1989.

[11] In this study of Pankhurst, the term 'conservative evangelicalism' is used as a more general term than 'fundamentalism' and therefore all 'fundamentalists' automatically qualify as 'conservative evangelicals'.

[12] Bebbington, 'Martyrs for the Truth', pp. 419–20.

[13] George M. Marsden, *Understanding Fundamentalism and Evangelicalism*, Grand Rapids: William B. Eerdmans, 1991, p. 1.

comments is that it is all too easy for the tail to start wagging the dog so that instead of continuing to investigate what fundamentalists were actually like, a definition becomes enshrined that causes one simply to deny the label 'fundamentalist' to everyone who does not conform to a pre-existing fixed standard in the mind of the scholar. Bebbington comes close to reasoning that various people could not have been fundamentalists because they took a moderate tone, when it is equally possible that his standard is what needs to be questioned rather than their status. The most fruitful way to proceed would be to continue to examine groups that accepted the label 'fundamentalist', or who were well accepted as like-minded Christians by groups that did.

Pankhurst and Fundamentalism in Britain

In order further to grasp and evaluate Pankhurst's status as a fundamentalist, it would be useful to take a tour of her more important connections while simultaneously assessing their significance and status. Her primary British sponsor, F. B. Meyer (1847–1929), was a leading conservative evangelical statesman. He was one of the most eminent Baptist – indeed even Nonconformist or evangelical – ministers of his generation, and an immensely popular preacher and devotional author. He was a favourite speaker at, and one of the most well-known ambassadors of, the Keswick holiness convention, which, as has been mentioned, is considered a wellspring of fundamentalism. He was also closely identified with the eminent American evangelist D. L. Moody, and Meyer was a speaker at Moody's Northfield conferences, another seedbed of the movement. Indeed, Meyer was a frequent speaker in many parts of America and his ministry there was deeply admired in fundamentalist circles. In Britain, he was a founder and the chairman of the Advent Testimony (eventually 'and Preparation') Movement, which began in 1917. This put him at the head of the kind of millenarian interests that Sandeen identifies as central to fundamentalist identity. Bebbington records that Meyer had backed American fundamentalism in 1923, Pankhurst's crucial first full year of ministry and the year that her first religious book was published: 'Our brethren in America are lifting up a standard against the inrush of a mighty host of deserters from the truth – God bless them! We extend to them the right hand of sympathy, for we are face to face with the same conflict here.'[14] Bebbington also credits Meyer with having written a fundamentalist creed in 1920 as a parallel to American developments.[15] In short, if Meyer was only an occasional fundamentalist according to

---

[14] Bebbington, 'Baptists and Fundamentalism', p. 312.
[15] Bebbington, 'Martyrs for the Truth', p. 425.

Bebbington, he was nevertheless the best British ambassador to the world of American fundamentalism that one could hope to find: the more thorough-going fundamentalists were lesser men, less well-known, whose endorsements would have counted for less. Consequently, Meyer was the ideal figure in Britain to put Pankhurst's credentials in order in fundamentalist circles on both sides of the Atlantic.

Meyer's backing of Pankhurst was generous and unwavering. As we have seen, it would appear that Meyer helped connect Pankhurst with the fundamentalist circuit when she first came to America in 1921–22. More crucially, he wrote the foreword for her first religious book, thus endorsing her as a genuine and sound fellow-believer:

> The events that are transpiring around us to-day are exactly such as the Master's words taught us to expect, as preparing His pathway; and new voices, from unexpected quarters, are crying *Ecce venit*; amongst which we greet that of *Christabel Pankhurst*, to whom this message has been entrusted, and who, turning from all other methods of world-renewal, bids us lift up our heads and rejoice, because the Redeemer draweth nigh.[16]

As a director of the evangelical Morgan & Scott publishing company he undoubtedly found her publisher for her and convinced the firm that she was trustworthy, and then continued to see that her ministry and writings were given maximum publicity in Morgan & Scott's widely circulated newspaper, the *Christian*. Meyer continued to open doors for her and publicly to endorse her ministry as the decade progressed. He ensured that letters she wrote to him were published in the evangelical press.[17] The *Advent Witness* reported in 1924: 'We shall look forward with pleasure to reading Miss Pankhurst's new book for which Dr Meyer is writing a foreword.'[18] He duly wrote the foreword to her second religious book just as he had done for her first, citing his 'personal acquaintance with the Authoress'.[19] F. B. Meyer's introduction also appeared in the American version of this book.[20] By her third religious book, *The World's Unrest*, it would seem that Meyer, Pankhurst, and Morgan & Scott Ltd now considered a foreword by Meyer superfluous, but the Baptist minister was still helping behind the scenes, as well as publicly promoting it in other ways. The *Christian* told its readers, 'Dr Meyer informs us that he has had the first reading, and he considers it quite the best of Miss Pankhurst's three

---

[16] Pankhurst, *'The Lord Cometh'*, p. iv.
[17] See, for example, *Christian*, 24 January 1924, p. 19; *Advent Witness*, November 1924, p. 131; *Advent Witness*, February 1926, p. 31.
[18] *Advent Witness*, November 1924, p. 131.
[19] Pankhurst, *Pressing Problems*, p. iii.
[20] Christabel Pankhurst, *Some Modern Problems in the Light of Bible Prophecy*, New York: Fleming H. Revell, 1924.

books on the subject of present day conditions.'[21] Also, when the time came, he reviewed it, arguing that Pankhurst was 'in the foremost rank' of those who proclaimed the vital truth that these are the end times.[22] Meyer arranged for Pankhurst to be one of the speakers in a major national series of meetings held by the Advent Testimony and Preparation Movement from September 1926 to February 1927. She proved a good draw at these meetings, speaking in Scotland, Wales, and Ireland, as well as in many English cities. At the Queen's Hall, London, Meyer, as chairperson, commented: 'Miss Pankhurst has already rendered invaluable service to the cause of the Master by her eloquent platform ministry.'[23] There had been such a demand for tickets to this event that they had already arranged for her to speak in the Royal Albert Hall in January 1927. Thus the apex of the tour came when 'she twice filled to overflowing' the 'ten-thousand capacity Royal Albert Hall'.[24] The *Advent Witness* enthused: 'Never before have such crowds gathered to witness to the "blessed hope" of Christ's return along sound and sober evangelical lines. The over-shadowing presence of God was most marked all through.'[25] The *Christian* remarked: 'The statement of Dr Meyer, from the chair, that the meeting was probably the largest ever held since the early days of the Church, to consider the doctrine of the Blessed Hope, and to voice the prayer, "Come, Lord Jesus," is doubtless true to the very letter.'[26]

F. B. Meyer, by then an octogenarian, died on 28 March 1929. Pankhurst's tribute to him (apparently written as a letter to a friend of his) was printed in the *Christian*. Resourcefully, she managed to extract a final, posthumous plug for her latest book from him while simultaneously paying her respects:

> Though 'Seeing the Future' was primarily written for them that are outside, I naturally rejoice that believers should find it acceptable. Dr Meyer was able to read my book during his last days, and twice wrote to express his satisfaction with it.
>
> With yourself and others, who worked side by side with our saintly Dr Meyer during many years, I feel the deepest sympathy. His friendship I prized so very greatly that I can the better understand what this bereavement means to you as a friend of long standing.[27]

[21] *Christian*, 1 July 1926, p. 10.
[22] *Christian*, 15 July 1926, p. 20.
[23] *Christian*, 11 November 1926, p. 6.
[24] *Evangelical Christendom*, 27 January 1927, p. 40. She also addressed crowds at the Queen's Hall and the Royal Albert Hall during the Suffragette campaign.
[25] *Advent Witness*, March 1926, p. 48.
[26] *Christian*, 27 January 1927, p. 4.
[27] *Christian*, 18 April 1929, p. 6.

No one could be considered outside the movement whose ministry had been so forcefully and persistently sanctioned by Meyer.

Pankhurst's role as a spokesperson for the Advent Testimony and Preparation Movement is worth underlining. When she died in 1958, the organization still remembered her service to them in that great tour:

> All old friends of the Movement will remember Miss Pankhurst and her association with the Movement in its early days. . . . In 1926–27 at the invitation of Dr Meyer, Dame Christabel came to England from the United States, and with Dr F. B. Meyer, Mr A. Lindsay Glegg and others, addressed a wonderful series of meetings all over the country (including the Queen's Hall in London): they were deeply inspiring and met with great response.[28]

When the organization published an official history in the late 1960s, Pankhurst had still not been forgotten. In addition to including a photograph of her and listing her as one of the outstanding speakers associated with the cause, the tour was again remembered fondly:

> So strong was the conviction that the evangelistic appeal must accompany the preaching of the hope that Dr F. B. Meyer, the Rev E. L. Langston and Miss Christabel Pankhurst toured Britain, heralding the Coming and preaching the gospel to crowded meetings at Bristol, Birmingham, Liverpool, Manchester, Glasgow and Edinburgh. Hundreds of their hearers turned to Christ for salvation, and thousands of Christians rededicated their lives to God.[29]

The Bible Testimony Fellowship was founded in the 1920s from a classic fundamentalist impulse to defend the scriptures against modernist attacks. Following the same strategy as the Advent Testimony tour a decade earlier, the Bible Testimony Fellowship sponsored a campaign involving numerous speakers in many different venues across Britain in the last months of 1937 and the first months of 1938. Pankhurst was one of the most prominent speakers in this 'Nation-Wide Witness Through the British Isles'. While she was speaking on the main platform for the organization's 'Tenth National Bible Day' in 1937, the noted American fundamentalist, Dr Will Houghton, was reduced to addressing those who had failed to secure a seat to hear her and who had therefore been ushered off into an overflow room.[30] Despite having enlisted the speaking services of thirty-eight Anglican clergymen and fifty-five Free Church ministers for the tour, the Bible Testimony Fellowship's journal announced when reporting on the success of this venture: 'Dame Christabel Pankhurst's

---

[28] 'The Homecall of Dame Christabel Pankhurst', *Prophetic Witness*, March 1958, p. 47.
[29] F. A. Tatford, *The Midnight Cry: The Story of Fifty Years of Witness*, Eastbourne: Bible and Advent Testimony Movement, n.d. [c. 1967], p. 81.
[30] *Quarterly Paper of the Bible Testimony Fellowship*, 10, 3 (July–September 1937), p. 3.

photograph appears on the previous page as a "representative" of the panel of speakers by right of her many (and important) engagements throughout the Campaign.'[31] Her strategic and high-profile role in this Bible Testimony Fellowship initiative is solid proof that she was, beyond all doubt, 'one of them'.

It would be tedious to chronicle exhaustively all Pankhurst's contacts in her native land, but it might serve to round off the British part of this tour to mention that both D. M. McIntyre and H. Tydeman Chilvers endorsed Pankhurst in reviews of *The World's Unrest*. McIntyre was the principal of the Bible Training Institute in Glasgow, a rare British equivalent to the influential fundamentalist Bible schools in North America. H. Tydeman Chilvers was the minister at Spurgeon's Metropolitan Tabernacle, and a thorough-going British fundamentalist leader even by the most exacting definition. Nevertheless, his endorsement of Pankhurst was determined and unequivocal:

> the Lord has laid His hand upon Miss Pankhurst, and not only given her hope of salvation in Christ, but has made her a herald of the Glorious Appearing of our Lord and Saviour Jesus Christ. . . . It is remarkable how much knowledge of divine things in so short a time has been acquired by the author of this notable book . . . She has evidently been under the very close tuition of the Holy Spirit, and a diligent student of the Bible . . .[32]

He went on to quote passages from the book on 'the Cross of Christ and personal salvation by the Blood' in order to prove that she was sound on touchstone fundamentalist doctrines. Even a strict fundamentalist leader in Britain was willing to recognize wholeheartedly that Pankhurst not only belonged to the movement, but was a valuable member.

Pankhurst and Fundamentalism in North America

It is undoubtedly easier to know who were full-blooded fundamentalists in North America than in Britain, and therefore Pankhurst's contacts there are even more revealing. As has been shown already, Pankhurst began her public ministry by speaking at Knox Presbyterian Church in Toronto, a conservative evangelical bastion; this opportunity arose through her having won the backing of A. B. Winchester (1858–1943), Knox's former pastor and minister-at-large. Winchester's endorsement was also unequivocal. Not only did he clearly take pride in being able 'to introduce a new member to the family circle of redeemed ones', but he

---

[31] *Quarterly Paper of the Bible Testimony Fellowship*, 11, 1 (January–March 1938), p. 6.
[32] *Christian*, 26 August 1926, p. 14.

also established hers as a legitimate ministry: once Knox had thrown wide open its pulpit for her to offer numerous addresses there, the invitations started to pour in.[33] Winchester's name was an impressive calling card. Not only was he a fundamentalist, he was also a widely known speaker and a prominent leader in crucial fundamentalist ventures. Winchester addressed the founding conference of the World's Christian Fundamentals Association, and he served that organization faithfully thereafter. At the same time that he was helping to establish Pankhurst's ministry, he was also co-founding the institution that came to be known as Dallas Theological Seminary, which quickly became a stronghold of the movement. Winchester's credentials as a leading fundamentalist in the 1920s are impeccable, and he zealously endorsed Christabel Pankhurst's ministry.

It is difficult to overestimate how crucial the Bible institutes – centres for training Christian workers in a context of theologically conservative convictions – were in American fundamentalism. According to Sandeen, 'The simplest way to explain the function of the Bible institute within the Fundamentalist movement is to compare its role to that of the headquarters of a denomination.'[34] Sandeen has also argued that 'Fundamentalism owed its survival to the Bible institutes.'[35] By the 1920s, one could find a Bible institute in a wide variety of places in North America, but the Moody Bible Institute in Chicago, founded by D. L. Moody himself, was the greatest of them all.

In the September 1923 issue of the *Moody Bible Institute Monthly* there was an account of 'Miss Pankhurst's Conversion'.[36] Within six months, this journal was reporting on an address that Pankhurst had given at the institute. Moreover, the *Chicago Tribune* revealed that she was also 'speaking at the Moody Tabernacle', a premier city congregation known today as Moody Memorial Church.[37] The *Sunday School Times* observed in 1940 that 'Dame Christabel is now in the United States, and has been asked to be one of the speakers at the great Founder's Week Conference at the Moody Bible Institute in Chicago in February', but it would appear that she was unable to attend this still popular annual event.[38]

---

[33] *Christian*, 29 March 1923, p. 20.
[34] Sandeen, *Roots of Fundamentalism*, pp. 241–2.
[35] Sandeen, *Roots of Fundamentalism*, p. 183. For a study of the Bible institutes, see Virginia Lieson Brereton, *Training God's Army: The American Bible School, 1880–1940*, Bloomington, IN: Indiana University Press, 1990.
[36] *Moody Bible Institute Monthly*, September 1923, p. 14.
[37] *Moody Bible Institute Monthly*, March 1924, pp. 337–9. It is indicative of how foreign this world has been to scholars who have studied Pankhurst hitherto that Pugh could claim that she spoke at 'Moody Tabernacle in New York', a phrase that would sound to those with a general knowledge of American Protestantism comparable to saying 'Westminster Abbey in Edinburgh'. Pugh, *Pankhursts*, p. 384.
[38] *Sunday School Times*, 14 December 1940, p. 1025.

In 1924, Pankhurst spoke at the Bible Institute of Los Angeles (Biola), another one of the more prominent of the Bible institutes.[39] Moreover, because Moody and Biola were major institutes that published their own journals (and because both institutions still exist) they are the kind of places most likely to have left a record of Pankhurst's ministry. In other words, it is probable – given the fact that we know, for example, that she was on the itinerant speaking circuit for six-month tours in North America repeatedly – that Pankhurst spoke at numerous other Bible institutes as well. For example, because the *Christian* happened to reprint her speech, we have a record of the fact that Pankhurst spoke at the National Bible Institute in New York.[40]

Charles Gallaudet Trumbull (1872–1941) was a fundamentalist who edited the popular *Sunday School Times*. He was the main American promoter of the kind of spirituality arising from the Keswick conferences in England and therefore, in that respect, a parallel figure to F. B. Meyer. He also wrote a biography of C. I. Scofield, the man who had done so much to popularize dispensational premillennialism through his reference Bible. Pankhurst's *The World's Unrest* was published in America by Trumbull's Sunday School Times Company. Letters and articles by her consistently appeared in the *Sunday School Times*, as did news items about her ministry. The *Sunday School Times* had a circulation of around 80,000.[41] It was proud to wear the label 'a Fundamentalist religious newspaper',[42] and it repeatedly used special deals ('Ten Weeks Get Acquainted series') tied into a 'Pankhurst series' in order to endeavour to increase the number of its subscribers.[43] The paper was glad to be able to boast that 'Miss Pankhurst is writing several new articles exclusively for the TIMES'.[44]

Not unlike Trumbull, Fleming Hewitt Revell (1849–1931) was a leading publisher in fundamentalist circles. His brother-in-law and friend had been the evangelist D. L. Moody. Revell's publishing company had been a major influence in the effort to shift the conservative evangelical world toward premillennialism. It was the only large commercial firm in America that was committed to fundamentalism.[45] In 1924, the Fleming H. Revell Company (of which Revell himself was still president) published for the American market Pankhurst's *Pressing Problems of the Closing Age* under the title *Some Modern Problems in the Light of Bible Prophecy*.

---

[39] *King's Business*, September 1924, pp. 553, 597–600.
[40] *Christian*, 3 July 1924, p. 5.
[41] Joel A. Carpenter, *Revive Us Again: The Reawakening of American Fundamentalism*, New York: Oxford University Press, 1997, p. 26.
[42] *Sunday School Times*, 3 January 1931, p. 2.
[43] See, for example, *Sunday School Times*, 23 October 1926, p. 615.
[44] *Sunday School Times*, 7 September 1929, p. 485.
[45] Carpenter, *Revive Us Again*, p. 25.

A book of hers on this topic would not have been issued from such a publisher unless the firm was confident that it would contain premillennial teaching deemed sound from a fundamentalist perspective.

Pankhurst was one of the speakers at the Christian Fellowship Bible Conference held in the Los Angeles area in 1943. This conference was organized by Westmont College, one of the new educational ventures that fundamentalists were embarking upon in order to supply their constituency with a liberal arts education.[46] There were eleven speakers – including Pankhurst – who were highlighted (including photographs and biographical summaries) in the conference brochure. Many of the other speakers were leading figures in American fundamentalism, including Lewis Sperry Chafer, the president of Dallas Theological Seminary; Charles E. Fuller, a beloved radio evangelist; Clarence Mason, a Baptist minister and popular speaker; John Bradbury, editor of the *Watchman-Examiner*, the conservative Baptist newspaper that had coined the word 'fundamentalist'; John Mitchell, vice-president of Multnomah School of the Bible in Oregon; and Henry C. Thiessen, a New Testament scholar at Wheaton College, Illinois, another acceptable place for fundamentalists to receive a liberal arts education.[47] In short, Pankhurst shared the platform at this conference with some of the most respected Bible teachers on the fundamentalist circuit. It would be safe to say that the organizers thought that they had an all-fundamentalist platform.

The Bible conferences were opportunities for thousands of the faithful to gather together to hear leading fundamentalists preach. The annual conference at Winona Lake, Indiana, was the most popular of such events in this period. Pankhurst was one of twenty-three main speakers at the forty-seventh annual Winona Lake Bible Conference in 1941. Once again, those with whom she shared the platform locate her ministry at the heart of the fundamentalist circuit. Some of the other speakers included H. A. Ironside, Lewis Sperry Chafer, W. B. Riley, and Bob Jones, Jr. Ironside was the pastor of Moody Memorial Church in Chicago and a celebrated dispensationalist teacher. W. B. Riley ran a great fundamentalist empire in Minneapolis, Minnesota. He is widely considered one of the most influential fundamentalist leaders of his generation. George W. Dollar, an historian from inside the fundamentalist tradition, identified Riley as one of four 'Prima Donnas of Fundamentalism' during the 1920s and '30s.[48] C. Allyn Russell chose Riley as one of seven fundamentalist

---

[46] Carpenter, *Revive Us Again*, p. 21.
[47] *Christian Fellowship Bible Conference Under the Auspices of Westmont College. July 11–18 [1943] Inclusive. Over sixty churches participating, representing sixteen denominations at six locations.*
[48] George W. Dollar, *A History of Fundamentalism in America*, Greenville, South Carolina: Bob Jones University Press, 1973, chapter 7.

leaders that he highlighted in order to explore 1920s fundamentalism.[49] Bob Jones, Jr, however, is the most interesting of them all. His father had founded Bob Jones College, a bastion of fundamentalism, and Bob Jones, Jr would emerge as a leading champion of the decidedly separatistic or sectarian version of fundamentalism. Pankhurst was sharing the limelight with the prima donnas of the movement.

The third annual Fundamentalist Rally and Prophetic Conference was held at a Baptist church in Atlantic City, New Jersey, in September 1932. It was sponsored by a regional fundamentalist body, the Interstate Evangelistic Association. A full list of speakers has not been discovered but – beside the prominent place offered to Pankhurst – the speakers that the *Atlantic City Press* chose to cover included Howard C. Fulton, Will H. Houghton, and Cortland Myers.[50] Fulton, a minister in Chicago, that very same year would chair a separatistic meeting that created a new fundamentalist denomination, the General Association of Regular Baptist Churches.[51] Houghton was, at the time of this conference, the pastor of Calvary Baptist Church in New York City, a fundamentalist flagship congregation, and a few years later he became the president of Moody Bible Institute. Myers was a Baptist pastor in California who had played a prominent role at numerous key fundamentalist gatherings. Dollar, who did not give his approval readily, deemed Myers to be: 'One of the most stimulating and hard-hitting Fundamentalists of his day.'[52]

John Roach Straton (1875–1929) was the pastor of Calvary Baptist Church in New York City, and no one would deny that he was one of the most important leaders of American fundamentalism in the 1920s. In fact, he has sometimes been dubbed the 'Pope of fundamentalism'.[53] He is one of Russell's seven leaders of fundamentalism in the 1920s and one of Dollar's four 'Prima Donnas of Fundamentalism'.[54] Straton was the pre-eminent fundamentalist in the northeastern part of the United States in the 1920s. In 1922, he founded the Fundamentalist League of Greater New York. Straton was also a principal supporter of Christabel Pankhurst and he frequently relinquished his pulpit at Calvary Baptist Church in order that his large congregation might benefit from her ministry.

---

[49] C. Allyn Russell, *Voices of American Fundamentalism: Seven Biographical Studies*, Philadelphia: Westminster Press, 1976.
[50] *Atlantic City Press*, 24 September 1932, p. 10; 26 September 1932, p. 1; 27 September 1932, p. 1; 28 September 1932, pp. 1 and 4; 29 September 1932, p. 1.
[51] Dollar, *History of Fundamentalism*, p. 171.
[52] Dollar, *History of Fundamentalism*, p. 346.
[53] R. L. Peterson, 'John Roach Straton (1875–1929)', in Reid (ed.), *Dictionary of Christianity*, p. 1138.
[54] Russell, *Voices of American Fundamentalism*, chapter 3; Dollar, *History of Fundamentalism*, chapter 7.

For example, she preached there on Sunday 9 March 1924.[55] In 1926, the *Manchester Guardian* gave its readers in Pankhurst's home town an update on her current activities in which it reported, 'For several years past she has delivered addresses every season at the headquarters of Fundamentalism in New York, the Calvary Church, of which the famous Dr J. R. Straton is minister.'[56] In New York, if not everywhere, he was the pontiff of fundamentalism, and Pankhurst had his blessing.

The capstone of this whole line of argument is that Pankhurst was one of the main speakers at the annual conference of the World's Christian Fundamentals Association when it met in Philadelphia in May 1931. There is no organization at that time that had a greater right to be considered the centre of American fundamentalism than this one. As it was a unifying forum for fundamentalists across America, a speaker who would have been unacceptable to a certain segment of fundamentalists would not have been chosen. In other words, her appearance as a main speaker at the W.C.F.A. is a clear indication that her ministry was approved of and owned by American fundamentalism generally. Other speakers at the 1931 annual conference included H. A. Ironside, W. B. Riley, Will H. Houghton, Lewis Sperry Chafer, J. Oliver Buswell, Jr (president of Wheaton College, Illinois), Arno C. Gaebelein (a dispensational teacher and the editor of *Our Hope*), and Paul W. Rood (a pastor in California who, a few years later, became the president of the Bible Institute of Los Angeles). On the first full day of the conference, Pankhurst was given the choicest spot on the programme: she was the last evening speaker (having already spoken in the afternoon as well), sharing the platform with Will H. Houghton, whose address preceded hers.[57] This slot was not only the best attended one, but it was also the only segment (that is, the last of the two evening addresses) on the daily programme that was aired on the radio.[58] There were only six such slots in the conference programme. Her message was also selected for reprinting in the W.C.F.A.'s journal, the *Christian Fundamentalist*.[59]

This is by no means an exhaustive tour of Christabel Pankhurst's engagements on the fundamentalist circuit or her connections with respected fundamentalist leaders. Many other lesser places where she stopped that already have been discovered have not been mentioned, and as Pankhurst made a career of ministering in this milieu, local investigations would undoubtedly turn up numerous additional venues. Given the *New York Times'* role as a 'local' paper, for example, it is also known that

[55] *New York Times*, 10 March 1924, p. 17.
[56] 'Miss Christabel Pankhurst as Evangelist', *Manchester Guardian*, 20 August 1926.
[57] See the *Christian Fundamentalist*, April 1931, pp. 363–5; and May 1931, pp. 403–8.
[58] *Christian Fundamentalist*, August 1931, p. 55.
[59] *Christian Fundamentalist*, July 1931, pp. 5 and 9.

she spoke at the popular Old Tent Evangel there, and that she spoke at A. C. Gaebelein's prophetic conference at Stony Brook, New York.[60] Nevertheless, the evidence that has been given here is more than sufficient to prove that Pankhurst was not only a fundamentalist, but also that her ministry was highly valued and honoured by other leading fundamentalists, and by the fundamentalist community in general.

[60] *New York Times*, 16 August 1923, p. 15; 19 August 1923, p. 13.

Chapter Six

FUNDAMENTALISM AND FEMINISM IN SOCIETY

Fundamentalism and Women's Suffrage

Of all the things that contemporary society thinks it knows about fundamentalism, perhaps the notion that it is opposed to feminism is one of the most prominent. This general impression has also been adopted by scholars. Bruce B. Lawrence, for example, in his *Defenders of God: The Fundamentalist Revolt Against the Modern Age*, pronounces confidently when expounding the nature of historic fundamentalism in America that 'Secondary male elites provided their leadership, extolling women as mothers and custodians of family values but never recognizing an individual woman as authoritative teacher.'[1] This is a typical assessment, but it is simply not true. 'Authoritative teacher' is a slippery category for fundamentalists, as they believed that the Bible was the true authority and that no human being had the right to dictate to others how it was to be interpreted, but, beyond an *a priori* assumption that it just could not have been so, it does not seem demonstrable that Pankhurst was any less an 'authoritative teacher' than the males on the fundamentalist circuit. Nor is her case singular. Attitudes toward women in the life and ministry of the church and attitudes toward women in society in general are naturally entwined – in reality as well as in the scholarly literature – but, for the purpose of clarity of analysis and presentation, this chapter will focus on fundamentalism and women in society, leaving a full discussion of women in ministry and fundamentalism for the next chapter.

The most important book making the case that fundamentalism in the 1920s was a movement especially hostile to women is Betty A. DeBerg's *Ungodly Women: Gender and the First Wave of American Fundamentalism*.[2] Repeatedly, DeBerg makes her case by the simple expedient of only citing the evidence in its favour, and then pronouncing the picture thereby

[1] Bruce B. Lawrence, *Defenders of God: The Fundamentalist Revolt Against the Modern Age*, San Francisco: Harper & Row, 1989, p. 230.
[2] Betty A. DeBerg, *Ungodly Women: Gender and the First Wave of American Fundamentalism*, Minneapolis: Fortress, 1990.

assembled as the monolithic fundamentalist view. Although this will be demonstrated more fully as different specific issues are addressed below and in the next chapter, it is worth observing here that despite the fact that she wrote an entire monograph on gender and fundamentalism that is centred chronologically in the 1920s, DeBerg never once even referred to Christabel Pankhurst. As this study ought to have already sufficiently illuminated, this omission would be surprising if one were merely discussing fundamentalism in the 1920s at book length, but for a monograph addressing the issue of gender and fundamentalism in that period it is a truly stunning feat. Scholars have been largely content to latch upon the evidence that indicates that fundamentalists were misogynist and to leap to the assumption that the whole movement was uniformly and exceptionally hostile to women.

For example, as to the main issue at hand, DeBerg confidently declares: 'Premillennialists also attacked "the emancipation of woman" as a "bad sign" that we are "living in the last days, the perilous times." Suffrage was singled out.'[3] This is profoundly misleading. Whatever individual fundamentalists believed they were apt to articulate by quoting Scripture, so it is not surprising that those who happened to disapprove of women's suffrage did so. The more important point, however, is that DeBerg has neglected to add the crucial word 'some' at the start of her sentence that would have instantly and accurately reduced her point almost to a banality. Women's suffrage divided most subgroups of society at that time and her evidence reflects no more than that very obvious fact. On the same basis – statements made by members of a particular group in society condemning the enfranchisement of women – one could equally assert that almost any group attacked women's suffrage, including, of course, women. DeBerg's statement is calculated to give the impression that fundamentalists were uniformly or exceptionally opposed, yet she does not offer evidence that would substantiate such a claim.[4]

---

[3] DeBerg, *Ungodly Women*, p. 126.
[4] In an earlier chapter, DeBerg does concede in passing that some fundamentalists were pro-women's suffrage, but then adds 'antisuffrage statements in popular fundamentalist periodicals outnumbered prosuffrage statements by a ratio of more than ten to one' (DeBerg, *Ungodly Women*, p. 51). A number of points need to be made about this statement. Even if it was demonstrated that this statistic reflected accurately the views on each side of this issue in the movement as a whole, it should be noted that close to ten per cent is a sizeable group: it means that women's suffrage was not an issue where there was a fundamentalism 'position' in the way that there was one on social issues such as abortion or homosexuality. Moreover, one would then need to compare it with statistical studies of other groups in American society at that time in order to discover whether or not fundamentalists were exceptionally anti-women's suffrage. More importantly, however, it can by no means be assumed that this statistic accurately reflects the convictions of fundamentalists in general. As fundamentalists – owing to their eschatological vision – were more apt to highlight developments in the wider culture that they deemed alarming rather than welcome, it would have been much more natural for the antis than

In fact, many fundamentalists supported women's suffrage, and it is possible that those in favour of this cause were the more influential camp within the movement. One of the great nineteenth-century champions of women's suffrage, the evangelical Frances E. Willard, was invited by D. L. Moody to work with him as a fellow evangelist (and, for several months, she did). Moody encouraged her in her suffrage work. The movement for women's suffrage made major inroads into the conservative evangelical camp through the arguments of temperance reformers such as Willard. When Viola D. Romans was one of the main speakers at Winona Lake Bible Conference in 1914 she told her audience of fundamentalists (or proto-fundamentalists) a classic suffragist story about how she felt when her younger brother gained the right to vote and yet she – older and just as politically aware – was still deprived of it. More importantly, however, she assumed that most of her audience was in agreement with her: 'Now, I am a suffragist. Maybe you have suspected that from the things I have said. I understand most of you here are suffragists.'[5] When Pankhurst spoke at the third annual Fundamentalist Rally and Prophetic Conference in Atlantic City in 1932, another speaker at the conference was Lucy Waterbury Peabody. Beyond merely believing in women's suffrage, she was amassing the fundamentalist troops to wield their power: 'And the votes of women, who see in prohibition their greatest protective law, will make both repeal of the 18th Amendment and modification of the Volstead Act an impossibility.'[6]

A study has been made of references to women in society (and in church life) in the *Christian* newspaper for the year 1920. The *Christian* was the English religious paper that was most widely read by conservative evangelicals. 1920 was chosen because it falls before Pankhurst's conversion had been made public – and thus the possibility that the paper was bending its policy in order to court her is ruled out – but this date is also close enough to the time when she became a prominent figure to make the assumption that no dramatic change of directions had taken place in its editorial views a safe one. Not one statement opposed to equality for women in society has been found in the *Christian*, and several have been found that distinctly expressed that the paper was in favour of it. For example, Lady Astor's maiden speech in the House of Commons was received with

the pros (on any social or political issue) to find an occasion to air their ideas in print. Furthermore, presumably one periodical regularly denouncing women's suffrage would quickly accumulate a lot of 'statements' even though they reflected the views of only one editor. Most of all, the evidence offered in this chapter leads to a different conclusion from the one indicated by DeBerg's statistic.

[5] Viola D. Romans, 'The Nation's Call', *Winona Echoes: Forty-five Notable Addresses Delivered at the Twentieth Annual Bible Conference. Winona Lake, Indiana, August, 1914*, 1914, pp. 345–56.

[6] *Atlantic City Press*, 24 September 1932, p. 10.

enthusiasm: 'The ultra-conservative people who imagined that the introduction of women legislators would jeopardize the social fabric, will, we
hope, live long enough to learn how mistaken they were.'[7] The news that
women could now receive the Victoria Cross was welcomed: 'All
women – and surely all men – will learn with pleasure that women are in
future to be eligible for the Victoria Cross.'[8] There was also an article
resolutely and forthrightly in favour of gender equality in higher education:

> Those educationalists who have championed the women's cause will
> be happy – and properly so – that the Oxford University has at last
> admitted women to its degree honours. The fight has been a long one,
> and against immense prejudice and opposition. . . . The real truth is
> that there still lingers an unreasonable prejudice against admitting
> women to the rights which their abilities have won for them. It is a sex
> prejudice, pure and simple, but upon the old false idea that a woman
> must necessarily be inferior to a man. Little by little, however, the
> fight has been won, and commonsense has triumphed.[9]

Christabel Pankhurst, at the height of the Suffragette campaign, could
hardly have written it better herself. There is no evidence that the paper
was fighting a brave battle against the sensibilities of its readers on this
issue; the obvious explanation is that many conservative evangelicals
believed in these campaigns for promoting gender equality in society.

This study is not the place to offer a systematic survey of fundamentalist
attitudes toward women's suffrage, but it is readily apparent that many
fundamentalist leaders supported the movement. For example, the great
fundamentalist statesman in the first half of the 1920s (he died in 1925),
William Jennings Bryan – the voice of the anti-Darwinian troops at the
famous Scopes trial – was an advocate of women's suffrage.[10] Billy Sunday
(1862–1935) who, at the height of his ministry, was unquestionably the
most popular fundamentalist evangelist, was 'a persistent and outspoken
supporter of women's suffrage'.[11] In fact, in some prominent instances,
Pankhurst's new friends in the world of fundamentalism were old friends
of women's suffrage. John Roach Straton, 'the Pope of fundamentalism',
for example, had been an advocate of women's suffrage before he had ever

---

[7] *Christian*, 4 March 1920, p. 3.
[8] *Christian*, 24 June 1920, p. 4.
[9] *Christian*, 21 October 1920, p. 3.
[10] Russell, *Voices of American Fundamentalism*, p. 179. It should also be noted that
votes for women came to the congregational lives of many Baptists and
Congregationalists a long time before the issue became prominent in politics. See, for
example, Timothy Larsen, '"How Many Sisters Make A Brotherhood?" A Case Study
in Gender and Ecclesiology in Early Nineteenth-Century English Dissent', *Journal of
Ecclesiastical History* 49, 2 (April 1998).
[11] Lyle W. Dorsett, *Billy Sunday and the Redemption of Urban America*, Grand
Rapids: William B. Eerdmans, 1991, p. 153.

become a champion of Pankhurst's ministry.[12] This was also the case with Pankhurst's English sponsor, F. B. Meyer. Ian Randall has observed that 'Equality for women was also part of Meyer's message. . . . Against the background of the campaign for votes for women, Meyer stated in *The Times* [in] 1913: "Woman suffrage has got to come."'[13] Likewise J. D. F. Inkpin in a recent Ph.D. thesis on Christianity and the women's suffrage movement in Britain comments that 'Within its ranks the F.C.L.W.S. [Free Church League for Women's Suffrage] also included more sober and orthodox figures such as the Reverend F. B. Meyer, a leading figure in both the Baptist Union and the National Free Church Federation.'[14] It might be that this stance forms part of the background to a remark that Pankhurst once made about her relationship with Meyer: 'By name Dr Meyer was, of course, always well known to me, as to every one, but I had never met him until my return from the United States and Canada some years ago.'[15] While not wishing to discount Meyer's general level of fame, and it would have been natural for her to have also heard his name owing to his role as general secretary of the Free Church Council, it seems more than likely that Pankhurst would have especially registered the names of those prominent ministers who had endorsed women's suffrage. In short, supporting the enfranchisement of women was a perfectly acceptable stance for a fundamentalist leader to take. There was no need or requirement for Pankhurst to abandon or suppress her commitment to women's suffrage in order for her to join the fundamentalist circuit. Nor did she.

Pankhurst the Fundamentalist on Women and Social Reform

Pankhurst's life has been insufficiently studied in general, and her life beyond 1922 has been woefully neglected. Nevertheless, in the few sources that do discuss her life, the impression is repeatedly given that she abandoned her commitment to feminism once she entered the world of fundamentalism. Rita Pankhurst (Sylvia Pankhurst's daughter-in-law), for example, claimed in 1987 in the introduction to a new edition of Christabel Pankhurst's account of the Suffragette movement, *Unshackled*: 'By 1921, three years after women broke through to obtain a limited

---

[12] Russell, *Voices of American Fundamentalism*, pp. 58, 76.

[13] Ian M. Randall, 'The Social Gospel: A Case Study', in John Wolffe (ed.), *Evangelical Faith and Public Zeal: Evangelicals and Society in Britain 1780–1980*, London: SPCK, 1995, pp. 167–8.

[14] Jonathan David Francis Inkpin, 'Combatting the "Sin of Self-Sacrifice": Christian Feminism in the Women's Suffrage Struggle: (1903–18)', unpublished Ph.D. thesis, University of Durham, 1996, p. 233. It would appear that he is using the word 'orthodox' to indicate that Meyer was a conservative evangelical.

[15] Fullerton, *F. B. Meyer*, p. 160.

franchise, she had turned away from feminism.'[16] This is a slippery statement that is – to say the least – highly likely to mislead. It is accurate enough, in a technical sense, if it means no more than that Pankhurst was no longer devoting her time to working for an organized women's pressure group, but the same could be said for the vast majority of other Suffragettes. 'Feminism', however, at least the version of it that Pankhurst had always championed, is a conviction regarding how society ought to be – that it ought to be marked by gender equality before the law – and Christabel Pankhurst never turned away from that conviction. A worse misrepresentation has been made by Barbara Castle, in one of the very few studies of Pankhurst's life (although, given the ever-growing list of studies of Sylvia Pankhurst, this one predictably is a joint study of the two sisters). Castle asserts (falsely) that Christabel Pankhurst's religious writings revealed 'the complete reversal of her views on the women's struggle'.[17] Pugh has recently remarked that 'Christabel even went so far as to repudiate the whole suffrage cause after 1920.'[18] Therefore, there is a widespread assumption that Pankhurst spent the second half of her life rejecting the very feminism that she had stood for in the first half.

This impression seems to have developed through a hurried reading of some of Pankhurst's comments as a fundamentalist, perhaps coupled with an inability to understand fundamentalist theological and biblical lines of thought. Castle cited Pankhurst's book *Some Modern Problems in the Light of Bible Prophecy* as the one that most clearly reveals her alleged complete reversal. This is undoubtedly the most accessible place to start for anyone wanting to make a judgment on Pankhurst's view, as a fundamentalist, of her Suffragette work, as she handily inserted a whole section conveniently labelled 'The Votes of Women'. The first paragraph of this section is as follows:

> Various reasons forbid us to expect that, when other means are failing to save the world situation, the votes of women will succeed. Some of us hoped more from woman suffrage than is ever going to be accomplished. My own large anticipations were based partly upon ignorance, which the late war dispelled, of the magnitude of the task which we women reformers so confidently wished to undertake when the vote should be ours. Even had one suspected in the days of the struggle for the vote, how vastly is the task beyond human power, whether of women or men, one would still have been without a better hope, because

---

[16] Rita Pankhurst, 'Introduction to the Cresset Women's Voices Edition', Dame Christabel Pankhurst, *Unshackled: The Story of How We Won the Vote*, London: Cresset Women's Voices, 1987, p. [10].
[17] Barbara Castle, *Sylvia and Christabel Pankhurst*, Harmondsworth, Middlesex: Penguin, 1987, p. 158.
[18] Pugh, *Pankhursts*, p. xv.

of the ignorance of or indifference to Bible prophecy, from which, grievous to say, some politicians have not, even now, freed themselves.[19]

The content of the rest of the chapter unfolds this argument in more detail. Pankhurst made statements like this repeatedly in her speeches and writings over many years. The point was very simple: she had learned that votes for women was not a panacea that could save society. She had also learned, of course, that Jesus was the one and only panacea that could save society. In other words, her comments about votes for women were not specific to that cause, but the application of a general assessment of all human efforts. The section just before the one on votes for women in that same book explained why democracy could not save society, but it would be absurd to argue that she had 'turned her back' on democratic government or had made a 'complete reversal' of her former views regarding elected leaders as if to imply that she had moved toward some alternative such as fascism.[20] She applied her new insight into the limits of human achievement to women's suffrage because she had once viewed it as a potential solution to the world's problems. It is possible that she constructed for rhetorical effect an imagined, naïve past that she never really lived, but there is some evidence that she was recounting her experience with some accuracy. She had, after all, argued that votes for women would be a major part of the solution to the problem of the spread of venereal diseases.[21] She once expressed her new awareness of the limitations of what women could achieve thus: 'They say, "can't the women do something?" but the women are, as George Eliot said, "fools, too, for the Lord A'mighty made 'em to match the men."'[22] Again, her point was that *all* human efforts were insufficient in the face of the world's problems. In a speech in 1926, for example, she discoursed on the millennial period of human peace and happiness:

> How is it to come? Human hands cannot bring it. I thought once that women would do it. But no! The world is in revolt. The Kingdom must come, or the universe will not be safe! The Church cannot build or bring it. Learned ecclesiastics cannot do it. We will be content with no kingdom till the King brings it Himself.[23]

The contrast between human and divine power is the point of such a statement. To read it as a rejection of feminism is misguided. It is no more a statement against the women's movement than it was a statement

---

[19] Christabel Pankhurst, *Some Modern Problems in the Light of Bible Prophecy*, New York: Fleming H. Revell, 1924, pp. 42–3.
[20] Pugh nevertheless levels this charge as well: Pugh, *Pankhursts*, p. 342.
[21] Christabel Pankhurst, *The Great Scourge and How To End It*, London: E. Pankhurst, 1913.
[22] *New York Times*, 16 August 1923, p. 14.
[23] *Christian*, 28 October 1926, p. 21.

against 'learned ecclesiastics' (her dear friend, Dr F. B. Meyer being in the chair as a sort of visual aid), or a statement against church work.

Moreover, her disillusionment regarding what the women's movement (again, or any movement) could achieve was not prompted by embracing fundamentalism, but rather by the reality of the Great War. She recollected in 1923: 'I think that it was through the war that I came to the conclusion that things were wrong. The women were no sooner prepared to vote than there came up great questions that could not be settled by vote.'[24] A summary of a speech she gave in the Queen's Hall, London, in 1926 said: 'The Great War brought disillusionment and made it clear that however good were the intentions of the advocates of equal rights for women, they had overlooked the fact that what mankind needs is not a change of conditions but a change of heart.'[25] Another summary in a different journal of the same sermon reported that she was:

> not so much disappointed as disillusioned. She had cherished theories of gradual evolution toward peace and perfection . . . And then she made a discovery – that what is wrong with the world is inherent sin, which makes impossible all genuine progress, and must always result in strife and unrest. The War shattered her ideals, and she found herself without a philosophy of life . . . [26]

The pious appeal to changing hearts might grate, and it is hard to remember Christabel Pankhurst in her W.S.P.U. days as someone committed to *gradual* improvement but, be that as it may, it is worth recalling once again that this was by no means a unique response to the Great War.[27] It was neither a betrayal of the cause nor a crankish turn for Pankhurst to conclude that – a prospect that seemed much more probable than in the past – if human violence could erupt on a massive scale and sweep away democracy as a whole – or even western civilization itself – then the right to participate in that democracy and that civilization could not be the guarantor of future justice. She was surely not merely projecting her own experiences on others when she averred: '"Progress" and "evolution" are disappearing from current philosophies of the future. The world-war and after-war experience have convinced many that progress is not sure and continual.'[28] In fact, her comments – stripped of the eschatology, of course – are no different from

[24] *New York Times*, 16 August 1923, p. 15.
[25] *Advent Witness*, December 1926, pp. 191–2.
[26] *Christian*, 11 November 1926, p. 6.
[27] In 1932, Pankhurst wrote an article on 'The Hopelessness of the Intellectuals'. She reviewed current American literature, the British writer John Galsworthy, Aldous Huxley's thought (contrasting it with the Darwinian optimism of his grandfather, T. H. Huxley), and ended with sections arguing that 'Even [H. G.] Wells and [Bernard] Shaw are disheartening their disciples by bitter doses of pessimism' *Sunday School Times*, 19 November 1932, p. 599.
[28] *Present and Future*, May 1934, p. 1.

those of some other leaders in the cause of women's suffrage. Charlotte Despard, for example, told the Women's Freedom League in 1927: 'I have no confidence in the future of parliamentary democracy.'[29] Even Christabel Pankhurst's own mother, Emmeline, reflected on votes for women in language almost identical to her daughter's in an interview in 1926: 'We thought a miracle was going to happen – all reformers think that. We thought it was going to bring Utopia, but we left human nature out of the question.'[30] As for Sylvia Pankhurst, Pugh has written that she 'eventually became sceptical about the vote and Parliamentary politics in general'.[31] Christabel Pankhurst can hardly be credited with rejecting feminism merely for observing that votes for women was not a solution to all society's ills.

It is fair to say that at times – in the early years – she sounded as though she was dismissing all movements for reform. This, it would seem, was the kind of unbalanced enthusiasm often associated with the zeal of a new convert. It is important to emphasize, however, that this was a comprehensive reaction and therefore not an expression of a new attitude toward women's movements in particular. Pankhurst could bat away the contentious issue of the revision of the Anglican Prayer Book (a cause that evangelicals viewed as an Anglo-Catholic plot) with a dose of end-times expectations: 'even if a generally acceptable revision were possible, *the time has gone by* for revision of the Prayer Book'.[32] Her new impatience with reform efforts could also have been fuelled by her suspicion that Grattan Guinness might have been right and therefore it was certain that the age would come to an end in a handful of years. However, as the years came and went, and she matured as a believer, Pankhurst began to make more room in her thinking for the practical work that still needed to be done in this world. In May 1934, to a Manchester audience, she is reported to have given a more measured assessment:

> At the afternoon meeting Miss Pankhurst said her work in the women's suffrage movement had taught her how much could be done by human agency and how much could not. Everywhere one saw evidence of noble endeavour and self-sacrifice, but everywhere also were evidences of the adverse side of human nature, which handicapped the best aspirations and finest ideals.[33]

That same week she wrote to Winston Churchill. Her letter betrays a growing awareness that just because she was called to spend her life

[29] David Mitchell, *The Fighting Pankhursts: A Study in Tenacity*, New York: Macmillan, 1967, p. 192.
[30] 'Mrs Pankhurst Comes Back', *Daily Chronicle*, 28 January 1926.
[31] Pugh, *Pankhursts*, p. 311.
[32] *Christian*, 17 February 1927, p. 14
[33] 'Word and Theocracy. Miss Christabel Pankhurst's Sermons', *Manchester Guardian*, 14 May 1934.

proclaiming the second coming of Christ that did not mean that it was the Almighty's will for everyone to live that way: 'My own turning from politics to prophecy is definitive, but I recognise that some, & especially those having your experience of office, may have to *unite* the political and prophetic roles.'[34] By the time she wrote *The Uncurtained Future*, she was preaching against the notion that the message of Jesus' return entailed an abandonment of reform work: 'Sometimes, but mistakenly, it is said that looking forward to the second advent means indifference and inaction in face of social and international wrongs. The classical disproof of this is Lord Shaftesbury, who, deeply interested in the second advent doctrine, was also a pioneer of social reform.'[35] By 1943, she had worked her way over to the notion that the church was actually the fount of it all: 'All social reforms sponsored by statesmen, originated in the Christian church.'[36] Pankhurst's views on the importance of reform movements did contract after her conversion, but they did not remain as narrow as they started.

The Question of Immorality in the Roaring Twenties

A central thesis of DeBerg's *Ungodly Women* is that fundamentalists in the 1920s were preoccupied with what they viewed as alarming moral developments because of new habits of behaviour amongst young women – the flapper in particular – such as wearing short skirts. She even goes so far as to claim repeatedly that the fundamentalist emphasis on the authority of the Bible may be seen as a by-product of their desire to force women to conform to the old patterns:

> it is readily apparent that the Bible was not defended, revered, or exegeted simply for its own sake nor for the sake of abstract theological disputations. The Bible was of such concern to these conservative evangelical Protestants because they saw in it the basis for a set of eternal and unchanging social norms, most of which set boundaries on private, gender-related behaviors and attitudes. . . . The divine origin and verbal accuracy of the Bible were important to these conservative religious leaders because it was upon scriptural authority that the fundamentalists defended their standards of morality – the social conventions of the late-Victorian middle-class to which they

[34] Churchill Archives Centre, Churchill College, Cambridge: Christabel Pankhurst to Winston Churchill, 14 May 1934.
[35] Pankhurst, *Uncurtained Future*, pp. 142–3. Shaftesbury's case was also cited earlier: 'Belief in the ultimate solution of the world's problems by the Second Advent was firmly held by the famous social reformer, Lord Shaftesbury' (*Present and Future*, June 1934, p. 8). The first mention of Shaftesbury in this regard would appear to be the following one: Pankhurst, *World's Unrest*, p. 120.
[36] 'British Suffrage Leader Here for Religion Talks', *Los Angeles Times*, 9 July 1943.

belonged. . . . They needed an infallible Bible because their defense of Victorian social and sexual conventions depended heavily on the authority of divine revelation – in this case, divine revelation of social relations and morality.[37]

Christabel Pankhurst was not attracted to the notion of an infallible Bible for this reason. She found the idea compelling because it guaranteed that the Bible could be a reliable guide to current and forthcoming events and that its promise that Christ would return to usher in the millennium would be fulfilled. It seems probable that numerous other pre-millennialists found the doctrine of biblical inerrancy appealing for the same reasons.

Moreover, DeBerg's assumption that critiquing the new morality was a misogynist stance is questionable. It is more accurate to recognize that feminists have often disagreed on issues of morality. Christabel Pankhurst, as has already been shown, positioned herself as a Suffragette within the sexual purity tradition of feminist thought. Her comment on 'a supposed "new morality"' in *The World's Unrest* could just as well have been made in her pre-conversion days: 'the old disaster is only too often the result, especially for the women'.[38] The really fascinating point, however, is how little Pankhurst had to say about immorality; it was simply not one of her preoccupations. This is particularly interesting given the fact that it was one of the biblical signs of the times:

> This know also, that in the last days perilous times shall come. For men shall be lovers of their own selves, covetous, boasters, proud, blasphemers, disobedient to parents, unthankful, unholy, without natural affection, trucebreakers, false accusers, incontinent, fierce, despisers of those that are good, traitors, heady, highminded, lovers of pleasure more than lovers of God . . . (2 Timothy 3:1–4 Authorized Version)

A rather propitious text, should one be inclined to argue that the younger generation was going to the dogs. As a portion of scripture on a main theme of her ministry – the signs of the times – Pankhurst could not really ignore these verses, but nevertheless this theme clearly was not very appealing to her. She only gestured at it occasionally, in a perfunctory way. In *'The Lord Cometh'* she noted in passing: 'the social, moral and religious signs of the Age-end are predicted in the Second Epistle to Timothy, to which I refer you'.[39] The impression that David Mitchell gives – namely, that Pankhurst went out of her way to attack the new sexual and moral climate – is inaccurate.[40] In fact, Pankhurst classified the signs of the times in a way that minimized the place of any supposed rise

---

[37] DeBerg, *Ungodly Women*, pp. 128, 129, and 134.
[38] Pankhurst, *World's Unrest*, p. 214.
[39] Pankhurst, *'The Lord Cometh'*, p. 100.
[40] Mitchell, *Queen Christabel*, p. 301.

of immorality in the scheme. In her three-point pattern, the third sign was the restored Roman empire and the second sign was the Jews in Palestine. The first sign was as follows: 'Firstly, there is the general disturbance of the nations and of nature, expressing itself in warfare and the rumour thereof, in social unrest, in earthquake, storm, and flood.'[41] If the 2 Timothy passage was thought of at all in her scheme, therefore, it must be subsumed in this list under the vague phrase 'social unrest'. Even if there, however, it rarely saw the light of day. Her weekly column, 'On the Watchtower', which she wrote in 1926–27, had as its theme current events in line with the signs of the times. In twenty-six columns she never once brought forward any issue of mores as reflecting the signs of the times. Wars and rumours of wars, freakish weather, Zionism, and developments that might point to a new Roman empire, however, were all dealt with over and over again. Indeed, her lack of interest in supposedly immoral literature and youthful excesses may be contrasted with her careful tracking of notable storms: a meteorologist might find her column a decent source for reconstructing macro-weather patterns during these years. Here is a standard specimen:

> From Cuba came this message: 'During the past week the population of Oriente Provino have been in a state of constant terror owing to recurring earthquake-shocks. The fifteenth shock in three days was reported at Santiago this evening.' The recent Japanese earthquake was one of the most violent and destructive on record, 'a revisitation with quadrupled force', says one newspaper correspondent, comparing it with a past visitation.[42]

In the early days, her enthusiasm for seismic activity was rather too unchecked: 'I rejoice when I see in the signs of the times any fulfilment of prophecy in a mild degree. I don't want any one to be hurt, but when I read (as I did this morning, for instance) of an earthquake in England, I am delighted.'[43] When Pankhurst did address the moral degeneration sign it would appear that it was for the sake of comprehensiveness. In *Present and Future*, she offered an article on 'Some Signs of the Times', which did make a breezy attempt at the full tour; not just rumours of war and Zionism and 'the recent Indian earthquake', but even a half-hearted effort to deal with the (not very forthcoming) sign of famine. On the immorality issue, she wrote:

> Pagan pleasures have lately been under condemnation; displays of animal ferocity; pictorial reports of the accidents and agonies of humankind; sordid fiction; unsavoury dramas on film, or in flesh and

---

[41] *Christian*, 5 May 1927, p. 12.
[42] *Christian*, 17 March 1927, p. 12.
[43] *King's Business*, September 1924, pp. 553, 597–600.

blood; painting, scupture [*sic*] and music not escaping the epidemic. In short, it is protested that 'cruelty, immorality, and other vices' are made the stuff of entertainment. Does not this find some prophetic reflection in the Apostle's anticipation of disturbed social conditions in the latter days![44]

Far from betraying a preoccupation with the expression of sexuality, this reads as a rather perfunctory passage that comes alive in the more vivid denunciations of examples of the glorification of gore and violence.

Fundamentalist Comments on Pankhurst's Suffragette Work

When introducing Christabel Pankhurst to a fundamentalist audience or readership it was natural to allude to her past work on behalf of women's enfranchisement as she had acquired so much fame in that context. It is a revealing fact, however, that not a single such introduction has been found that disparaged or critiqued her Suffragette work, or even one that indicated embarrassment regarding it. On the other hand, on numerous occasions, more generous language than the situation necessitated was used. *Moody Bible Institute Monthly* introduced Pankhurst's ministry to its readers for the first time in 1923 through a reprint of an article from another Chicago fundamentalist publication, *The Jewish Era: A Christian Quarterly*. In an extraordinary appropriation of complimentary Christian language, this report identified her as 'the great apostle of woman suffrage'. The article went on to eulogize her as follows:

> Those who have heard this brave, heroic woman do not doubt the sincerity of her purpose and aim. As a politician and militant suffragette she showed her willingness to endure scoffs, jeers, imprisonment and suffering of every kind. Now the Man of Galilee has so gripped her heart that she sees as a student of the Word . . .[45]

The English fundamentalist, H. Tydeman Chilvers, minister at Spurgeon's Metropolitan Tabernacle in London, introduced her thus: 'Miss Christabel Pankhurst is a "miracle of grace" of the twentieth century. It seems but as yesterday since she was booming the Suffragette Movement by very formidable means.'[46] When A. B. Winchester wrote to the *Christian* in order 'to introduce a new member to the family circle of redeemed ones' he declared that she had worked 'for the sake of obtaining justice for her sex', a phrase that has as its plain meaning the assumption that her cause was indeed

---

[44] *Present and Future*, May 1934, pp. 5–6.
[45] 'Miss Pankhurst's Conversion', *Moody Bible Institute Monthly*, September 1923, p. 14.
[46] *Christian*, 26 August 1926, p. 14.

right.[47] The fundamentalist community did not exhibit a desire to apologize for Pankhurst's past work in the cause of women's suffrage.

Pankhurst's Links with the Women's Movement

It is also apparent that Pankhurst did not sever her links with the women's movement and with her Suffragette colleagues when she became a fundamentalist. For example, she was publicly approached by the notable women's organization, the Six Point Group, in 1926 and asked to run for Parliament again. By 1926, of course, her fundamentalist ministry was well known and firmly established. Viscountess Rhondda and Lady Astor were both there to press the case, Lady Astor even going so far as to offer to vacate her own seat in order to make room for Pankhurst. Pankhurst's response to this request made it clear that she did rule out serving in this way:

> 'My answer,' replied Miss Pankhurst, 'is the answer that I have always tried to give to those who want me to do something. If you want me there and you think I can help make it easier for women and men, especially for the young, I will go there if I am sent there. But, touched as I am by Lady Astor's offer to give me her seat, I must decline, because if I go to Parliament I must win my seat.'[48]

Christabel Pankhurst, of course, wrote her retrospective defence of the Suffragette movement that was published posthumously under the title, *Unshackled: The Story of How We Won the Vote*, after she had already been pursuing her fundamentalist ministry for some years. The manuscript was not dated. Lord Pethick-Lawrence, an old colleague in the W.S.P.U. who edited it for publication, claimed in the preface that it had 'apparently been written about twenty years previously' (that is, before her death), which would date it as c. 1938.[49] Certainly, she could not have finished it earlier than the summer of 1928, as the manuscript includes an account of her mother's funeral which took place on 17 June 1928.[50] David Mitchell's biography reveals that Pankhurst was often staying with or meeting up with friends, colleagues or acquaintances from her W.S.P.U. days. Pankhurst used her rhetorical powers in order to honour the American champion of women's suffrage, Susan B. Anthony, at a meeting commemorating her life in 1948.[51] Finally, despite having immersed herself in the fundamentalist world for decades, Christabel Pankhurst

---

[47] *Christian*, 29 March 1923, p. 20.
[48] *New York Times*, 5 March 1926, p. 6.
[49] Pankhurst, *Unshackled*, p. 13.
[50] Pankhurst, *Unshackled*, pp. 298–9.
[51] Mitchell, *Queen Christabel*, p. 314.

named as the executor for her will, not a fundamentalist friend, but rather the Suffragette Grace Roe.[52]

Testifying to the Suffragette Truth

Far from having changed her mind about feminism, Christabel Pankhurst repeatedly went out of her way when addressing fundamentalist audiences or in her religious writings to reaffirm her commitment to gender equality before the law. This was often done in incidental comments, but as gender equality was not a theme of her books or addresses the fact that it was done at all required a degree of deliberate intention. The fact that these comments are so embedded in her discussions of religious themes explains why scholars who are primarily interested in her as a Suffragette have not apparently discovered them hitherto. In her first religious book, 'The Lord Cometh' (1923), Pankhurst asserted: 'Assuredly our political enfranchisement was a necessary measure of justice.'[53] In 1924, she testified to the usefulness of the Bible from her personal perspective at that time as 'a woman of progressive mind and modern thought'.[54] In response to the question of whether she was disappointed with votes for women, she told an audience in 1926: 'I am as disappointed with votes for women, as I am with votes for men. I am disappointed with us all. I have discovered that there is something wrong with human nature.'[55] That expresses her decreased faith in human ability precisely. Of course, she did not have second thoughts on votes for women any more than she had now decided to campaign to disfranchise men; the vote was all well and good, but humanity needed divine help.

She told another audience, 'We went forward with great trouble, to ourselves and to other people, to get votes for women. Well, we succeeded; but we find it is not enough, and we find that *we* are not enough! If you place your ideals lower than Christ you will be disappointed.'[56] Pankhurst was sufficiently at peace with her past in order to be able to use it for humour. The *Moody Bible Institute Monthly* reported a speech that she gave in London at 'the annual meeting of the International Christian Police Association'. This is how she began her address:

> When I was asked to speak at this meeting of the International Christian Police Association, I consented. I was acquainted with

[52] Pankhurst, *Unshackled*, p. 13.
[53] Pankhurst, *'The Lord Cometh'*, p. 6.
[54] *Christian*, 3 July 1924, p. 5.
[55] *Christian*, 14 October 1926, p. 37.
[56] *Christian*, 21 October 1926, p. 24.

the police. We have had, some of us – well, – we have worked together, haven't we? (Laughter.)[57]

Moreover, this fundamentalist journal added as a subtitle to one section of the reported speech: 'Proud of Her Sex'. In that section, Pankhurst exhorted 'we must feel proud of being women'. Moreover, on the theme of the limits of what politicians can achieve, she asserted:

> And whether it be a Lloyd George or a Macdonald, a government violently Red or ultra-conservative or moderate or liberal, or a government of women – and you know we may some time have a government of women even – any British government in these days will have a burden upon its shoulder which can only be borne by the Son of God of whom it is said by the prophet that when He comes the government shall be upon His shoulder.

Her letting the audience know that she could envision a government of women in Britain was a purely gratuitous aside; she could not resist informing them that such a thought was not so absurd as they might assume. In *Seeing the Future* she encapsulated her true point in a single sentence that also disentangled it from any misguided impression that she had repented of her feminism: 'Emphatically, we are not disappointed in votes for women; but government, in this modern world especially, is a more than superhuman task: it is truly a task beyond all save God in person.'[58] Later in that book she claimed that women politicians would also reflect human limitations as do men, although she again separated this point from any supposed backtracking on women's rights by observing parenthetically that although women therefore did not hold out the promise of solving the world's problems they, nevertheless, would not do 'one bit worse' than the men.[59] This is a true vision of gender equality. In a section on Zionism, she spoke with pride of her Suffragette achievement:

> The writer of these pages is better qualified by experience, than some, to judge the significance and the prospects of Zionism, having been concerned in another movement, which began as a weak and small thing and eventuated in the enfranchisement of millions of women who, from being politically non-existent, became numerically predominant, with a corresponding change in their whole social influence. As great a transformation in human institutions as the world has ever known! . . . Just in the same way women's enfranchisement in Great Britain, now a great accomplished fact, was an idea in a few minds for twice as long, forty years and more, before the

---

[57] 'Christabel Pankhurst to the London Police', *Moody Bible Institute Monthly*, September 1927, pp. 10–14.
[58] Pankhurst, *Seeing the Future*, p. 116.
[59] Pankhurst, *Seeing the Future*, p. 208.

phase of realisation began in the first decade of the present century, and ended in victory in the second decade. Modern Zionism has followed a like course. One well remembers the day when, from women themselves, the idea of voting, because unfamiliar, met with indifference, and even, where some were concerned, resistance. They were accustomed to being voteless: why not, thought many of them, leave things alone, especially as success was in their view doubtful, and even if realised might mean the loss of some existing privilege. Exactly the same indifference, and even greater resistance, have many Jews shown toward Zionism. Exactly in the same way will their indifference and resistance be overcome. A conquering idea is the return to Zion![60]

This is the kind of embedded piece of commentary that is typical of her. While the subject is clearly Zionism (a standard one for pre-millennialist writers), she is also reflecting that votes for women was a great, conquering idea that achieved much. In a letter to Churchill in 1934 she expressed gratitude for his comments on the women's suffrage campaign in an article he had written reflecting on the last twenty years: 'I appreciate your generous allusion to women's emancipation & achievement.'[61] She had achieved something as a Suffragette and she was grateful for recognition of that fact.

Her last religious book, *The Uncurtained Future* (1940), was the one that contained the most substantial reflections of her women's suffrage days. Here is a passage in which she catalogued what the W.S.P.U. accomplished for the war effort:

> We claimed and gained a wider sphere for women's war-work, advocated conscription of man-power, food rationing, unity of command; a mission to America was undertaken; inter-allied friendship was promoted; a war-time industrial crisis was averted by a call to the women munition workers; individual Suffragettes were active in many fields.[62]

In another section, Pankhurst argued that she had not abandoned the cause, but rather won it:

> It was decided to dissolve the Suffragette organisation which had achieved its original object of enfranchising women, and had played no small part in helping to win the war, and opening the post-war chapter. I decided to retire from politics. I had never cared for the climate of politics. It was only the cause of women's enfranchisement that had or could have drawn me into politics: this cause had now

[60] Pankhurst, *Seeing the Future*, pp. 269–70.
[61] Churchill Archives Centre, Churchill College, Cambridge: Christabel Pankhurst to Winston Churchill, 14 May 1934.
[62] Pankhurst, *Uncurtained Future*, p. 24.

triumphed. The winning of votes for women might have taken a lifetime, and the campaign for the vote could never have been abandoned until victory. But now victory had come, one was free to retire from the political field.[63]

In a later chapter, she paid tribute to the Suffragettes and savoured the victory they had won:

> Human agency I again saw at its best during our Suffragette campaign, in the unselfish devotion of numberless women, many of unknown or to-day forgotten name, to a movement which, to them personally, brought only sacrifice and loss. . . .

> The son of the Prime Minister who held office during the Suffragette campaign has made an *amende honorable* in the following words: 'Most people would now believe that the militants had a well-founded grievance against the way in which the Constitution was working in their own case. . . .' . . . Then followed the long sequence of protests and imprisonments which is now part of history and which ended happily in the completion of the British Constitution by the enfranchisement of women.

> There can never have been a political movement more earnest, more united, more inspiring. It was exacting, too, for added to its more dramatic events were thousands of meetings and other propaganda activities. Here, in fact, was human agency at its very best! Mother, true to her watchword of former days, 'Down with private interest, up with the public good,' put her health and her life in the balance, that the women of future generations might be free. . . . Greatly should I wish here to name and pay full tribute to our colleagues of those days![64]

Here are not only fond memories and a recollection of the perspective of the Suffragettes, but also a clear statement that what they had achieved was the removal of a real grievance, freedom for future generations of women, and 'the completion of the British Constitution'. Christabel Pankhurst, although a fundamentalist, was nevertheless still a feminist.

[63] Pankhurst, *Uncurtained Future*, p. 27.
[64] Pankhurst, *Uncurtained Future*, pp. 44–8.

Chapter Seven

FUNDAMENTALISM AND FEMINISM IN THE CHURCH

Fundamentalists and Women in Ministry

As the question of women's suffrage was settled so long ago – and apparently for henceforth and forever more – the truism that fundamentalism is opposed to women in ministry is the one that is more prominent today. A standard source to cite in order to substantiate that view is John R. Rice's *Bobbed Hair, Bossy Wives, and Women Preachers* (1941).[1] Rice, a separatistic Baptist, was a leading fundamentalist voice through the power of his popular journal, the *Sword of the Lord*. One reason why this book is so often referred to by scholars is because its evocative title neatly attacked allegedly wayward women on three different fronts in three curt phrases (the social/societal, the domestic/familial, and the ministerial/ecclesiastical). 'Women preachers' are the relevant target for this chapter. Rice offered a synopsis of each theme in the table of contents, and his summary on women in ministry begins:

> Human opinions differ. Questions cannot be settled by logic, by opinion, nor by feeling. Impressions that are contrary to the Bible not from the Spirit of God. 1 Timothy 2:11–15 says no women to teach or usurp authority over men. Based on fundamental differences in man and woman since creation. Women permitted to teach younger women, to teach children, to win souls, but to be in silence as far as teaching men or the whole church, or having any place of authority over men or over the church. Pastors have authority from God to rule, so no woman could be a bishop or pastor. Evangelists were to 'command and teach,' so Bible forbids woman to be evangelist. 1 Corinthians 14:34, 35 commands women to be silent in the church. Addressed to all Christians everywhere, therefore binding today. Women forbidden to have authority in the church, likewise commanded to be silent in other mixed gatherings, as far as official

[1] John R. Rice, *Bobbed Hair, Bossy Wives, and Women Preachers: Significant Questions For Honest Christian Women Settled by the Word of God*, Wheaton, Illinois: Sword of the Lord Publishers, 1941.

121

teaching or preaching is concerned. There were no women pastors, evangelists, Bible teachers or preachers in New Testament times. . . .[2]

This is often considered the unanimous opinion of the fundamentalist world, an impression that led Bruce B. Lawrence to declare confidently that fundamentalism never recognized 'an individual woman as authoritative teacher'.[3] The true picture is actually much more interesting and complex. Even if one were to assume that Rice's opinion was the uniform judgment of the whole fundamentalist movement, it is important to recognize that Rice's book was published in 1941. It is therefore anachronistic to assume that this was the opinion of fundamentalists in the 1920s.

In fact, Janette Hassey has done a fine job of documenting the openness to women in ministry that fundamentalists had in the 1920s (and their precursors in the decades before).[4] Hassey was an evangelical writing for evangelicals through the medium of an evangelical publisher: the title, *No Time For Silence*, itself indicates that she was raising a prophetic voice in the camp about its contemporary views toward women in ministry. This context has meant that her book is not as well known or as often cited in the wider world of scholarship as it deserves. Moreover, the import of her work has not always been fully recognized. Betty A. DeBerg, for example, describes Hassey's volume in a footnote as a 'study of the steadily deteriorating support of church women by fundamentalists between 1880 and 1930', thereby passing over the remarkable place in ministry that women once had in fundamentalism in order to head straight to the story of the erosion of that tradition.[5] It is the assumption of this study of Christabel Pankhurst that DeBerg's point (that some fundamentalists are opposed to feminism) is not news, but that Hassey's rediscovery of the way in which the first generation of fundamentalists often affirmed women in ministry still is. Religion and gender are now frequent subjects for discussion and research. Margaret Lamberts Bendroth and Edith L. Blumhofer have offered surveys of fundamentalism and feminism in the twentieth century that take a stand between the argument that DeBerg makes and the more revisionist view that is being offered here (with Blumhofer's article coming closer to the latter and Bendroth's book closer to the former).[6] In the revisionist

[2] Rice, *Bobbed Hair*, pp. [5–6].
[3] Bruce B. Lawrence, *Defenders of God: The Fundamentalist Revolt Against the Modern Age*, San Francisco, 1989, p. 230.
[4] Janette Hassey, *No Time For Silence: Evangelical Women in Public Ministry Around the Turn of the Century*, Grand Rapids: Academie Books (Zondervan), 1986.
[5] DeBerg, *Ungodly Women*, p. 7.
[6] Margaret Lamberts Bendroth, *Fundamentalism and Gender, 1875 to the Present*, New Haven: Yale University Press, 1993; Edith L. Blumhofer, 'A Confused Legacy: Reflections on Evangelical Attitudes toward Ministering Women in the Past Century', *Fides et Historia*, 22, 1 (Winter/Spring 1990), pp. 49–61.

tradition, Michael S. Hamilton has raised the hard questions that expose the weaknesses in the standard presentations of fundamentalists as exceptionally misogynist, and provides a telling survey of some of the evidence to the contrary.[7] How difficult it is for scholars to accept this view, irrespective of the evidence, is illustrated by an article by David G. Hackett published in 1995 that surveyed the current state of the literature on gender and religion. In a three-sentence summary of Hamilton's argument, Hackett's first and last word is 'ironically', which he apparently uses as a way of saying that the evidence Hamilton has offered must be bracketed and put aside because we all 'know' that fundamentalists are misogynist.[8] The notion that fundamentalists might have been open to women in ministry in the 1920s has not yet been assimilated, despite the evidence that has already been offered by some scholars and the arguments that they have made.

It is not an intention of this study, of course, to argue that the fundamentalism of the 1920s was marked by gender equality; that could not be said of any major Christian branch or denomination in that period, and very few major groups of any sort. The more telling question is not whether or not fundamentalism discriminated against women (it most certainly did), but whether in the context of that time it offered more restrictions, or alternatively greater freedom, than other groups. Given the kind of evidence of women in ministry in fundamentalism that is already widely available, the argument that fundamentalism was exceptionally oppressive to women is usually structured by admissions followed by 'buts' that supposedly indicate the true test that gives the most revealing reading. The arguments run like this: it is true that women did a lot as missionaries, but what could they do on the home field? it is true that women could preach, but could they teach? it is true that women could teach, but could they administer the sacraments? it is true that women could evangelize, but could they pastor a local church? it is true that some women served as local pastors, but could they be ordained? it is true that women were very active in ministry in Holiness and Pentecostal churches, but what about in Baptist and Presbyterian churches? The effect of all this is to discount some really extraordinary opportunities for women by continually shifting the definition of 'real' ministry in an effort to bolster the assumption that fundamentalists were misogynist.

To begin with the last distinction listed, Bendroth argues that:

> Although many holiness and pentecostal groups may rightly assume the fundamentalist label, the two groups parted ways decisively in

---

[7] Michael S. Hamilton, 'Women, Public Ministry, and American Fundamentalism, 1920–1950', *Religion and American Culture*, 3, 2 (Summer 1993), pp. 171–96.
[8] David G. Hackett, 'Gender and Religion in American Culture, 1870–1930', *Religion and American Culture*, 5, 2 (Summer 1995), p. 131.

regard to the 'woman question.' For the purposes of my argument, I have chosen to differentiate the main body of fundamentalists from their charismatic conservative brethren. For although to outsiders they appeared nearly indistinguishable, fundamentalists abhorred the use of women preachers in holiness churches almost as vehemently as they opposed the practice of speaking in tongues.[9]

This methodology is problematic. While in the first sentence she concedes that holiness Christians and pentecostals were fundamentalists, by the third sentence the word 'fundamentalist' is being used in contrast to them. Therefore, Bendroth produces a major volume on fundamentalism and gender that intentionally excludes a significant part of fundamentalism on the grounds that it was known to be open to women in ministry, tailoring her study in order to leave the impression that fundamentalism was more opposed to women in public church life than in fact it actually was. Most notably, it neatly excludes the case of Aimee Semple McPherson (1890–1944), who not only was the most popular evangelist in America for some years, but who also was the local pastor of her own large congregation where she administered the sacraments, and the founder and president of her own denomination, the Four Square Pentecostal Church, and her own Bible institute, L.I.F.E., and thus the spiritual head of numerous men in ministry.[10] More to the point, however, this divide does not account for Pankhurst's ministry. Christabel Pankhurst was totally and unequivocally aligned on the so-called 'fundamentalist' side. No occasion has been found when she ever spoke in a Methodist, Holiness, or Pentecostal church or for a conference or organization sponsored by one of those groups. As has been shown, her public ministry began with a series of addresses in a Presbyterian church, Knox Presbyterian Church, Toronto, a congregation that she was invited back to repeatedly over the years; and Knox was not the only Presbyterian church to invite her. Her main constituency, however, was probably Baptist. It has already been noted that Pankhurst filled the pulpit at John Roach Straton's great fundamentalist stronghold in New York, Calvary Baptist Church, on numerous occasions. One could go on to discuss numerous less well-known churches, but it should suffice here to note the general pattern: Pankhurst ministered in Reformed or Baptist contexts often, but apparently never in the Holiness or Pentecostal orbits.

Having conceded that fundamentalist women were sometimes preachers and evangelists, DeBerg defines true ministry as that undertaken by ordained local pastors, a status rarely granted to women:

> No matter what the position expressed concerning women speaking in the church or in any other mixed assembly, all writers and editors

[9] Bendroth, *Fundamentalism and Gender*, pp. 4–5.
[10] For her life, see Edith L. Blumhofer, *Aimee Semple McPherson: Everybody's Sister*, Grand Rapids: William B. Eerdmans, 1993.

of these magazines opposed ordaining women to traditional parish ministry. . . . In the context of this debate, fundamentalists stressed a 'priestly' understanding of the ordained ministry, the authority of the clergy over the laity. . . . so they encouraged women only as lay workers . . . so did ordination remain, except in rare circumstances, an unbreachable barrier against women's participation . . . [women were active in some ways but] seldom the 'core' Protestant ministerial duties of shepherding a congregation.[11]

It is certainly true that women were seldom ordained ministers or local pastors in the fundamentalism of the 1920s, but how significant is this fact for determining the movement's attitude toward women? Bendroth has observed that:

The ideal fundamentalist minister was vigorous and energetic, following the masculine model of the evangelist rather than the feminized one of the church pastor. . . . The highest calling, therefore, was that of an evangelist. 'One can be a modernist and be a pastor,' Rice commented. 'But one cannot be a modernist and be a real evangelist. . . .'[12]

Following the standard approach of pointing toward the (alleged) boundary as all that matters, Bendroth then goes on to claim: 'Within the masculine realm of evangelistic preaching, women were clearly subordinate.'[13] The more revealing point, however, is that women were unequivocally given the title of 'evangelist' and recognized in that ministry in fundamentalist circles, despite the fact that it was the 'highest calling'. An article in the *Advent Witness* in 1933 discussed the nature of ministry. The article followed the structure of a list of ministries given in a passage of the Bible:

(. . . He that descended is the same also that ascended up far above all heavens, that he might fill all things.) And he [Christ] gave some, apostles; and some, prophets; and some, evangelists; and some, pastors and teachers; for the perfecting of the saints, for the work of the ministry, for the edifying of the body of Christ . . . (Ephesians 4:10–12 Authorized Version)

The author reasoned that the first two ministries, apostles and prophets, were no longer for today. This thereby gave the ministry of evangelist primacy of place in the modern hierarchy of ministry. Moreover, the author asserted that all these ministries were open to women: 'But let none impose upon the Church the yoke of the University – let none refuse to recognise nor to employ the gifts which come from God Himself – let

[11] DeBerg, *Ungodly Women*, pp. 79–83.
[12] Bendroth, *Fundamentalism and Gender*, p. 77.
[13] Bendroth, *Fundamentalism and Gender*, p. 77.

none discourage the men and women who, being converted to the Lord, whether young or old, beyond school age, feel called of God.'[14] The fundamentalist leader John Roach Straton was even willing to waive the 'beyond school age' caveat and concede that a fourteen-year-old girl, Uldine Utley, was a true evangelist. Giving weight to his conviction, Straton turned his pulpit over to Utley's ministry.[15]

Despite Lawrence's assertion, women were not automatically excluded from the ministry of teacher either. The *Christian Fundamentalist*, for example, carried an article in 1931 puffing the ministry of 'Mrs Carl Gray': 'Mrs Gray is a woman of national reputation as a Bible teacher.'[16] The evangelist Paul Rader's *World-Wide Christian Courier* promoted the ministry of numerous women, including 'Mrs A. M. Johnson' whose Sunday sermons at the Chicago Gospel Tabernacle were broadcast over the radio.[17] Moody Bible Institute was proud of the popular class on Paul's Epistles taught by Iris Ikeler McCord that was a highlight of its 'Radio Bible Study'.[18] Moreover, it would be wrong to assume a boundary has been found in the 'Mrs' and conclude that a woman might teach if she was demonstrably under the control of a husband. Pankhurst, of course, was a woman in ministry who never married, and her case was not *sui generis*. For example, when she spoke at the World's Christian Fundamentals Association annual conference, there were two other women with the title 'Miss' on the programme, the more famous one being Elizabeth Knauss, who had built up a very popular ministry by criticizing Bolshevism 'from the Biblical standpoint'.[19] Pankhurst was not the only single woman on the platform at Winona Lake Bible Conference in 1941 either, as Ruth Paxson was also a featured speaker.[20] Paxson had written a three-volume work of systematic theology that the influential fundamentalist R. A. Torrey endorsed in a way that made it apparent that the doctrinal teaching of this single woman could be taken to be just as authoritative as a man's:

> A remarkable book – one of the most satisfying I have ever read. It deals pretty much with all the great fundamentals of the Christian faith: – the absolute authority of the Bible; the humanity and deity of Jesus Christ, His Incarnation, the Virgin Birth, Atoning Death, Resurrection and Ascension; Sin; the Forgiveness of Sin; and others . . . all in a Scriptural way, a thorough way, and rings true every time.[21]

[14] *Advent Witness*, 1 August 1933, pp. 132–3.
[15] Hassey, *No Time For Silence*, pp. 189–210.
[16] *Christian Fundamentalist*, June 1931, p. 447.
[17] See, for example, *World-Wide Christian Courier*, January 1928, p. [2].
[18] *Sunday School Times*, 14 September 1929, p. 504.
[19] *Christian Fundamentalist*, May 1913, pp. 404, 408.
[20] *Winona Echoes 1941*, Grand Rapids: Zondervan, n.d.
[21] *Sunday School Times*, 24 November 1928, p. 705.

The Bible Testimony Fellowship endorsed and praised the ministries of 'Miss E. M. Perry' and 'Miss Dorothy M. Graves', both of whom taught mixed assemblies in churches.[22] The *Advent Witness* repeatedly ran articles by and about the missionary to China, Gladys Aylward.[23] Aylward's ministry was eventually considered sufficiently inspiring by the wider culture to warrant a major Hollywood film with Ingrid Bergman in the leading role: *The Inn of the Sixth Happiness* (Twentieth Century Fox, 1958). Another single woman, Gladys M. Phipps, repeatedly wrote Bible teaching articles for the *Advent Witness*.[24] Agnes Scott Kent wrote a regular column, 'The Sign of the Fig Tree', for the *Evangelical Christian*.[25] She was thereby pursuing a ministry of analysing the signs of the times similar in kind to Pankhurst's, demonstrating that the Suffragette was not an exception to some men-only rule owing to her personal fame. In a study of the *Christian* newspaper for 1920, not only was the newspaper uniformly and vocally in favour of gender equality in society, but the paper was also invariably supportive of women preachers. It answered the question 'Shall Women Preach?' in an issue in June in the affirmative, huffing indignantly at the end: 'And some say that women should not speak in the Churches!'[26] As the most obvious person who had dared to say such a thing was apparently the apostle Paul, this is a rather remarkable turn of phrase. Though less common than fundamentalist women preachers, evangelists, and Bible teachers, cases of women being ordained or serving as local pastors in fundamentalist or proto-fundamentalist circles have been documented by Hassey.[27] Women were certainly engaged in prominent ministries in fundamentalism in the 1920s.

Pankhurst's Ministry

Christabel Pankhurst's ministry was not only well-received by fundamentalists, it was also given significant scope. She was appreciated for her evangelistic abilities. A report of her address at St John's Presbyterian Church, Toronto, for example, enthused: 'Miss Pankhurst has evangelistic passion. She is out for souls.'[28] The *Christian* declared in 1926: 'Miss Pankhurst is

---

[22] *Quarterly Paper of the Bible Testimony Fellowship*, 11, 2 (April to June 1929), p. 4; 9, 2 (April to June 1936), p. 4.
[23] See, for example, *Advent Witness*, 1 June 1935, p. 111; October 1938, p. 186.
[24] See, for example, *Advent Witness*, 1 December 1935, p. 226; May 1936, pp. 90–1; and November 1939, p. 216.
[25] See, for example, *Evangelical Christian*, September 1937, p. 417.
[26] *Christian*, 17 June 1920, p. 6.
[27] Hassey, *No Time For Silence*.
[28] *Christian*, 29 March 1923, p. 6.

undoubtedly an able evangelist, and many will no doubt look expectantly for further service from her along that line.'[29] The Advent Testimony Movement remembered her ministry primarily and fondly as the key guest ministry in their great evangelistic campaign of 1926–27.[30] She was also appreciated for her Bible teaching. An article in the *Christian* commented: 'Those who read *The Lord Cometh*, recognised in Miss CHRISTABEL PANKHURST one to whom the Lord had given a marvelous grasp of revealed truth.'[31] In a daring as well as generous identification of her ministry gift, the *Sunday School Times* deemed her to be 'a true prophetess to our generation'.[32] The *King's Business* claimed that she was one of the 'Defenders of the Faith' and, no doubt, she was gratified to take her place alongside the monarchs of Great Britain.[33]

Fundamentalists instinctively went to the Bible to find great women with whom to compare Pankhurst. An article in the *Christian* in 1923 declared: 'As we consider her work, conviction grows that she has been raised up for such a time as this.'[34] There is, as the biblically literate already know, a phrase of Scripture embedded in this statement that would have caused the newspaper's readers to recognize instantly that 'Queen Christabel' was being compared with Queen Esther. A favourite was Deborah. As a prophet and a judge (ruler) who had led the whole people of Israel, Deborah was a particularly promising example. Dr A. H. Burton, a popular dispensational teacher in England, ended a review of Pankhurst's *The World's Unrest* with the words: 'At any rate, it is time for a Deborah to be raised up.'[35] This sentiment is in marked contrast to DeBerg's picture of dispensationalists viewing women in leadership as a negative sign of the times. F. B. Meyer pronounced Pankhurst to be 'the Deborah of this movement'.[36] The prophet Anna was another common biblical comparison. Anna was an apt choice because she proclaimed the first advent of Christ and therefore, as a woman in ministry declaring the second advent, Pankhurst made a neat parallel. In a review of *The World's Unrest*, F. B. Meyer argued that there 'was an Apocalypse, some nineteen centuries ago, heralded by Mary and

[29] *Christian*, 21 October 1926, p. 23.
[30] F. A. Tatford, *The Midnight Cry: The Story of Fifty Years of Witness*, Eastbourne: Bible and Advent Testimony Movement, n.d. [c. 1967], p. 81. Pankhurst, reflecting her personal experience, frequently connected adventist teaching and evangelism. For example, she once remarked, 'We must preach the Lord's coming because that is the effective evangelization for to-day . . . Once they understand and rejoice in that truth it is for them but a step to the understanding of the Gospel as it applies to the individual.' *Sunday School Times*, 24 October 1925, p. 664.
[31] *Christian*, 8 July 1926, p. 2.
[32] *Sunday School Times*, 31 January 1925, p. 72.
[33] *King's Business*, September 1924, p. 553.
[34] *Christian*, 12 July 1923, p. 1.
[35] *Christian*, 12 August 1926, p. 5.
[36] *Christian*, 28 October 1926, p. 21.

Elizabeth, Simeon and Anna, and others. There is a second Apocalypse, near at hand. Many voices announce it, and among them, in the foremost rank, will be this remarkable book by Miss Christabel Pankhurst.'[37]

In her *Who's Who* entry – in language that had the distinct ring of having been written by herself – Pankhurst was said to be 'now active in heralding the personal, visible, and powerful Second Coming of the Lord Jesus Christ as foreshown by the present signs of the times'.[38] The entry was altered in the early 1950s – obviously it was time for a more objective voice – and the old wording was replaced with the cold and curt phrase 'Religious Propagandist'.[39] Pankhurst's own apologetic for women in ministry will be offered below, but it is worth mentioning here that she was probably quite content to think of herself as a herald of her King. Nevertheless, the fundamentalist world allowed her to be more than that. A delightful example of this is a 'Meeting for Ministers' in Cardiff at which Pankhurst was the co-speaker with the Revd W. M. Robertson[40] (not the only ministerial gathering that she addressed). Beyond being merely a preacher, Pankhurst took on the self-imposed task of training other preachers, including a whole chapter in one of her books on 'How to Preach Prophecy'.[41] An even more revealing event is that Pankhurst gave the address at a Communion Service at Knox Presbyterian Church, Toronto, on 10 December 1922. Pankhurst began her message with the words:

> The prince of this world invites men to a table prefigured by Belshazzar's feast, and the Spirit invites regenerate men to the Lord's Supper. It is not because of any virtue and wisdom in ourselves that we have left the world's table, and gained the right to partake of the emblems of our Lord's broken body and shed blood, for it is God who hath called us to repentance.[42]

Fundamentalism was the kind of world in which a single woman with a controversial past, and without a single day of formal theological or ministerial training, could end up as a central figure at a sacramental occasion in one of the largest and most prominent churches in a major city.

Mainline Protestantism and the Anglican Context

Fundamentalists had limits on what kind of ministries women could usually pursue, and there is no doubt that women who wished to minister

---

[37] *Christian*, 15 July 1926, p. 20.
[38] See, for example, *Who's Who 1938*, London: A. & C. Black, p. 2591.
[39] See, for example, *Who's Who 1957*, London: Adam and Charles Black, p. 2311.
[40] *Christian*, 14 October 1926, p. 37.
[41] Pankhurst, *Uncurtained Future*, chapter 11.
[42] *Christian*, 29 March 1923, p. 24.

experienced discrimination in significant ways, but this was also true of all major branches of Christianity (and most secular professions). The vast Roman Catholic and Eastern Orthodox traditions did not have a place for women preachers in the church in any way comparable to what was happening in fundamentalism. Most of the major Protestant denominations did not allow women to be ordained, and it is arguable that those that did had fewer women in ministry and women who were generally less prominent than in fundamentalist circles. Maude Royden had an outstanding ministry in England based at the City Temple, a large Congregational church in London, but if one were to match her with Aimee Semple McPherson (who undoubtedly had a far more influential ministry) and then start to evaluate the rest of the women in ministry in mainline churches against fundamentalist ones it seems certain that fundamentalism would end up with a far better record for making room for women.[43] Studies by those who wish to expose fundamentalists as misogynist generally fail to examine a control group by which it might be demonstrated that they were more or less so than other large Christian bodies (or, indeed, large non-religious bodies in society). When Pankhurst spoke in Glasgow, the Moderator of the General Assembly of the Church of Scotland, the Revd Dr J. D. McCallum, and the Moderator of the General Assembly of the United Free Church of Scotland, the Revd Dr George H. Morrison, presided. It is readily apparent that Pankhurst had more scope for ministry on the fundamentalist circuit than in either of those distinguished denominations. The obvious control group, however, is her own denomination: Anglicanism.

Throughout her ministry, Pankhurst always considered herself an Anglican. When she launched her journal, *Present and Future*, she declared that it was edited 'by one who is simply a member of the Church of England'.[44] Upon her death in February 1958, the local paper where she lived (Santa Monica, California) reported that she was 'an active member of the Episcopal Church'.[45] Her writings are filled with references to the thoughts and actions of bishops, archbishops, Church commissions, and the like. In a matter of a few pages, for example, in *Seeing the Future*, there are references to the dean of Westminster, the archbishop of York, and the bishop of Durham, the fact that the book was published only in America notwithstanding.[46] If one is inclined to find the limits for women in ministry then it is hard to overlook the fact

---

[43] For Maude Royden, see Sheila Fletcher, *Maude Royden: A Life*, Oxford: Basil Blackwell, 1989.
[44] *Present and Future*, May 1934, p. 2.
[45] 'Dame Pankhurst, Noted Suffrage Leader, Dies', *Evening Outlook*, 14 February 1958.
[46] Pankhurst, *Seeing the Future*, pp. 241–4.

that no woman has ever been appointed a bishop in the Church of England – yet that church is not usually thought of as misogynist today, and it certainly has not generated the kind of lengthy, passionate denunciations by historians for its discrimination against women that fundamentalism in the 1920s has. What is certain is that fundamentalism offered Pankhurst scope as a woman with a call to ministry that was not available in the Anglicanism of her day. Revealing a culture of confining women far more strictly than the world of fundamentalism, the *New York Times* reported in 1923 on Pankhurst's ministry: 'She has spoken in churches of practically all denominations and in halls connected with the Anglican Churches, where women are not allowed to speak in the church proper.'[47] In all the reports of Pankhurst's ministry throughout the years, the only time that her supposed 'lay' status was made explicit was in the context of the Anglican communion. A report on her ministry in Ascension Memorial Episcopal Church in New York said: 'As a lay preacher she delivered the first of a series of talks on world events.'[48] And this, of course, was a rare event, illustrating the Anglican tradition at its most generous and accommodating extreme on the issue of women in ministry. At the Church of England's Church Congress in Bristol in 1938: 'Dame Christabel Pankhurst took advantage of the invitation, open to any member of the Congress, to speak to the limit of five minutes.'[49] This event was reported in the *Church Times*' account of the congress under the extraordinary subheading 'A Woman Speaks'. The fundamentalist conferences and rallies that Pankhurst addressed would never have reported her words under such a heading – as if it was news that a woman happened to speak! But it was news in an Anglican context. Maude Royden, after all, had this much in common with Pankhurst: they were both Anglicans who had to pursue their ministries outside their own denomination. Sean Gill, in his study of *Women and the Church of England*, records that

> The restrictions imposed in 1920 were made even clearer in 1922 when the Lower House of Canterbury Convocation passed two amendments prohibiting deaconesses from reading morning and evening prayer and from leading in prayer and preaching at church services.[50]

In other words, in the very year that Christabel Pankhurst began a preaching ministry in major fundamentalist churches, the Church of England was firmly closing its own doors on the very possibility of

---

[47] *New York Times*, 19 August 1923, p. 13.
[48] *New York Times*, 5 January 1925, p. 9.
[49] *Church Times*, 7 October 1938, p. 858.
[50] Sean Gill, *Women and the Church of England: From the Eighteenth Century to the Present*, London: SPCK, 1994, p. 219.

women having such a ministry. In fact, if Pankhurst had spent her whole Christian life in an Anglican context, she almost certainly would have never even heard a woman preach, let alone have become a preacher herself. Brian Heeney demonstrated the deep hostility that there was within the established church in the 1910s and 1920s regarding the notion of women preaching. In 1916 the wartime situation raised the possibility that women might read the lesson in places where no man was available: 'There followed over a month of warm correspondence, much of it hostile on the ground that "universal custom" forbade women to take such a public ecclesiastical role.'[51] Later that year, the possibility was raised that women might speak as part of the National Mission of Repentance and Hope. The reaction was so vehement that the bishop of London, who had already agreed to women speakers for the work of the mission in his diocese, was forced to rescind his approval. A modest proposal to allow some women speakers in some tightly prescribed circumstances a few years later was still too controversial: 'Debated continually from 1919 to 1922, it finally emerged in a weakened form: women's right to speak and lead prayers in consecrated buildings was "normally" to be confined to congregations of women and children.'[52] Things did not improve during Pankhurst's active years of ministry; fundamentalism offered her freedom in ministry that was simply not available in her own denomination.

The Bible and Women in Ministry

It has often been assumed that an evangelical or fundamentalist approach to the Bible – one that sees every passage as the binding word of God for today – makes a rejection of women in ministry almost inevitable. DeBerg, as has already been shown, goes so far as to argue that fundamentalists were attracted to a doctrine of biblical inerrancy precisely because it bolstered a misogynist stance. Bendroth recognizes an older tradition in evangelicalism that endeavoured to handle the Bible in a way that allowed women in ministry, but she sees this as totally incompatible with a fundamentalist approach:

> Though the battle for the Bible proved somewhat inconclusive in regard to the woman question, dispensational premillennialism, the theological system fundamentalists adhered to, offered an air-tight argument for feminine subordination. Taken in isolation, the numerous biblical texts on women's role could be a matter of endless

---

[51] Brian Heeney, *The Women's Movement in the Church of England, 1850–1930*, Oxford: Clarendon Press, 1988, p. 121.
[52] Heeney, *Women's Movement*, p. 124.

debate; however, within the more rigid schema of dispensational interpretation all controversy ceased, for their meaning was clear.[53]

Bendroth here is presenting an illuminating viewpoint on how a certain dispensational logic worked against women in ministry, but the impression that this was a monolithic perspective held by all dispensationalists is over-played. Pankhurst, of course, was a dispensationalist who believed in both the inerrancy of the Bible and women in ministry. In the very same address, for example, she once remarked both that 'the Bible is unerring' and that 'this age of dispensation is drawing to a close'.[54] Bendroth's assessment is based on an emphasis upon female subordination as part of the creation order, but Pankhurst emphasized that it was part of humanity's curse, rather than its creation: '"He shall rule over thee" – the ancient curse, pronounced upon the woman.'[55] Moreover, as has already been shown, many of the fundamentalist leaders who supported her ministry were also dispensationalists who affirmed women in ministry. It is instructive that John R. Rice felt a need to criticize the Scofield Bible – that benchmark teaching text for dispensational fundamental-ists – in order to strengthen his case against women preachers.[56] If dispen-sationalism was incompatible with an affirmation of women in ministry, many of the first generation of fundamentalists were unaware of this fact.

There was always an internal debate within evangelicalism regarding the role of women in ministry. This debate was usually conducted as an exercise in understanding the Bible, as the Bible was the authority to which evangelicals appealed. Although every scripture verse that in any way might seem relevant was brought into the debate at various points, the discussion primarily revolved around a few verses that might be called 'keynote' texts. Those who believed that women should be restricted, focused on two primary keynote texts:

> Let the woman learn in silence with all subjection. But I suffer not a woman to teach, nor to usurp authority over the man, but to be in silence. For Adam was first formed, then Eve. And Adam was not deceived, but the woman being deceived was in the transgression. (1 Timothy 2:11–14 Authorized Version)

> Let your women keep silence in the churches: for it is not permitted unto them to speak; but they are commanded to be under obedience, as also saith the law. And if they will learn any thing, let them ask their husbands at home: for it is a shame for women to speak in the church. What? came the word of God out from you? or came it unto you only? (1 Corinthians 14:34–6 Authorized Version)

---

[53] Bendroth, *Fundamentalism and Gender*, p. 41.
[54] *New York Times*, 5 January 1925, p. 9.
[55] Pankhurst, *Seeing the Future*, p. 119.
[56] Rice, *Bobbed Hair*, p. 51.

According to this view, these two texts expressed the Bible's 'true' teaching on the subject, and any other verses of Scripture that seemed to offer a different perspective ought to be interpreted so as to make them compatible with the 'clear' teaching of these keynote texts.

Advocates of women in ministry, however, had two keynote texts of their own. They were:

> And it shall come to pass in the last days, saith God, I will pour out of my Spirit upon all flesh; and your sons and your daughters shall prophesy, and your young men shall see visions, and your old men shall dream dreams: And on my servants and on my handmaidens I will pour out in those days of my Spirit; and they shall prophesy. (Acts 2:17–18 Authorized Version)

> For ye are all the children of God by faith in Christ Jesus. For as many of you as have been baptized into Christ have put on Christ. There is neither Jew nor Greek, there is neither bond nor free, there is neither male nor female: for ye are all one in Christ Jesus. (Galatians 3:26–8 Authorized Version)

Those who argued in favour of women preachers and ministers claimed that these two texts (individual advocates usually found one or the other to be the more telling one) offered the Bible's general judgment on this subject, and that therefore any verses that appeared to offer a more restricting word must be interpreted so as not to override the Bible's 'final' or 'general' word on the subject offered in these keynote texts.

Interestingly, no example has been found of Pankhurst ever quoting or referring to either of the first two texts which so often set the context for arguments against women in ministry. Her response to the two restrictive passages would seem to have been merely to ignore them. She spent her time in what to her were far more fascinating portions of the Bible – the visions of the future in the books of Daniel and Revelation. Moreover, only one instance has been found of her quoting either of the two standard keynote texts in favour of women in ministry and that is the earliest apologetic for her ministry that has been found, an interview in the *Toronto Daily Star* in November 1922:

> 'You believe, then, in women taking their place in the pulpit?' suggested The Star. 'Don't we find something about sons and daughters testifying, in the Bible?' replied Miss Pankhurst. 'It has always been open to women to do this. In the early church women played a great and honored part. That is what I shall do. I shall testify to my experience.'[57]

---

[57] *Toronto Daily Star*, 18 November 1922, p. 20.

After that, however, Acts 2 and Galatians 3:28 are nowhere to be found in her writings and speeches. Nevertheless, this does not mean that she failed to offer any biblical defence of women in ministry. In fact, Pankhurst found her own keynote text, and she came back to it again and again. It was the following passage in the narrative in Matthew's Gospel of Christ's resurrection:

> In the end of the sabbath, as it began to dawn toward the first day of the week, came Mary Magdalene and the other Mary to see the sepulchre. And, behold, there was a great earthquake: for the angel of the Lord descended from heaven, and came and rolled back the stone from the door, and sat upon it. His countenance was like lightning, and his raiment white as snow: And for fear of him the keepers did shake, and became as dead men. And the angel answered and said unto the women, Fear not ye: for I know that ye seek Jesus, which was crucified. He is not here: for he is risen, as he said. Come, see the place where the Lord lay. And go quickly, and tell his disciples that he is risen from the dead; and behold, he goeth before you into Galilee; there shall ye see him: lo, I have told you. And they departed quickly from the sepulchre with fear and great joy; and did run to bring his disciples word. (Matthew 28:1–8 Authorized Version)

The result of the events presented in this passage is recorded in Luke's Gospel, in a passage recounting the words of the disciple Cleopas before he had become convinced of the resurrection:

> Yea, and certain women also of our company made us astonished, which were early at the sepulchre; And when they found not his body, they came, saying, that they had also seen a vision of angels, which said that he was alive. (Luke 24:22–3 Authorized Version)

Pankhurst did not discover these passages for the first time, of course, as they often had been quoted by those in favour of women in ministry, but she is a rare, if not singular, example of someone who put all her eggs in this Easter basket.

The significance of this keynote text is the gender role reversal. The 'disciples' to whom the women are instructed by the angel to bring the message of the resurrection include, of course, the men, the apostles, Peter, James, John, and the rest. 'Apostle' means 'sent one' and thus the women received a divine commission to be apostles to the apostles, teachers to the teachers, evangelists to the evangelists, preachers to the preachers. Tellingly, the only ministry from the classic list of ministries in Ephesians chapter four for which one cannot make an obvious case from this keynote text is pastor. Only one instance has been found when Pankhurst appeared to concede that full gender equality in Christian ministry was not appropriate, and that was on the ministry of the pastor. She is reported to have said in her address to the Moody Bible

Institute in 1924:

> I want to name the name of Christ where it has never yet been
> named. Is that not so with you? Women cannot be pastors. They can
> tell the good tidings like the other women who make the men aston-
> ished. I cannot help rather liking that. We are neither bond nor free.
> If the Son has made you free you shall be free indeed. We don't need
> to antagonize.[58]

The intent of her words is clearly to encourage women in ministry:
women do not need to start an internecine war in the Christian camp by
a confrontational attitude, they can just stand in the freedom Christ has
given them and go on to minister in a way that astonishes the men. It is
tempting to wonder if her concession of the pastorate was only tactical;
thus the passage would read something like: '[They say that] women
cannot be pastors, [but I say] they can tell the good tidings like the other
women . . .' It would be anachronistic, however, to demand that feminism in the 1920s meant an appreciation that women ought to have the
right to be pastors or ordained ministers. No doubt many women who
were committed Suffragettes or Suffragists never contemplated such a
possibility.[59] The truth, however, is probably that Pankhurst was not
thinking systematically about women in ministry at all. She knew what
she wanted to do in ministry and it was certainly not pastor a local church
or take on the mundane life and duties of a vicar: she wanted to preach,
to teach, to evangelize, and she had found the argument she needed to
justify her own aspirations and calling. In a speech that she gave in 1931,
Pankhurst tacitly argued that her own ministry was greater than that of
ordained liberal pastors and ministers: 'Ours be the privilege (since there
are Christian leaders who still renounce it) to be the ones that "publish
peace, and bring good tidings of good, that publish salvation." '[60]

The women at the tomb were commissioned to do all that she wanted
to do, that was the great fact that quickly settled in her mind. It is there
right in the very introduction to her first religious book, *'The Lord
Cometh'*: 'But somehow one is constrained to tell other people. Just as did
the women at the tomb whom the risen Jesus bade to go and tell the news,

---

[58] *Moody Bible Institute Monthly*, March 1924, pp. 337–9. Although it was stated
earlier that she does not refer to the Galatians 3:28 passage, there is arguably an echo
of it embedded in this quotation.
[59] Rather than some of the boundaries such as the local pastorate or ordination representing what was prized most by male ministers who are therefore seen as guarding their
choice preserve, it is possible that, in some instances, it was what they prized least, and
therefore a token terrain in which to bury the awkward Bible texts that appeared to say
something restrictive about women in ministry while still allowing women the freedom
to engage in all the forms of ministry that mattered most.
[60] *Christian*, 9 June 1932, p. 22.

so those who see the truth as it is in Christ Jesus have been telling it out to others ever since.'[61] (This quotation and the following one are informed by another verse: 'Now when Jesus was risen early the first day of the week, he appeared first to Mary Magdalene', Mark 16:9 Authorized Version.) Later in the same book, she exclaims while discussing Christ's resurrection: 'They *saw* Him after His resurrection. The women saw Him first.'[62] In *Seeing the Future* she exclaimed:

> Nearest to the cross, earliest at the tomb, first with the news that He was risen – loyal women have a like privilege to-day: Now, as then, it is theirs to see; it is theirs to 'Go quickly and tell!' . . . 'Yea, and certain women also . . . made us astonished,' but we 'found it even so as the women had said.' (St Luke 24:22, 24) [ellipsis in original][63]

The women who were the heralds of Christ's resurrection became a keynote text that enabled her to find biblical warrant for women in ministry.

It is also worth observing that Pankhurst was drawn to the female characters in the Bible, and references to them appear far more frequently in her writings than one might otherwise expect. In the very introduction to one of her books, for example, there is a paragraph about a prophecy by Huldah, a female prophet from the Old Testament who is such a minor character that few evangelical preachers can have found occasion to mention her in one of their books or sermons in a lifetime of ministry.[64] The woman at the well was one of her favourites. One suspects that Pankhurst liked this passage because it presented a woman in deep conversation with Jesus himself. For example, the woman at the well shows up in two separate chapters in *Pressing Problems of the Closing Age*, despite the fact that it is not a passage that one would think to go to when discussing biblical prophecy, the end times, or the return of Christ.[65] The woman at the well also reappeared in *The World's Unrest*.[66] Just as Pankhurst ignored hell and judgment and preached Christ the ultimate panacea, so her approach to the debate about women in ministry was simply to ignore those passages that seemed to be pessimistic about it and to proclaim her great text of liberation.

Opening the Professions for Women

One of the goals of the feminist movement has been to open up the professions to women. The lives of women who were pioneers in fields

[61] Pankhurst, *'The Lord Cometh'*, p. ix.
[62] Pankhurst, *'The Lord Cometh'*, p. 116.
[63] Pankhurst, *Seeing the Future*, p. 120.
[64] Pankhurst, *Pressing Problems* , p. 8.
[65] Pankhurst, *Pressing Problems*, pp. 48, 146.
[66] Pankhurst, *World's Unrest*, p. 188.

such as medicine or science are often celebrated by feminists. As one of the first women in Britain to receive a law degree, the young Christabel Pankhurst is often viewed as in this same pioneering tradition. One suspects that many feminists who have thought about Pankhurst's life have wished that she would have used the second half of her life to blaze a trail for women in the legal profession. Alternatively, she might have kept trying to secure a seat in Parliament and then, having succeeded, gone on to make a mark for women in that male bastion, along with Lady Astor and the others. Although it is hard to know what precisely he means, Pugh has pronounced condescendingly that 'In spite of her undoubted talents and her prominence, Christabel never quite achieved all that she was capable of during her adult life.'[67] It is true that Pankhurst did not choose for herself the life of a lawyer or politician in the end. That does not mean, however, that she refused the role of pioneer. The Christian ministry, after all, is also one of the classic male professions. For those who view the stance that the church historically has taken in the world as one that is particularly hostile to feminism, then, for them, surely the Christian ministry is the one that is most badly in need of being wrested away from a male hegemony. Speaking of Maude Royden, Brian Heeney reports that 'In her draft autobiography she wrote of the "singularly nauseous quality" of the opposition to women preachers, an unpleasantness "which exceeded anything I had met with in the fight for the vote."'[68] Pankhurst went into a profession that was male dominated – the Christian ministry – and carved out a place for herself in that world, not just as a participant, but as a star.

[67] Pugh, *Pankhursts*, p. 36.
[68] Heeney, *Women's Movement*, p. 125.

Epilogue

FORGETTING AND REMEMBERING

Many feminists have not known what to do with Christabel Pankhurst's religious turn. The result has been a tendency simply to ignore it. This trend began as soon as she was dead, if not even before, as can be seen in an article 'In Memoriam' written by 'Mrs Kent Allen' that was printed in the *Los Angeles Times* just two weeks after Pankhurst's death. It is worth including the whole article in order to gain the full effect:

> Feb. 13 Dame Christabel Pankhurst, crusader in the suffragette cause, passed from our midst.
>
> This noble lady, who fought so valiantly for women's right to vote, always admonished us to use our votes for the betterment of humanity. We who knew her feel her going is a great loss to the world as well as to her personal friends.
>
> Dame Christabel was a great humanitarian. Among her many kind deeds, there is one outstanding in my memory: when she nursed a blind woman night and day for months with dedicated devotion until Dame Christabel herself became ill from exhaustion but would not leave the blind woman until someone capable could take over.
>
> Dame Christabel's interest in good statesmanship never ceased. She also devoted time in her later years to the study of drawing, painting and music.
>
> A noble crusader has gone home. Sweet be her well-earned rest and blessed be her memory in the pages of history as well as in the hearts of us whose privilege it was to know her and love her.[1]

This is a tribute that not only completely ignores a spectacular career in active Christian ministry and the writing of a handful of popular Christian books – replacing them with a vision of a gentlewoman dabbling in the arts – but also one that so totally censors any mention of religion that one does not even have sufficient information to discover whether or not Pankhurst was an atheist.

---

[1] 'In Memoriam', *Los Angeles Times*, 27 February 1958.

Joyce Marlow has recently observed that Sylvia Pankhurst is 'the most popular Pankhurst for latterday feminists (Christabel's and Emmeline's wartime jingoism and postwar activities are difficult subjects)'.[2] Likewise, Martin Pugh has noted, 'Surprisingly, there is still no good, scholarly biography of either Emmeline or Christabel Pankhurst.'[3] One wonders whether Pugh decided that the solitary biography of Christabel Pankhurst, David Mitchell's *Queen Christabel* (1977), was not 'good' or not 'scholarly'.[4] Certainly, Mitchell was not an academic, and feminists have not been fond of his book. Barbara Castle has called it 'bitchy and prejudiced'.[5] Olive Banks has claimed that it 'is biased by Mitchell's failure to understand feminism'.[6] Marie Mulvey Roberts has dubbed it 'his misogynistic biography', arguing that it 'reveals more about himself than about his subject'.[7] Those with an interest in religious history have no reason to celebrate *Queen Christabel* either: Mitchell was so uninterested in the kind of questions that an historian of religion would ask that he did not even bother to mention Pankhurst's denominational identity. Martin Pugh's recent volume, *The Pankhursts*, largely relies on Mitchell's research when addressing Christabel Pankhurst's Christian ministry and does not overcome the weaknesses of that earlier book when it comes to this aspect of his subject area.[8] Betty A. DeBerg has written an entire volume on 'Gender and the First Wave of American Fundamentalism', a work centred on the 1920s, and yet she did not mention Pankhurst even once. One cannot help but wonder if she felt that Pankhurst's case would overly complicate her narrative of fundamentalists as misogynist.[9] In Margaret Lamberts Bendroth's *Fundamentalism and Gender: 1875 to the Present*, a book that also seeks to highlight hostility toward women in

---

[2] Joyce Marlow (ed.), *Votes for Women: The Virago Book of Suffragettes*, London: Virago Press, 2000, p. 293.

[3] Martin Pugh, *The March of the Women: A Revisionist Analysis of the Campaign for Women's Suffrage, 1866–1914*, Oxford: Oxford University Press, 2000, p. 2. Since Pugh wrote that, a major, scholarly biography of Emmeline Pankhurst has appeared: June Purvis, *Emmeline Pankhurst: A Biography*, London: Routledge, 2002.

[4] David Mitchell, *Queen Christabel: A Biography of Christabel Pankhurst*, London: Macdonald and Jane's, 1977.

[5] Barbara Castle, *Sylvia and Christabel Pankhurst*, Harmondsworth, Middlesex: Penguin, 1987, p. 158.

[6] Olive Banks, *The Biographical Dictionary of Feminists, Volume I: 1800–1930*, New York: New York University Press, 1985, p. 149.

[7] Marie Mulvey Roberts, 'Introduction', in Christabel Pankhurst, *The Militant* [a reprint of *Unshackled*] (eds Marie Mulvey Roberts and Tamae Mizuta), London: Routledge/Thoemmes Press, 1995, pp. xii–xiii.

[8] Martin Pugh, *The Pankhursts*, London: Allen Lane Penguin Press, 2001.

[9] Betty A. DeBerg, *Ungodly Women: Gender and the First Wave of American Fundamentalism*, Minneapolis: Fortress Press, 1990.

fundamentalism, Pankhurst is named as a speaker twice and quoted once, but her ministry is never discussed.[10]

This study of Pankhurst's ministry has sought to help to recover a period in history when fundamentalism and feminism could be in coalition, and, in the thoughts, actions and attitudes of individual fundamentalist leaders, sometimes were. In the first third of the twentieth century, there were fundamentalist leaders who believed in the causes of votes for women and women in ministry. There is no doubt that fundamentalist attitudes toward the role of women narrowed as the twentieth century progressed, going a long way toward squeezing out the more supportive stances taken by some fundamentalist leaders in the 1920s. Therefore, historians within the fundamentalist camp have not known what to do with Christabel Pankhurst any more than feminist scholars. For example, Pankhurst is not once mentioned in that hefty, encyclopaedic volume written by a professor of church history at the fundamentalist stronghold, Bob Jones University: George W. Dollar, *A History of Fundamentalism in America* (1973).[11] Dollar offers no less than seventy-five pages of text-filled, usually three-or-four-line, biographical sketches of fundamentalists, yet did not choose to include one on Pankhurst, despite the fact that hers was one of the more popular and high-profile ministries on the fundamentalist circuit in the 1920s.

Pankhurst has made a brief appearance in the works of some evangelical historians. Janette Hassey provided one page on Pankhurst. This is apparently the fullest summary of Pankhurst's ministry to appear in any work of religious history, but the only source footnoted is David Mitchell's earlier book, *The Fighting Pankhursts* (1967). Nevertheless, Hassey's conclusion on the turn away from women in ministry in fundamentalism is probably accurate: 'In a sense, Christabel Pankhurst represented the end of an era.'[12] In a book on the history of the pre-millennialist movement, Timothy P. Weber spent two pages on Pankhurst. The sources cited are (again) Mitchell's *The Fighting Pankhursts*, as well as some of Pankhurst's religious books.[13] Dwight Wilson introduced Pankhurst briefly in his polemical study of the history of the pre-millennialist movement in order to denounce her as 'a false prophetess'.[14] It would appear that, in complete contraposition to this study, Wilson was unsympathetic to both fundamentalism and

---

[10] Margaret Lamberts Bendroth, *Fundamentalism and Gender, 1875 to the Present*, New Haven: Yale University Press, 1993.
[11] George W. Dollar, *A History of Fundamentalism in America*, Greenville, South Carolina: Bob Jones University Press, 1973.
[12] Hassey, *No Time For Silence*, p. 136.
[13] Timothy P. Weber, *Living in the Shadow of the Second Coming*, Grand Rapids: Academie Books (Zondervan), 1983.
[14] Dwight Wilson, *Armageddon Now! The Premillenarian Response to Russia and Israel Since 1917*, Grand Rapids: Baker Book House, 1977, p. 64.

feminism. Wilson's book, in turn, is the only source cited for the page and a half on Pankhurst in a semi-popular guide to historical movements regarding eschatology published in 1999.[15]

Substantial books reflecting the highest standards of scholarship on themes directly relevant to this study have somehow not found a place for Christabel Pankhurst in their discussions. George M. Marsden's study of American fundamentalism to 1925 does not mention her once; and neither does Joel A. Carpenter's monograph that picks up the story starting at 1930.[16] Neither Brian Heeney's *The Women's Movement in the Church of England, 1850–1930* (1988), nor Sean Gill's *Women and the Church of England: From the Eighteenth Century to the Present* (1994), mentions Christabel Pankhurst, although she was arguably the most significant Anglican female preacher after Maude Royden in the first half of the twentieth century.[17] In short, despite the fact that Pankhurst's religious ministry once attracted great crowds and was promoted in the fundamentalist press, it has been neglected by historians to a remarkable extent.

Although feminists have sometimes wished to forget that one of their more celebrated leaders from the past became a fundamentalist, and fundamentalists have wished to forget that one of their more popular ministries was that of a woman (and a feminist), yet the story of fundamentalism and feminism in coalition is one well worth telling. This study has been written in order to tell it. Christabel Pankhurst passionately gave her life to two major causes: feminism and fundamentalism. Although the 'In Memoriam' piece in the *Los Angeles Times* already marked the neglect that was to come of Pankhurst's Christian ministry, her obituary in her local paper in Santa Monica, California, got it right: 'Dame Christabel Pankhurst, militant campaigner for Christ and women's suffrage, is dead.'[18]

[15] Robert G. Clouse, Robert N. Hosack, and Richard V. Pierard, *The New Millennium Manual: A Once and Future Guide*, Grand Rapids, MI: Baker Books, 1999, pp. 121–2.
[16] George M. Marsden, *Fundamentalism and American Culture: The Shaping of Twentieth-Century Evangelicalism, 1870–1925*, Oxford: Oxford University Press, 1980; Joel A. Carpenter, *Revive Us Again: The Reawakening of American Fundamentalism*, New York: Oxford University Press, 1997.
[17] Brian Heeney, *The Women's Movement in the Church of England, 1850–1930*, Oxford: Clarendon Press, 1988; Sean Gill, *Women and the Church of England: From the Eighteenth Century to the Present*, London: SPCK, 1994. It should be noted, however, that Heeney died before he could oversee a final version of his manuscript.
[18] 'Dame Pankhurst, Noted Suffrage Leader, Dies', *Evening Outlook*, 14 February 1958.

WORKS CITED

Primary Sources

Unpublished Sources

Binfield, Clyde. Notes from 'Union Chapel Oxford Road and Union Chapel Fallowfield Church Register, 1842 – February 1977'.

King, Louise. Churchill Archives Centre, Churchill College, Cambridge. Information provided by e-mail, 2001.

Knox Presbyterian Church Archives, Toronto: 'Annual Report 1922 Knox Church Toronto', [1923].

Pankhurst, Christabel. Letters to Winston Churchill. Churchill Archives Centre, Churchill College, Cambridge.

Pankhurst, Richard. E-mail correspondence with the author, 2001.

Newspapers and Journals

Advent Witness
Atlantic City Press
Christian
Christian Fundamentalist
Church Times
Daily Chronicle
Evangelical Christendom
Evangelical Christian and Missionary Witness
Evening Outlook
King's Business
Los Angeles Times
Manchester Guardian
Moody Bible Institute Monthly
New York Times
Present and Future
Prophetic Witness
Quarterly Paper of the Bible Testimony Fellowship
Sunday School Times
Toronto Daily Star
Weekly Dispatch
World-Wide Christian Courier

Books and Other Printed Material

Christian Fellowship Bible Conference Under the Auspices of Westmont College, July 11–18 [1943] Inclusive. Over sixty churches participating, representing sixteen denominations at six locations.

The Constitution of the Elim Pentecostal Church (Elim Foursquare Gospel Alliance): Deed Poll and General Rules, Cheltenham: Elim Pentecostal Church, 1975.

Dallas Theological Seminary 2000–2001 Catalogue.

Who's Who 1938, London: A. & C. Black.

Who's Who 1957, London: Adam and Charles Black.

Winona Echoes 1941, Grand Rapids: Zondervan, 1941.

Cox, Herbert W. *Epochs Connected with the Second Coming of Christ*, London: Marshall, Morgan & Scott, 1928.

Dickens, Charles *A Christmas Carol and Other Christmas Stories*, New York: Signet Classic (Penguin), 1984 [originally 1843].

Fullerton, W. Y. *F. B. Meyer: A Biography*, London: Marshall, Morgan & Scott, [1930].

Gaebelein, Arno Clemens *Half a Century: The Autobiography of a Servant*, New York: Our Hope Offices, 1930.

Guinness, H. Grattan *The Approaching End of the Age Viewed in the Light of History, Prophecy, and Science*, twelfth edition, London: Hodder and Stoughton, 1894.

Leith, John H. (ed.) *Creeds of the Churches: A Reader in Christian Doctrine from the Bible to the Present*, third edition, Atlanta: John Knox Press, 1982.

Mann, A. Chester *F. B. Meyer: Preacher, Teacher, Man of God*, London: George Allen & Unwin, 1929.

Nicolson, Nigel (ed.) *The Sickle Side of the Moon: The Letters of Virginia Woolf, Volume V: 1932–1935*, London: The Hogarth Press, 1979.

Niebuhr, Reinhold *The Nature and Destiny of Man: A Christian Interpretation*, 2 volumes, London: Nisbet & Co., 1941.

Packer, J. I. *'Fundamentalism' and the Word of God: Some Evangelical Principles*, Leicester: InterVarsity Press, 1996 [originally 1958].

Pankhurst, Christabel *The Great Scourge and How to End It*, London: E. Pankhurst, 1913.

Pankhurst, Christabel *'The Lord Cometh': The World Crisis Explained*, London: Morgan & Scott, 1923.

Pankhurst, Christabel *'The Lord Cometh': The World Crisis Explained*, revised edition, London: Marshall, Morgan, & Scott, 1934.

Pankhurst, Christabel *Pressing Problems of the Closing Age*, London: Morgan & Scott, 1924.

Pankhurst, Christabel *Seeing the Future*, New York: Harper & Brothers, 1929.

Pankhurst, Christabel *Some Modern Problems in the Light of Bible Prophecy*, New York: Fleming H. Revell, 1924.

Pankhurst, Christabel *The Uncurtained Future*, London: Hodder and Stoughton, 1940.

Pankhurst, Christabel *Unshackled: The Story of How We Won the Vote*, London: Cresset Women's Voices, 1987 [originally published posthumously, in 1959].

Pankhurst, Christabel *The World's Unrest: Visions of the Dawn*, London: Morgan & Scott, 1926.

Pankhurst, E. Sylvia *The Suffragette Movement: An Intimate Account of Persons and Ideals*, London: Virago, 1977 [originally 1931].

Rice, John R. *Bobbed Hair, Bossy Wives, and Women Preachers: Significant Questions for Honest Christian Women Settled by the Word of God*, Wheaton, IL: Sword of the Lord Publishers, 1941.

Romans, Viola D. 'The Nation's Call', in *Winona Echoes: Forty-five notable addresses delivered at the twentieth annual Bible Conference. Winona Lake, Indiana, August, 1914*, 1914.

Scofield, C. I. (ed.) *The Scofield Reference Bible*, New York: Oxford University Press, 1917.

Tatford, F. A. *The Midnight Cry: The Story of Fifty Years of Witness*, Eastbourne: Bible and Advent Testimony Movement, n.d. [c. 1967].

Torrey, R. A., and A. C. Dixon *The Fundamentals: A Testimony to the Truth*, Los Angeles: the Bible Institute of Los Angeles, 1917 (reprinted Grand Rapids: Baker Book House, 1988).

Secondary Sources

'Diary reveals lesbian love trysts of suffragette leaders', *Observer*, 11 June 2000.

Banks, Olive *The Biographical Dictionary of Feminists, Volume I: 1800–1930*, New York: New York University Press, 1985.

Bebbington, D. W. 'Baptists and Fundamentalism in Inter-War Britain', in Keith Robbins (ed.), *Protestant Evangelicalism: Britain, Ireland, Germany and America, c. 1750–c. 1950*, Oxford: Basil Blackwell for the Ecclesiastical History Society, 1990.

Bebbington, D. W. *Evangelicalism in Modern Britain: A History from the 1730s to the 1980s*, London: Unwin Hyman, 1989.

Bebbington, D. W. 'Martyrs for the Truth: Fundamentalists in Britain', in Diana Wood (ed.), *Martyrs and Martyrologies*, Oxford: Blackwell for the Ecclesiastical History Society, 1993.

Bendroth, Margaret Lamberts *Fundamentalism and Gender, 1875 to the Present*, New Haven: Yale University Press, 1993.

Blumhofer, Edith L. *Aimee Semple McPherson: Everybody's Sister*, Grand Rapids: William B. Eerdmans, 1993.

Blumhofer, Edith L. 'A Confused Legacy: Reflections on Evangelical Attitudes toward Ministering Women in the Past Century', *Fides et Historia*, 22, 1 (Winter/Spring 1990).

Brereton, Virginia Lieson *Training God's Army: The American Bible School, 1880–1940*, Bloomington, IN: Indiana University Press, 1990.

Bruce, F. F. *The English Bible: A History of Translations*, London: Lutterworth Press, 1961.

Bullock, Ian *Sylvia Pankhurst: From Artist to Anti-Fascist*, Basingstoke: Macmillan, 1992.

Carpenter, Joel A. *Revive Us Again: The Reawakening of American Fundamentalism*, New York: Oxford University Press, 1997.

Carson, D. A. *The King James Version Debate: A Plea for Realism*, Grand Rapids: Baker Book House, 1979.

Caplan, Lionel (ed.) *Studies in Religious Fundamentalism*, Albany: State University of New York Press, 1987.

Castle, Barbara *Sylvia and Christabel Pankhurst*, Harmondsworth, Middlesex: Penguin, 1987.

Clouse, Robert G., Robert N. Hosack, and Richard V. Pierard *The New Millennium Manual: A Once and Future Guide*, Grand Rapids: Baker Books, 1999.

Dangerfield, George *The Strange Death of Liberal England*, New York: Perigee Books, 1980 [originally 1935].

Davis, Mary *Sylvia Pankhurst: A Life in Radical Politics*, Sterling, Va.: Pluto Press, 1999.

DeBerg, Betty A. *Ungodly Women: Gender and the First Wave of American Fundamentalism*, Minneapolis: Fortress Press, 1990.

Dollar, George W. *A History of Fundamentalism in America*, Greenville, South Carolina: Bob Jones University Press, 1973.

Dorsett, Lyle W. *Billy Sunday and the Redemption of Urban America*, Grand Rapids: William B. Eerdmans, 1991.

Fitch, William *Knox Church Toronto*, Toronto: John Deyell, 1971.

Fletcher, Sheila *Maude Royden: A Life*, Oxford: Basil Blackwell, 1989.

Fox, Richard Wightman *Reinhold Niebuhr: A Biography*, San Francisco: Harper & Row, 1985.

Fulford, Roger 'Pankhurst, Dame Christabel Harriette (1880–1958)', *Dictionary of National Biography 1951–1960*, London: Oxford University Press, 1971.

Fussell, Paul *The Great War and Modern Memory*, London: Oxford University Press, 1975.

Gill, Sean *Women and the Church of England: From the Eighteenth Century to the Present*, London: SPCK, 1994.

146

Hackett, David G. 'Gender and Religion in American Culture, 1870–1930', *Religion and American Culture*, 5, 2 (Summer 1995).

Hamilton, Michael S. 'Women, Public Ministry, and American Fundamentalism, 1920–1950', *Religion and American Culture*, 3, 2 (Summer 1993).

Hardman, Keith J. *Charles Grandison Finney, 1792–1875*, Syracuse, NY: Syracuse University Press, 1987.

Hassey, Janette *No Time For Silence: Evangelical Women in Public Ministry Around the Turn of the Century*, Grand Rapids: Academie Books (Zondervan), 1986.

Heeney, Brian *The Women's Movement in the Church of England, 1850–1930*, Oxford: Clarendon Press, 1988.

Hoppen, K. Theodore *The Mid-Victorian Generation, 1846–1886*, Oxford: Clarendon Press, 1998.

Hutchison, William R. *The Modernist Impulse in American Protestantism*, Cambridge, MA: Harvard University Press, 1976.

Inkpin, Jonathan David Francis 'Combatting the "Sin of Self-Sacrifice": Christian Feminism in the Women's Suffrage Struggle (1903–18)', unpublished Ph.D. thesis, University of Durham, 1996.

Isichei, Elizabeth *Victorian Quakers*, London: Oxford University Press, 1970.

Johnson, Paul *Modern Times: The World from the Twenties to the Eighties*, New York: Harper & Row, 1983.

Larsen, Timothy '"How Many Sisters Make A Brotherhood?" A Case Study in Gender and Ecclesiology in Early Nineteenth-Century English Dissent', *Journal of Ecclesiastical History* 49, 2 (April 1998).

Lawrence, Bruce B. *Defenders of God: The Fundamentalist Revolt Against the Modern Age*, San Francisco: Harper & Row, 1989.

Lewis, Donald M. (ed.) *The Blackwell Dictionary of Evangelical Biography, 1730–1860*, 2 volumes, Oxford: Blackwell, 1995.

Lindsay, Andrea M. *The Role of Sylvia Pankhurst in the Italo-Abyssinian Conflict*, Ottawa: National Library of Canada, 1990.

Malmgreen, Gail (ed.) *Religion in the Lives of English Women, 1760–1930*, Bloomington: Indiana University Press, 1986.

Marlow, Joyce (ed.) *Votes for Women: The Virago Book of Suffragettes*, London: Virago Press, 2000.

Marsden, George M. *Fundamentalism and American Culture: The Shaping of Twentieth-Century Evangelicalism, 1870–1925*, New York: Oxford University Press, 1980.

Marsden, George M. *Understanding Fundamentalism and Evangelicalism*, Grand Rapids: William B. Eerdmans, 1991.

Marty, Martin E., and R. Scott Appleby (eds) *Fundamentalisms Observed*, Chicago: University of Chicago Press, 1991.

147

Mathers, Helen 'The Evangelical Spirituality of a Victorian Feminist: Josephine Butler, 1828–1906', *Journal of Ecclesiastical History*, 52, 2 (2001).

Mitchell, David *The Fighting Pankhursts: A Study in Tenacity*, New York: Macmillan, 1967.

Mitchell, David *Queen Christabel: A Biography of Christabel Pankhurst*, London: Macdonald and Jane's, 1977.

Murray, Iain H. *Jonathan Edwards: A New Biography*, Edinburgh: Banner of Truth, 1987.

Pugh, Martin *The March of the Women: A Revisionist Analysis of the Campaign for Women's Suffrage, 1866–1914*, Oxford: Oxford University Press, 2000.

Pugh, Martin *The Pankhursts*, London: Allen Lane Penguin Press, 2001.

Purvis, June, and Sandra Stanley Holton (eds) *Votes for Women*, London: Routledge, 2000.

Purvis, June 'A "Pair of . . . Infernal Queens"? A Reassessment of the Dominant Representations of Emmeline and Christabel Pankhurst, First Wave Feminists in Edwardian Britain', *Women's History Review*, 5, 2 (1996).

Purvis, June 'Christabel Pankhurst and the Women's Social and Political Union', in M. Joannou and J. Purvis (eds), *The Women's Suffrage Movement, New Feminist Perspectives*, Manchester: Manchester University Press, 1998.

Purvis, June *Emmeline Pankhurst: A Biography*, London: Routledge, 2002.

Randall, I. M. 'The Career of F. B. Meyer (1847–1929)', unpublished M.Phil thesis, CNAA, 1992.

Randall, Ian M. *Evangelical Experiences: A Study in the Spirituality of English Evangelicalism, 1918–1939*, Carlisle: Paternoster, 1999.

Reid, Daniel G. (ed.) *Dictionary of Christianity in America*, Downers Grove, IL: IVP, 1990.

Robbins, Keith *Churchill*, London: Longman, 1992.

Roberts, Marie Mulvey 'Introduction', in Christabel Pankhurst, *The Militant* [a reprint of *Unshackled*] (eds Marie Mulvey Roberts and Tamae Mizuta), London: Routledge/Thoemmes Press, 1995.

Romero, Patricia W. *E. Sylvia Pankhurst: Portrait of a Radical*, New Haven: Yale University Press, 1990.

Rosen, Andrew *Rise Up, Women: The Militant Campaign of the Women's Social and Political Union, 1903–1914*, Boston: Routledge & Kegan Paul, 1974.

Russell, C. Allyn *Voices of American Fundamentalism: Seven Biographical Studies*, Philadelphia: Westminster Press, 1976.

Sandeen, Ernest R. *The Roots of Fundamentalism: British and American Millenarianism, 1800–1930*, Chicago: University of Chicago Press, 1970.

Stackhouse, John G., Jr *Canadian Evangelicalism in the Twentieth Century: An Introduction to Its Character*, Vancouver: Regent College, 1999.

Taylor, Rosemary *In Letters of Gold: The Story of Sylvia Pankhurst and the East London Federation of the Suffragettes in Bow*, London: Stepney Books, 1993.

Weber, Timothy P. *Living in the Shadow of the Second Coming*, enlarged edition, Grand Rapids: Academie Books (Zondervan), 1983.

Willard, W. Wyeth *Fire on the Prairie: The Story of Wheaton College*, Wheaton, IL: Van Kampen Press, 1950.

Wilson, Dwight *Armageddon Now! The Premillenarian Response to Russia and Israel Since 1917*, Grand Rapids: Baker Book House, 1977.

Winslow, Barbara *Sylvia Pankhurst: Sexual Politics and Political Activism*, London: UCL Press, 1996.

Winter, Jay, Geoffrey Parker and Mary R. Habeck (eds) *The Great War and the Twentieth Century*, New Haven: Yale University Press, 2000.

Wolffe, John (ed.) *Evangelical Faith and Public Zeal: Evangelicals and Society in Britain, 1780–1980*, London: SPCK, 1995.

Index

Tower of London 7
Tractarians *see* Anglo-Catholics
Trafalgar Square 3, 5
Tribulation, The Great 32, 43–4, 79
Trinity 45
Trumbull, C. G. 98
Tuke, Mabel 5
Turkey 37, 74
Twentieth Century Fox 127

Uncurtained Future, The 28, 69, 71, 73, 76, 77, 82, 83, 86, 112, 119
Unshackled 107, 116
Union Chapel 17
Union Theological Seminary 87
United Free Church College 91
United Free Church of Scotland 130
United States 10, 24, 25, 27, 29, 33, 35, 36, 52 (n. 6), 61, 63, 66, 71, 78, 84, 86, 89, 90, 91, 92, 93, 95, 97–102, 103, 107, 116, 119, 130, 142
Utley, Uldine 126

Vandalism 4–5
Venereal diseases 11, 12, 109
Victoria Cross 106
Victoria University 3
Victorian era 11, 16, 30, 47, 65, 77, 112
Volstead Act 105

Wales 94, 67 (n. 62)
War, The Great vii, 6, 9, 15, 21, 37, 39, 60–1, 63, 65, 69–72, 75, 108, 110, 119
Wasserman, Oscar 63
Watchman-Examiner 89, 99
Webb-Peploe, W. H. 91
Weber, Timothy P. 54, 141
Weekly Dispatch 10

Weizmann, Chaim 63
Wells, H. G. 13, 110
Wesley, John 29
West, Rebecca 13
Westminster Abbey 9, 97 (n. 37)
Westminster Chapel 91
Westminster Confession 31
Westmont College 99
Wheaton College 34, 99, 101
Whitaker, Alma 10, 77
Whitefield, George 29
Whitelaw, Thomas 91
Who's Who 77 (n. 35), 129
Wilberforce, William 30
Willard, Frances E. 105
Wilson, Dwight 141
Wimbledon 66
Winchester, A. B. 25, 26, 31, 96, 97, 115
Winona Lake Bible Conference 99, 105, 126
Woman at the well 137
Women's Freedom League 111
Women's League for Palestine 64
Women's Social and Political Union vii, 1–9, 10, 11, 15, 16, 19, 110, 116, 119
Woolf, Virginia 11
World's Christian Fundamentals Association 89, 97, 101, 126
World's Unrest, The 27, 41, 44, 49, 51, 52, 53, 54, 76, 93, 96, 98, 113, 128, 137
World War I *see* War, The Great
World War II 63, 65
World-Wide Christian Courier 126

Zionism 62–3, 64, 114, 118, 119
Zionist Congress 63
Zionist Record 62
Zionist Review 62